THE ULTIMATE UCAS PERSONAL STATEMENT GUIDE

UniAdmissions

THE ULTIMATE UCAS PERSONAL STATEMENT GUIDE

DR. ROHAN AGARWAL

DR. DAVID SALT

UniAdmissions

ABOUT THE AUTHORS

Rohan is **Director of Operations** at *UniAdmissions* and is responsible for its technical and commercial arms. He graduated from Gonville and Caius College, Cambridge, and is now a doctor in Leicester. Over the last five years, he has tutored hundreds of successful Oxbridge and Medical applicants. He has authored twenty books on admissions tests and interviews.

He has taught physiology to undergraduates and interviewed medical school applicants for Cambridge. He has also published research on bone physiology and writes education articles for the Independent and Huffington Post. In his spare time, Rohan enjoys playing the piano and table tennis.

David is **Director of Services** at *UniAdmissions*, taking the lead in product development and customer service. David read medical sciences at Gonville and Caius College Cambridge, graduating in 2012, completed his clinical studies in the Cambridge Clinical School and now works as a medical doctor.

David is an experienced tutor, having helped students with all aspects of the university applications process. He has authored five books to help with university applications and has edited four more. Away from work, David enjoys cycling, outdoor pursuits and good food.

CONTENTS

INTRODUCTION

Good university courses are competitive. After a few years of lower application rates, the 2016 entry cycle received a record-breaking 592,290 applications through UCAS.

With so many aiming high for the university place they dream of, you need to find a way to distinguish yourself from other applicants – a way you can demonstrate your superior skills, motivation, and potential.

Although the personal statement is just one component of the applications process, for the vast majority of applicants it is the only component that provides the admissions tutor with information about the real you. Only the small proportion of courses that require an interview offer an additional opportunity to shine. The personal statement is your opportunity to show your reasons for choosing your subject, your motivation, and the personal skills that will help you succeed in your field in the future. The importance of the personal statement should never be underestimated.

This book first guides you through the process of writing your personal statement. The first section gives top tips and advice to help you show yourself in the best possible light whilst avoiding common pitfalls. There are then 100 successful personal statements from recent applicants. Each of these comes with a commentary showing you the strongest and weaker points of the statement, helping you hone the structure and content of your own. These personal statements cover all major subjects so you should find statements in your chosen subject here. But also read personal statements from similar subject areas – whilst the focus of the content will be different, the ways these successful applicants display their skills, interests and motivation can give you valuable ideas to incorporate into your own statement.

So, what are you waiting for?

THE BASICS

Your Personal Statement

Applying to university is both an exciting and confusing time. You will make a decision that will impact the next 3-6 years and potentially your entire life. Your personal statement is your chance to show the universities that you apply to who you *really* are. The rest of the application is faceless statistics – the personal statement gives the admissions tutor the opportunity to look beyond those statistics and focus on the real you, the person they may spend at least three years teaching.

You may hear some people telling you there is a certain right and wrong way to write a personal statement, but this is only partially true. There is a game to be played, but within the broad conventions of good personal statements laid out here, you have considerable flexibility with *what* you choose to talk about. One of the reasons we produced this collection is to show you the vastly different styles that successful personal statements have. While there are rules of thumb that can help you along the way, never lose sight of the fact that this is your opportunity to tell your story.

How Does The Process Work?

University applications are made through the online UCAS system. You can apply to up to 5 universities (4 for Medicine). After receiving the outcomes of all applications, you make a confirmed (i.e. first) and reserve choice. Entry to a university is only confirmed upon achievement of the conditions set out in the conditional offer. It is very important to remember that **the same application will be sent to all of your choices**. It is, therefore, a good idea to apply for similar courses rather than courses which are vastly different from one another. It will be very hard to complete an application for Chemistry, English, Art, Geography, and Engineering. However, applying for Chemistry and Biochemistry would be much more straightforward.

Other than exam marks, GCSE grades and teacher references, the only part of the application which you have direct control over is your personal statement. This is your chance to convince the reader (i.e. admissions tutor) to give you a place at their university. Although it's not a job interview, it is important to treat the personal statement with the respect it deserves. Many universities do not require applicants to attend interviews, in which case the personal statement is your **only chance** to show the admissions tutor who you are.

Deadlines

The final deadline is the 15th of January next year. For medicine, dentistry, Oxford, and Cambridge, be aware of an earlier deadline of the **15th of October** this year– if you don't get your application in on time it won't be considered. Remember that **schools often have an earlier internal deadline** so they can ensure punctuality and sort out their references in time. Different schools have different procedures, so it is very important that you know what the timescale is at your school before the end of year 12. Internal deadlines for the 15th October deadline can be as early as the beginning of September, which is only a couple of weeks after the summer break.

Early submissions are advised because **universities begin offering places as soon as they receive applications**. This is very important as those who submit their application before the final 15th of January deadline can be offered places before Christmas! Therefore, it is in your best interest to submit your application as early as possible – even if you're not applying for medicine or Oxbridge.

In addition, early submission frees up your time to concentrate on any admissions tests or interviews you may need to prepare for, and also your A Level studies.

What are the requirements?

- Maximum 47 lines
- Maximum 4000 characters
- Submitted by the deadline

I have the grades; do I need to worry about the statement?

In short - yes. Both are important. The grades are a foundation that tells the university your academic credentials are good enough to cope with the demands of the course. So achieving the entrance grades required is considered to be the basic requirement for successful applicants. The personal statement gives additional information, allowing the admissions tutor to assess your own personality and suitability for their course and style of teaching. If an applicant's personal statement isn't strong enough but they meet the minimum grade criteria, they may still be rejected.

What do Admissions Tutors look for?
Academic ability

This is the most obvious. Every university will have different entrance requirements for the same course titles, so make sure that you are aware of these. Some universities may have extra requirements, e.g. applicants for English at UCL require a minimum GCSE in a foreign language other than in English. It is your responsibility to ensure that you meet the entry criteria for the course that you're applying to.

Extra-curricular activities

Unlike in the US, the main factor in the UK for deciding between candidates for university places is their academic suitability for the course to which they have applied, and little else. This is especially true for Oxford. Whilst extra-curricular activities can be a positive thing, it is a common mistake for students to dedicate too much of their personal statement to these. There is, however, an important place for subject-related extra-curricular activities in a personal statement, like work experience.

Passion for your subject

This is the easiest part to get wrong in a personal statement, and it can be very important. This is what makes your statement personal to you and is where you can truly be yourself, so do not hold back! Whether you've dreamt of being a doctor since birth or a historian since learning to read, if you are truly passionate about your chosen subject this should shine through in the personal statement.

It is not necessary, however, for you to have wanted to do a particular subject for your entire life. In fact, it is entirely possible to choose a subject because you found a course that really appealed to you on a university open day. Whatever the case, you should find reasons to justify your decision to pursue a course that will cost a lot of time and money. If the personal statement does not convince the reader that you're committed to the academic pursuit of your chosen subject, then you'll likely be rejected.

It is important to remember that you are applying for undergraduate admission, not a job. Whilst it is not a bad thing to have an idea of potential career paths beyond university, writing a personal statement that bypasses the academic nature of university courses will be judged negatively.

Application Timeline

	Early Deadline	Late Deadline	
Research Courses	May + June	June + July	
Start Brainstorming	Start of August	Throughout August	
Complete First Draft	Mid-August	Early September	
Complete Final Draft	End of August	Late September	
Expert Checks	Mid-September	Early-October	
Submit to School	Late September	Late-October	**ASAP**
Submit to UCAS	Before 15th October	Before 15th January	

Researching Courses

This includes both online research and attending university open days. Whilst this has been more difficult than normal for the past couple of years, open days will be either virtual or in person and are always worth attending. Some of you reading this guide will already know exactly which course you want to apply for, but many will not have decided. Course research is still very important even if you're certain. This is because the 'same' courses can vary significantly between universities. As only one personal statement is sent to all universities that you apply to, it is important that you write in a way that addresses the different needs of each university.

If you cannot make it to university open days, you can usually email a department and request a tour. If you allow plenty of time for this, quite often universities are happy to do this. Be proactive – do not sit around and expect universities to come to you and ask for your application! The worst possible thing you can do is appear to be applying to a course which you don't understand or haven't researched.

As a result, we highly recommend that you research the content of courses which you are interested in. Every university will produce a prospectus, which is available in print and online. Take some time to compare modules between universities. This will help to not only choose the 4/5 universities which you apply for but also be aware of exactly what it is that you are applying for.

Start Brainstorming

At this stage, you will have narrowed down your subject interests and should be certain of which subjects to apply for. For applications which will include universities offering single and general subject areas such as individual Engineering disciplines/Sciences and universities offering general Engineering/Natural Sciences etc., it is important to plan a personal statement that fits both.

A good way to start a thought process that will eventually lead to a personal statement is by simply listing all of your ideas; why you are interested in your course, what makes you a good fit, and the pros and cons between different universities. If there are particular modules which capture your interest and are common across several of your university choices, do not be afraid to include this in your personal statement. This will not only show that you have a real interest in your chosen subject, but also that you have taken the time to do some research.

Complete First Draft

Once you have your list of ideas, you want to start fleshing these out. Think about how you would communicate each point to someone you don't know, and turn that list into a side of A4. This will not be the final personal statement that you submit. In all likelihood, your personal statement will go through multiple revisions and re-drafts before it is ready for submission. In most cases, the final statement is wildly different from the first draft.

The purpose of completing a rough draft early is so that you can spot major errors early. It is easy to go off on a tangent when writing a personal statement, with such things not being made obvious until somebody else reads it. The first draft will show the applicant which areas need more attention, what is missing, and what needs to be removed altogether.

Re-Draft

Once your first draft is finished and you've checked it over, you should show it to friends, teachers, or guardians. This will probably be the first time you receive any real feedback on your personal statement. Obvious errors will be spotted and any outrageous claims that sound good in your head, but are unclear or dubious, will be obvious to these readers. It is important to take advice from family and friends, however, with a pinch of salt. Remember that the admissions tutor will be a stranger and not familiar with your personality.

Complete Final Draft

This will not be the final product, and until now, you probably won't have had much real criticism. However, a complete draft with an introduction, main body, and conclusion is important as you can then build on this towards the final personal statement.

Expert Check

This should be completed by the time you return for your final year at school/college. Once the final year has started, it is wise to get as many experts (teachers and external private or NTP tutors) to read through the final draft personal statement as possible.

Again, you should take all advice with a pinch of salt. At the end of the day, this is your UCAS application and although your teachers' opinions are valuable, they are not the same as that of the admissions tutors. In schools that see many Oxbridge/Medical applications, many teachers believe there is a correct 'format' to personal statements and may look at your statement like a 'number' in the sea of applications that are processed by the school.

They are right, but only to a limited extent, and you shouldn't change your statement to something you aren't happy with beyond ensuring that you have clearly addressed all of the main criteria needed for a successful statement outlined in this guide.

At schools that do not see many Oxbridge/Medical applications, the opposite may be true. Many applicants are coerced into applying to universities and for courses which their teachers judge them likely to be accepted for. It is your responsibility to ensure that the decisions you make are your own, and you have the conviction to follow through with your decisions. If anyone is pressuring you not to apply to Oxbridge, but you are confident you will have the right grades and you personally want to go, then you should apply.

Final Checks

Armed with a rough draft and advice from friends, family, and teachers, you should be ready to complete your final personal statement.

Submit to School

Ideally, you will have some time between getting your final draft feedback and submitting your statement for the internal UCAS deadline. This is important because it'll allow you to look at your final personal statement with a fresh perspective before submitting it. You'll also be able to spot any errors that you initially missed. You should submit your personal statement and UCAS application to your school on time for the internal deadline. This ensures that your school has enough time to complete your references.

Submit to UCAS

That's it! Take some time off from university applications for a few days, have some rest, and remember that you still have A levels/IB exams to get through (and potentially admissions tests + interviews)!

GETTING STARTED

The personal statement is an amalgam of all your hard work throughout both secondary school and your other extra-curricular activities. It is right to be apprehensive about starting your application and so here are a few tips to get you started...

GENERAL RULES

If you meet the minimum academic requirements, then it is with the personal statement that your can stand out from the crowd. With many applicants applying with identical GCSE and A-level results (if you're a gap year student), the personal statement along with your reference (and maybe admissions test) are used to refine the list of applicants into a pool worth interviewing. As such, there is no concrete formula to follow when writing the personal statement and indeed every statement is different in its own right. Therefore, throughout this chapter, you will find many principles for you to adopt and interpret as you see fit whilst considering a few of these introductory general rules.

Firstly: **space is extremely limited**; as previously mentioned, a maximum of 4000 characters in 47 lines. Note that this includes line breaks - this often means that candidates write a solid block of text, or use indents to denote paragraphs instead of a line. However, doing this not only makes your statement hard to read (especially as most tutors will skim your introduction and conclusion when deciding whether or not to read the rest), but including line breaks in spite of the line limit is a good way to show your competence and organisational skill. Before even beginning the personal statement, utilise all available space on the UCAS form. For example, do not waste characters listing exam results when they can be entered in the corresponding fields in the qualifications section of the UCAS form.

This limited space does also mean there are certain things you should try and make sure you don't miss out (as many do), particularly your interest in the course, academic skills, valid life experience, and suitability for university.

Secondly: always remember **it is easier to reduce the word count than increase** it with meaningful content when editing. Be aware that it is not practical to perfect your personal statement in just one sitting. Instead, write multiple drafts, with your first draft being written *without even thinking about the size limits*. If you don't worry about those, you'll find its easier to articulate all the points you want to say, and you can introduce efficiencies later on. As such, starting early is key to avoiding later time pressure as you approach the deadline. Remember, this is your opportunity to put onto paper what makes you the best and a cut above the rest – you should enjoy writing the personal statement!

Lastly and most importantly: **your statement is just one of hundreds that a tutor will read**. Admissions Tutors are only human after all and their interpretation of your personal statement can be influenced by many things. So get on their good side and always be sympathetic to the reader, make things plain and easy to read, avoid contentious subjects, and never target your personal statement at one particular university.

WHEN SHOULD I START?

TODAY!

It might sound like a cliché, but the earlier you start, the easier you make it. Starting early helps you in four key ways:

1. The most important reason to start early is that it is the best way to analyse your application. Many students start writing their personal statement then realise, for example, that they haven't done enough research or work experience, or that their extra reading isn't focused enough. By starting early, you give yourself the chance to change this. Over the summer, catch up on your weak areas to give yourself plenty to say in the final version.

2. You give yourself more time for revisions. You can improve your personal statement by showing it to as many people as possible to get their feedback. Starting earlier gives you more time for this.

3. Steadier pace. Starting early gives you the flexibility of working at a steadier pace – perhaps just an hour or so per week. If you start later, you will have to spend much longer on it, probably some full days, reducing the time you have for the rest of your work and importantly for unwinding, too.

4. Prompt submission. Although the official deadline is the 15th January for most courses, it is often the case that courses will allocate some places before this. By submitting early, you make sure you don't miss out on any opportunities.

What people think is best:

What is actually best:

DOING YOUR RESEARCH

The two most important things you need to establish are: **What course? + What University?**

If you're unsure where to begin, success with the personal statement (like most things in life) begins with preparation and research.

The most obvious and useful first port of call is your teachers at school on the subjects that you enjoy. Not only will they have detailed knowledge of general course requirements; but if they have taught you for a few years, they will also know a lot about you. In many ways, teachers like this offer the most valuable information as they can describe the course in the context of your personality and be fairly sure of whether you are suitable for the course or not. Progressing from teachers, discuss your options with your parents and continue on to **university open days**. This is where the next problem arises: *which universities do I apply for?*

Your choice of university is entirely personal and similar to your course choice; it needs to be somewhere that you are going to enjoy studying. Remember that where you end up will form a substantial part of your life. This could mean going to a university with a rich, active nightlife or one with strict academic prowess or perhaps one that dominates in the sporting world. In reality, each university offers its own unique experience and hence the best approach is to attend as many open days as feasibly possible. By doing this, you will have the opportunity to meet some of your potential lecturers and tutors, talk to current students (who offer the most honest information), and of course, tour the facilities.

The best way to prevent future stress is to start researching courses and universities early, *i.e.* 12 months before you apply through UCAS. There is a plethora of information that is freely available online, and if you want something physical to read, you can request free prospectuses from most UK universities. It is important to remember that until you actually submit your UCAS application, **you** are in control. Universities are actively competing against one another for **your** application! When initially browsing, a good place to start is by simply listing courses and universities which interest you, and two pros and cons for each. You can then use this to shortlist a handful of universities that you should then attend open days for.

There are no right choices when it comes to university choices, however, there are plenty of wrong choices. You must make sure that the reasons behind your eventual choice are the right ones and that you do not act on impulse. Whilst your personal statement should not be directed at any particular one of your universities, it should certainly be tailored to the course you are applying for.

With a course in mind and universities shortlisted, your preparation can begin in earnest. Start by ordering **university prospectuses** or logging onto the university's subject-specific websites. For Oxbridge, you should make sure to check out their *Alternative Prospectuses* which are prepared by and for students for more accurate information about what each course and university is like. In each prospectus, you should be trying to find the application requirements. Once located, there will be a range of information from academic demands including work experience to personal attributes.

Firstly, at this point, **be realistic with the GCSE results you have already achieved and your predicted A-level grades**. Also, note that some courses require a minimum number of hours of work experience – this should have been conducted through the summer after GCSE examinations and into your AS year. Work experience is not something to lie about as the university will certainly seek references to confirm your attendance. If these do not meet the minimum academic requirements, a tutor will most likely not even bother reading your personal statement, so don't waste a choice.

If you meet all the minimum academic requirements, then focus on the other extra-curricular aspects. Many prospectuses contain descriptions of ideal candidates with lists of desired personal attributes. Make a list of these for all the universities you are considering applying to. Compile a further list of your own personal attributes along with evidence that supports each one. Then proceed to pair the points on your personal list with the corresponding requirements from your potential universities.

It is important to consider extra-curricular requirements from all your potential universities in the interest of forming a **rounded personal statement applicable to all institutions**. This is a useful technique because one university may not require the same personal attributes as another. Therefore, by discussing these attributes in your statement, you can demonstrate a level of ingenuity and personal reflection on the requirements of the course beyond what is listed in the prospectus.

Always remember that the role of the personal statement is to **show that you meet course requirements by using your own personal experiences as evidence**.

TAKING YOUR FIRST STEPS

A journey of one thousand miles starts with a single step...

As you may have already experienced, the hardest step of a big project is the first step. It's easy to plan to start something, but when it actually comes to writing the first words, what do you do? As you stare at the 47-line blank page in front of you, how can you fill it? You wonder if you've even done that many things in life. You think of something, but realise it probably isn't good enough, delete it, and start over again. Sound familiar?

There is another way. The reason it is hard is because you judge your thoughts against the imagined finished product. So don't begin by writing full, perfectly polished sentences. Don't be a perfectionist. Begin with lists, spider diagrams, ideas, rambling. Just put some ideas onto paper and **write as much as possible** – it's easy to trim down afterwards if it's too long, and generally doing it this way gives the best content. Aim to improve gradually from start to finish in little steps each time.

Your Personal Statement

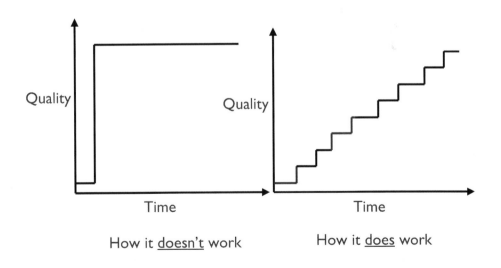

How it <u>doesn't</u> work   How it <u>does</u> work

The Writing Process

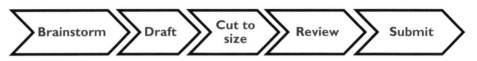

Brainstorm ⟩ Draft ⟩ Cut to size ⟩ Review ⟩ Submit

The Brainstorm

If writing prose is too daunting, start by using our brainstorm template. Write down just three bullet-points for each of the 12 questions below and in only twenty minutes you'll be well on your way!

Why did you choose this course?	**What features of each course interest you the most?**	**What are your three main hobbies and what skills have they developed?**
What have you chosen to read outside the A-level syllabus?	**Do you have any long-term career ideas/aspirations?**	**How have you learned about your chosen course?**
Have you won any prizes or awards?	**What is your favourite A Level subject and why?**	**What are your personal strengths?**
Have you attended any courses?	**Have you ever held a position of responsibility?**	**Have you been a part of any projects?**

Why did you choose this course?

What areas of your subject interest you the most?

What are your 3 main hobbies? What skills have they developed?

1.

2.

3.

What have you chosen to read outside the A-Level syllabus?

Do you have any long-term career ideas or aspirations?

What did you learn from your work experience?

Have you won any prizes or awards?

What is your favourite A-level subject and why?

What are your personal strengths?

What courses have you attended?

What positions of responsibility have you held?

What projects have you been involved in?

What is the Purpose of your Statement?

An important question to ask yourself before you begin drafting your personal statement is: "how will the universities I have applied to use my personal statement?" This can dramatically change how you write your personal statement. For the majority of courses, i.e. courses that don't interview, your personal statement is directly bidding for a place on the course. If this applies to you then you are in luck as these are the simplest to write. Just be aware that this is then your only opportunity to say what you want to say and space is much more of a commodity. In this instance, consider writing your reference with your teachers – more will be discussed on this later.

If, on the other hand, you are applying to a course that calls candidates in for an interview, writing your personal statement requires a little more thought and tactics. The first thing to establish is the role of the personal statement in the context of the interview. At this point, it is well worth going through the application procedures in prospectuses and on university websites.

The first option is that the personal statement is solely used for interview selection and discounted thereafter. In this case, the interviewer is going to want to discuss material that isn't included in your personal statement. As such, a tactical decision has to be made to withhold certain information in order to discuss at the interview. Of course, this is a difficult balance to strike; put too little into your personal statement and you won't get an interview; whereas if you put too much into the personal statement, you will lack original material to discuss within the interview. It is always better to tend towards putting a lot of effort into your personal statement to make sure of receiving an interview. Then, for the interview itself, read up on prominent topics within the academic field at the time in order to introduce new content for discussion at the interview. However, do be wary of discussing things that you know relatively little about – the interviewers are likely to be experts in the field after all!

Alternatively, the personal statement can represent a central component of the interview. Many institutions adopt an interview protocol whereby the interviewers run through the personal statement from start to finish, questioning the candidate on specific points. This technique has many benefits for the interviewer as it allows them to assess the presence of any fraudulent claims (it is very hard to lie to a tutor face-to-face when they start asking for specifics), it also gives the interview clear structure but also allows the interviewer to bring pre-planned questions on specific personal statement points.

However, from the candidate's point of view, this can lead to an oppressive, accusative, and intense interview. There are, however, techniques to take control back into your own hands like, for example, "planting" questions within your personal statement. This can be achieved in many ways, including unexplained points, ambiguous statements or just withholding information that can be added to previously mentioned points. In many ways, this protocol is easier to prepare for. There are accompanying risks however, and you must ensure that you do this carefully and considerately so that your statement doesn't seem too disjointed.

Finding the Right Balance

The balance of a personal statement can have a significant effect on the overall message it delivers. Whilst there are no strict rules, there are a few rules of thumb that can help you strike the right balance between all the important sections.

It's important that you focus primarily on academic matters. This means you need to tell a story – the story of how you developed sufficient interest in your chosen subject that you want to study it at degree level. If you are applying to study something you have studied in school like maths or geography, your story needs to start with the reasons you began to enjoy this subject. If it's a new subject such as medicine or engineering, you should explain what has led you to your chosen subject and what evidence you have that you'll enjoy it. You can then move on to talk about how you have investigated the subject, any extra work and projects, and how you have shown your aptitude for it. You may choose to include any work experience that you have done in this part, and you may also wish to give a perspective of any careers that interest you that this subject will help you achieve, taking care to support any opinions with reasons.

Extra-curricular activities are a great way of supporting your skills, however, you need to be careful that this is the supporting act and not the headliner. It is generally recommended to spend no more than a quarter of the personal statement discussing extra-curricular activities, leaving the other three-quarters for discussing academic matters.

The following template gives a suggestion of how to balance the different sections:

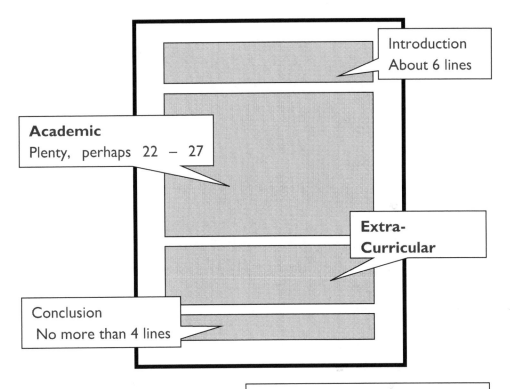

Introduction
About 6 lines

Academic
Plenty, perhaps 22 – 27

Extra-Curricular

Conclusion
No more than 4 lines

TOTAL: 47 lines; 4000 characters

STRUCTURING YOUR STATEMENT

This may sound obvious, but it's important to get the structure right as a good structure enhances the clarity of the content. Personal statements are not monologues of your life nor are they a giant list of your achievements. They are instead a formal piece of prose written with the aim of helping you secure a place at university.

THE INTRODUCTION

The Opening Sentence

Rightly or wrongly, it is highly likely that your personal statement will be remembered by its opening sentence. It must be something short, sharp, insightful, and catch the reader's attention. Remember that admissions tutors will read several hundred personal statements and often their first impression is made by your opening sentence which is why it needs to be eye-catching enough to make the tutor sit and pay particular attention to what you have written.

If this seems a daunting prospect (as it should!) then here are a few pointers to get you started:

- Avoid using overused words like "passion", "fascinating", and "devotion."
- Avoid using clichéd quotes like the infamous Coco Chanel's "fashion is not something that exists in dresses only."
- If you are going to use a quote, then put some effort into researching a less-well used one which is relevant to you and your application in a way you can personally – don't forget to include a reference.
- Draw on your own personal experiences to produce something both original and eye-catching.

In many ways, it is best that you save writing your opening statement till last; that way, you can assess the tone of the rest of your work but also write something that will not be repeated elsewhere.

If you are really stuck with where to begin, try writing down an experience and then explain how it has affected your relationship with your subject.

Whilst the opening statement is important, it is not something to stress about. Even if a strong opening statement can make your personal statement; a bad one will rarely break it.

Why Your Subject?

The introduction should answer the most important question of all:

Why do **YOU** want to study your subject?

The introduction does not need to be very long. It is generally a good idea to open the statement with something that sets the context of your application. For example, someone who is applying to study History may open: 'History is all around us', rather than 'I have always been interested in History because'. By the end of the introduction, the reader should know:

- What subject you are applying for.
- What motivated you to apply for that subject.

It is essential to show your genuine reasons and motivation. The first thing to consider is whether you genuinely want to study your subject at university. You need to be certain that your motivation comes from yourself and not from external sources such as teachers or family.

Try to avoid clichés; some people will say they've always wanted to study [subject] ever since they were born – but of course this simply isn't true and, therefore, isn't helpful. The admissions tutor wants to see a simple and honest story about your journey, helping them assess how carefully you have considered your choice and how suitable a choice it is. The exact phrase: "from a young age, I have always been interested in" was used more than 300 times in personal statements in a single year (data published by UCAS), and substituting "young" for "early" gave an additional 292 statements – these phrases can quickly become boring for admissions tutors to read!

There are certain things that raise red flags - phrases that will count against you if you write them. These include: saying that you want to study your subject for money, fame, family or because of other people telling you to. If any of these are true for you, do consider why *you* yourself want to do this, if you are struggling to find another reason, you may want another course!

THE MAIN BODY

In the rest of your text, your aim should be to demonstrate your suitability for the course by exemplifying your knowledge of the course structure and its requirements through personal experience. Again, there are no rigorous guidelines on how to do this and it is very much down to your own writing style. Whereas some prefer a strict structure, others go for a more synoptic approach, but always remember to be consistent in order to achieve a flowing, easy to read personal statement.

This point ties in closely with your writing style. You want one that the tutor will find pleasing to read, and as everyone prefers different styles the only way to assess yours accurately is to show your drafts to as many people as possible. That includes teachers, guardians, friends, siblings, grandparents – the more, the better - don't be afraid to show it around!

Despite the lack of a standardised writing method, there is, of course, a list of standard content to include. In general, you are trying to convey your academic, professional, and personal suitability for the course to the tutor. This needs to be communicated whilst demonstrating clear, exemplified knowledge of the course structure and your ability to meet its demands. The biggest problem in achieving these goals is originality, as almost all of the other candidates will be trying also trying to convey the same information, you need to produce an original personal statement and remain unique.

More practically, it is a good idea to split the main body into two or three paragraphs in order to avoid writing one big boring monologue.

Part One

This should cover why you are suited for your subject. This will include your main academic interests, future ambitions (related to the chosen degree), and what makes the course right for you, including what strengths you have which will serve you well on the course. It is a good idea for you to read the course syllabuses or outlines and find something that catches your interest for a particular reason. If you have read anything outside of the A-level/IB syllabus related to your chosen course which has inspired you (and hopefully you have), then this is the place to mention it. You should make sure that you avoid writing empty statements by backing everything up with facts. For example, someone applying to study History may write:

"'Reminisces of a Revolutionary War' by Ernesto Che Guevara provided a unique insight into the struggle against inequality in mid-20th century Latin America. Che's transformation from a doctor into a guerrilla leader completed his intellectual transition from an individual with a sense of duty to help others, into a soldier of totalitarian Marxism. Such transformations have influenced the modern world, and draw parallels with the world today. For this reason, understanding history is the key to understanding both the present and the future."

35

This shows that the applicant has read 'Reminisces of a Revolutionary War' by Ernesto Che Guevara, and truly believes in the importance that History has to the world today. This is much better than:

'I read Reminisces of a Revolutionary War by Ernesto Che Guevara. Studying History will allow me to understand the present and future by comparing to the past.'

Part Two

This section should still be about why you're suited to your chosen course. However, it can be less focused on academic topics. If you've had to overcome any significant challenges in life and wish to include these in your personal statement, this is normally the best place to do so. Similarly, any work experience or relevant prizes & competitions should be included here. However, it is important to remember not to simply list things. Ensure that you follow through by describing in detail what you have learned from any experiences mentioned.

Part Three

This is the smallest part of the main body and is all about extra-curricular activities. It is easy to get carried away in this section and make outrageous claims, e.g. claim to be a mountain climber if all you have ever climbed is a hill at the end your street etc. Lying is not worth the risk given that your interviewer may share the same hobby that you claim to be an expert in. So, don't be caught out!

Avoid making empty statements by backing things up with facts. For example: 'I enjoy reading, playing sports and watching TV', is a poor sentence and tells the reader nothing. The applicant enjoys reading, so what? Which sports? What is relevant to your course about watching TV? If the applicant is in a sports team or plays a particular sport recreationally with friends, then they should name the sport and describe what their role is. Likewise, the applicant should actually describe how their hobbies relate to them as a person and, ideally, their subject.

What to avoid

Whilst the points discussed previously can be interpreted and used as you see fit in order to produce your own unique personal statement; there are categorically certain things that you should avoid:

- Long complicated sentences
- Lack of reflection or self-awareness
- Lists
- Irrelevant/out of date examples – keep things recent (ideally the past two years)
- Negative connotations – always put a positive spin on everything
- Generic/stereotypical statements
- Controversy in whatever form it may come
- Repetition
- Overreliance on a single example or experience
- Inappropriate examples - ones which are unprofessional or not suitable for a model student.

What to Include

Still a little stumped? Well, here are a few must-haves in no particular order to get you started:

- Hobbies – these are particularly important for vocational courses like medicine, dentistry and law as they offer a form of stress relief amidst a course of intense studying whilst also demonstrating a degree of life experience and well-roundedness. By all means, discuss international honours, notable publications or even recent stage productions. Remember to reflect on these experiences, offering explanations of how they have changed your attitude towards life or how they required particular dedication and commitment.

- Musical instruments – Again, an excellent form of stress relief but also a great example of manual dexterity if your course requires this. Do not be afraid to mention your favourite musical works for that personal touch, but also any grades you have obtained, thus, demonstrating commitment and a mature attitude that can be transferred to any field of study.

- Work experience(s) – Don't bother wasting characters by citing references or contacts from your work experience, but rather discuss situations that you were presented with. Describe any situations where you showed particular maturity/professionalism and explain what you learnt from that experience. It is always advisable to discuss how your work experience affected your view of the subject field, either reinforcing or deterring you from your choice.

- Personal interests within the field of study – This is a really good opportunity to show off your own genuine academic interest within the subject field. Try to mention a recent article or paper; one that isn't too contentious but is still not that well-known to show depth of reading. Reflect on what you have read, offering your own opinions, but be warned, you will almost certainly be called upon this at the interview if you have one.

- Personal attributes – exemplify these through your own personal experiences and opinions. As mentioned previously, many courses will list "desired" personal attributes in their prospectus - you must include these as a minimum in your personal statement. Try to add others of your own choice that you think are relevant to the subject in order to achieve originality – here are a few to inspire you:
  o Honesty
  o Communication skills
  o Teamwork
  o Decision making

- o Awareness of limitations
- o Respect
- o Morality
- o Ability to learn
- o Leadership
- o Integrity

- Awards – be they national or just departmental school awards, it is always worth trying to mention any awards you have received since about the age of 15/16. A brief description of what they entailed and what you learnt from the experience can add a valuable few lines to your personal statement. Providing proof of long-term dedication and prowess.

Together, discussion of all these points can demonstrate reasoned consideration for the course you have applied for. This is particularly appealing for a tutor to read as it shows a higher level of thinking by giving your own reflection on the course requirements.

THE CONCLUSION

The conclusion of your personal statement should be more about leaving a good final impression than conferring any actual information. If you have something useful to say about your interest and desire to study your subject, you shouldn't be waiting until the very end to say it!

Admissions tutors will read hundreds of personal statements every year, and after about the fifth one, they all start looking very much the same. You should try to make your statement different so it stands out amongst the rest. As the conclusion is the last thing the admissions tutor will read, it can leave a lasting influence (good or bad!) The purpose of a conclusion is to tie up the entire statement in two or three sentences.

A good conclusion should not include any new information, as this should be in the main body. However, you also need to avoid repeating what you have said earlier in your personal statement. This would be both a waste of characters and frustration for the tutor. Instead, it is better to put into context what you have already written and, therefore, make an effort to keep your conclusion relatively short – no more than four lines.

The conclusion is a good opportunity to draw on all the themes you have introduced throughout your personal statement to form a final overall character image to leave the tutor with. Unless there is anything especially extraordinary or outrageous in the main body of your personal statement, the tutor is likely to remember you by your introduction and conclusion. The conclusion, therefore, is a good place to leave an inspiring final sentence for the tutor.

Some students will make a mention in here about their career plans, picking up on something they have observed in work experience or have encountered during reading. This can be a good strategy as it shows you're using your current knowledge to guide your future aspirations. If you do this, try to do so with an open mind, suggesting areas of interest but being careful not to imply you are less interested in others. You don't want to sound like you are interested in X-Ray Crystallography and *only* X-Ray Crystallography, this will tell the admissions tutor that you may be quite short on real-world experience and will likely struggle on their course. You have to spend a long time at university and your interests are likely to change depending on your experiences. Thus, admissions tutors need to be certain your interest extends into all areas. Secondly, don't sound too fixed about your plans, there is a lot more to see before you can make an informed career choice so by all means show your particular interests but avoid sounding as though you are closing any options off.

It is also very important to avoid sounding too arrogant here and over-selling yourself. Instead, adopt a phrase looking forward in time – perhaps expressing your excitement and enthusiasm in meeting the demands of your course requirements, or looking even further ahead, the demands of your career. E.g. *'driven by my love of medicine, I am sure that I will be a successful doctor and take full advantage of all opportunities should this application be successful'*, rather than *'I think I should be accepted because I am very enthusiastic and will work hard'*. The sentiment behind both of these statements is positive, however, the second sounds juvenile compared to the first.

Depending on the situation, it may be possible to end a personal statement with a famous quote or saying. If you decide to do this, ensure that you don't quote anything outrageous or controversial!

Extra Reading
Reading beyond what you would need to for your school studies is a great way to show genuine enthusiasm; a good personal statement will include at least some discussion of extra reading.

It also has the added benefit of suggesting your areas of particular interest which can help guide the interview discussion to your strongest topics.

Make sure you don't fall into the trap of thinking a long list of books will impress – this isn't the point, the admissions tutors will already know that you can read books. **The idea is you show what you have learned** from each of the books and how it has influenced your decision to study your chosen course. This shows that you haven't just looked at the pages of the text as you've turned them over, but rather that you have understood and thought about them. When discussing your learning, try to make specific points rather than generic ones.

For example, a weaker statement might say: "I read Thinking Fast and Slow by Daniel Kahneman, which helped me understand the way by which decisions are made"

Whereas a stronger statement may say: "I particularly enjoyed Thinking Fast and Slow by Daniel Kahneman, which made me realise the importance of shortcuts in making quick and accurate decisions."

Extra-Curricular

It is important to show you are a balanced person and not someone whose only focus is work. Extra-curricular activities can really strengthen your personal statement by showcasing your skills. Remember that there is no intrinsic value in playing county-level rugby or having a diploma in acting – you will not win a place on excellence in these fields. The value comes from the skills your activities teach you. Regardless of whether you're outstanding at what you do or you just do it casually, remember to reflect on what you've gained from doing what you do. There will always be something good to say and it may be more valuable than you think.

There are three important ways that extra-curricular activities can strengthen your application:

I. You should use your extra-curricular activities to highlight skills that will help with your degree. You play football – talk about how this has helped your teamwork; you play chess – surely this has improved your problem-solving? By linking what you do to the skills you've developed, you take a great opportunity to show the admissions tutor just how well-rounded you are. By showing how you have developed these critical skills, you can demonstrate that you're a strong applicant.

2. Interests outside work give you a way to relax. University studies can be stressful, and admissions tutors have a duty of care towards students. By accepting someone who knows how to relax, they are ensuring you'll strike the right balance between studies and relaxation, keeping yourself fresh and healthy through difficult times.

3. Showing that you have enough time for extra-curricular activities can support your academic capabilities. If you are a member of an orchestra, a sports team, and you keep a rock collection, you were clearly not pushed to the absolute limit to get the top grades you achieved. For a student without other interests, it might suggest to the admissions tutor they are struggling to keep up with the current workload and may not be able to cope with the additional demands of higher education.

WORK EXPERIENCE

Work experience is a great way to demonstrate your commitment to your subject. For many vocational courses like medicine, dentistry, law, and veterinary sciences, work experience must form a core component of the personal statement. Studying such courses is a significant life decision and the course tutors want to see that candidates have made an informed decision on their career path. It is, of course, useful to conduct work experience for other courses simply for your own information and to see what you enjoy.

WHY WORK EXPERIENCE?

Universities value work experience so highly because it shows you have essential traits:

Work experience shows you're informed. So, you're deciding what you want to do for the rest of your working life, how do you know you'll like it? Rather than choosing your subject simply due to the media or stories you hear from others, the best way to convince the admissions tutor you know what the job actually entails is to go and experience it for yourself. Getting as much varied work experience as possible to show that you have a realistic understanding of the profession better than any words can. If you have good work experience, admissions tutors are confident you're choosing your subject for the right reasons.

Work experience shows you're committed. Arranging work experience can be hard – you may need to approach multiple people and organisations before you get a yes. Therefore, if you have a good portfolio of work experience, it shows you have been proactive. It shows you have gone to effort for the sole purpose of spending your free time in a caring environment. This shows drive and commitment – impressive qualities that will help you gain that valuable place!

44

Arranging Work Experience

Arranging work experience can be hard. If you're finding it difficult to get exactly what you want, please don't be disheartened. You are facing the same difficulty that tens of thousands of students before you have faced.

With work experience, you're recommended to start early. The earlier you start making approaches to people, the more likely it is you'll get a yes in time. It is not really practical to start seeking work experience until after you turn 16 due to age restrictions within the workplace – especially where confidential information is concerned! So, conduct your work experience during the summer after your GCSE examinations and throughout your AS year. This can be achieved through private arrangements you yourself make but it is always worth consulting your school's careers officer as well.

Remember that any part-time/summer paid jobs also count as work experience and are definitely worth mentioning, as they show an additional degree of maturity and professionalism. In addition, if you are able to keep up a small regular commitment over a period of months it really helps to show dedication.

During the work experience itself, it is wise to keep a notebook or a diary with a brief description of each day, particularly noting down what events happened and, importantly, what you learnt from them. Whilst there is a designated section of the UCAS form for work experience details, the personal statement itself must be used to not only describe your experiences but also to reflect on them.

Make sure to discuss:

- How did certain situations affect you personally?
- How did the experience alter your perspective on the subject field?
- Were there particular occasions where you fulfilled any of the requirements listed within prospectuses?

45

- Most importantly, how did your experience(s) confirm your desire to pursue the field of study into higher education?

Applying for Different Subjects

Applicants who choose to apply for different subjects will have to address this in their personal statement as this is the only place in which the applicant can justify their choices to their chosen universities.

Applicants who decide to apply for different subjects fall into three categories. The first apply for multi-disciplinary subjects, where subject areas overlap. The second apply for dual honours degrees and the third apply for subjects which bear no relation to one another at all.

Multi-Disciplinary Subjects

The most common degree courses which fall into this category are subjects like Natural Sciences and Modern Languages. Multi-disciplinary degrees generally involve studying a broad range of subjects for the first one or two years of university and specialising in the third or fourth year. However, all of the subjects offered within the multi-disciplinary degree will be from the same broad subject area, like the sciences or humanities.

Applicants for such courses may decide to apply for multi-disciplinary degrees to some universities, and not others. In any case, it is important for applicants in this situation to mention in their personal statement their motivations for the parts of the multi-disciplinary degree relevant to their interests (therefore, covering the universities to which they have applied to study those single subjects) and to also state their desire to gain a broad understanding of their chosen subject area. This is because although applicants for such courses will almost certainly not have substantial experience in all of the subjects covered by their chosen multi-disciplinary degree, they will be required to complete all compulsory modules across all of the subject areas covered by the degree. The reader of the personal statement atm universities offering multi-disciplinary degrees must be left in no doubt that the applicant has the desire and capacity to learn about new subjects in addition to those they are familiar with, and those from universities offering single subjects must believe that the applicant is motivated to study their chosen individual subject at university.

DUAL HONOURS DEGREES

Unlike the US, dual honours degrees are not common in the UK. A few examples of dual honours degrees offered by UK universities include Physics & Philosophy (Oxford), PPE (Oxford), Maths & Computer Science (many). One notable exception to the general UK university trend is Keele University, which offers dual honours courses for all subjects.

Applications for dual honours degrees should be treated in the same way as those for a single subject, with the exception that equal attention should be given to both/all subjects in the degree. All dual honours degrees are different, and it is up to the applicant to ensure that they are aware of the make-up of their chosen degree. Some dual honours may be split 50/50 between two subjects, whereas others may have a major component and a minor component. This needs to be reflected in the personal statement.

Non-Related Subjects

This is undoubtedly the hardest situation for an applicant to prepare for. As the same personal statement will be sent to all universities, there will be parts of the personal statement that apply to some and not to others. For those in this situation, it will be necessary to sacrifice parts of the personal statement otherwise reserved for extra-curricular activities and interests for reasons to why each chosen course is applicable to the applicant.

If the courses chosen by the application fall within the same subject remit, e.g. Biology and Chemistry as separate subjects (but are both sciences) or English and History (but are both humanities), it is possible for the applicant to describe their interest in both, tactfully. Describing interest in areas of overlap between different subjects in addition to that for each individual subject is a safe way in which the applicant can ensure that their personal statement is applicable to all of their chosen universities.

THE REFERENCE

The UCAS reference is often neglected by many applicants; it's an untapped resource that can give you an edge over other applicants. In order to plan your use of the reference, you first need to establish how it will be used – again consult prospectuses or subject websites. Does it actually count towards your application score or rather is it only consulted in borderline candidates? Furthermore, the reference could certainly affect the way in which the tutor perceives what you have written and indeed what they infer from it.

Either way, in order to get the most out of your reference you need to actively participate in its creation. The best way to achieve this is to ask a teacher who you are particularly friendly with to write it. Even if this is not possible, ask for a copy of your reference before it is submitted to UCAS. This way you can ensure that the personal statement and reference complement one another for maximum impact.

The reference is best used for explanations of negative aspects within your application, like deflated exam results, family bereavements – or even additional information if you run out of space in your personal statement. In this respect, the reference is a backdoor through which you can feed more information to the tutor in order to strengthen your application.

If there is a teacher who is willing to go through your reference with you (this is particularly advisable for medicine, dentistry, law, and veterinary science applicants); complete a final draft of your personal statement first before starting on the reference itself. This way you will have a clear idea of the content and tone of the majority of your application as well as anything that may be missing which you would like to add.

The reference is the one place for your teachers to be completely unreserved - superlatives and compliments mean a lot more coming from someone other than yourself. One such example of this is the opportunity for your teachers to discuss how they have actively noticed your initiative and passion, going above and beyond in pursuing the subject in question.

Standing Out from the Crowd

Admissions tutors read hundreds of personal statements, so to be in with the best chance yours should offer something a bit different to leave a lasting good impression of yourself.

Now standing out from the crowd is easy, but the line between standing out for the right and the wrong reasons is a fine one and you have to be careful.

Many universities will score your personal statement based on a marking grid. You'll gain marks for evidence of performance in different areas depending on your assessed level of achievement. These areas may include interest in your subject, a variety of work experience, evidence of altruism/volunteering, communication skills, and general skills. It is a very good idea to get hold of these marking grids wherever possible and ensure you cover all the areas described in them. The best place to find them is the university website and failing that, you can email the admissions tutors at the university.

Proof-reading the personal statement is extremely important – not just by yourself, but also by friends, family, and teachers to get their opinions. Firstly, it's so easy to ignore your own mistakes because as you become familiar with your own work, you begin skimming through rather than reading in depth. But also, this allows people to assess the writing style – by gathering lots of opinions you can build up a good idea of the strongest areas (which you should expand) and the weakest areas (which you should modify and trim down).

Don't try to force anything into the personal statement. Allow it to grow and showcase your wide variety of skills. Make sure there is a smooth flow from one idea to the next. Allow it to tell your story. Make sure all the spelling and grammar is accurate. Then, your personal statement will shine out from the average ones to give you the best possible chance.

INTERVIEWS

In any interview, you can expect to be asked questions about the content of your personal statement – these could be on your work experience, your reading, your extra-curricular activities and so on. This makes it especially important to be completely honest. We don't mean just avoiding explicit lies – this includes all the little traps that are so easy to fall into – the book you intend to read, the course you'll probably attend and so on. That book you were genuinely planning to read might turn out to be terrible but you're then committed to reading it front to back in case your interviewer probes your interest in it.

But this isn't all bad news – **it can actually be a very positive thing**. By writing about all the subjects that interest you most in your personal statement, you have the opportunity to guide the interview towards those areas you love, know most about, and would enjoy discussing. By doing so, you give yourself an opportunity to show your knowledge and enthusiasm to the interviewer – traits which will go a long way in convincing them you are the right person to fill that elusive place.

Therefore, it is important that you use your personal statement as part of your interview preparation. Read and re-read your statement before the interview to make certain you are ready to talk about anything you may be asked questions about. Not only does this give you a great chance of answering these questions well, it can give you an overall feeling of assurance that you are well-prepared, lending confidence to make your overall performance more polished. What's more, if you have all your personal statement information at the front of your mind, answering general questions about your experiences is much easier as you have a great bank of information to quickly draw upon.

Omissions

It can be difficult to work out exactly where the line stands when it comes to omitting certain information.

Of course, you should only include things that emphasise your best points. But sometimes leaving certain things out can cause problems.

For example, let's imagine you worked for half an hour a month at a care home over a 6-month period. If you said in your personal statement you had worked at a care home for 6 months, you could reasonably expect interview questions on it. When it turns out you've only spent three hours there in total, the interviewer would not be impressed and would be left doubting the truthfulness of the whole personal statement. Far better to just say you arranged a few sessions helping in a care home, then discuss what you learned from it and avoid the risk of being left looking like a fool.

Another circumstance when not to omit details is when there is something that needs explaining. Perhaps you've taken a year out of the normal education pathway to do something different or because you were experiencing some difficulty. Whilst the personal statement is not the place to discuss extenuating circumstances, it should tell the story of your recent path through life. If there are any big gaps, it is likely to concern the person reading it that you have something to hide. Make sure you explain your route and the reasons for it, putting it in the context of your journey towards your chosen course and potentially beyond.

THINGS TO AVOID

Whilst there are no rights and wrongs to writing a personal statement, there are a few common traps students can easily fall into. Here are a few things that are best to be avoided to ensure your personal statement is strong.

Stating the obvious – this includes phrases like "I am studying A-level biology which has helped me learn about human biology in the human biology module". Admissions tutors can see from the UCAS form what A-level subjects you are studying. They know that most applicants study broadly similar A-levels so you don't stand out, and the statement about what you have learned is obvious. This does little to convince someone you are suited for your course, so therefore, it is a waste of words.

University names – the same personal statement goes to all universities, so don't include any university names. Only include specifics of the course if they are common to all the courses you are applying to.

Lists – everything needs to be included for a reason. Very few things have an intrinsic value, rather the value comes from the knowledge you gain and the skills you develop by doing the activities. Therefore, reeling off a long list of sports you play won't impress anyone. Instead, focus on specifics and indicate what you have learned from doing each thing you mention.

Flattery – this includes flattery of either people or universities. Saying how much you dream of studying your course, entering a certain career or how much you admire someone's work will not win you a place.

Harsh criticism – it's great to show two sides of anything and it's perfectly acceptable to disagree with things, however, it is wise to avoid excessively strong criticism of anything for two reasons. Firstly, you are still early in your academic journey. Questioning established knowledge makes a good student, but dismissing the work of eminent academics will make you seem ignorant and should be avoided. Secondly, you never know who is going to interview you – it could be the person you are criticising, or a close friend or work colleague of theirs. There have been multiple examples of Cambridge interviews where a student had strongly criticised a book in their personal statement, and guess who the interviewer turned out to be... This can sometimes be by design, a colleague will be the first to read your statement, and they'll pass it on to the book's author as a result of your critique.

Details about your A-level subjects – your A-levels are included on your UCAS form and admissions tutors know the content of different A-level courses. Admissions tutors are looking for ways you are unique and have differentiated yourself from others. Discussing normal school curricula does not achieve this. However, if you have been part of an interesting project/presentation or have won an award in one of your A-level subjects, then absolutely, you should discuss that.

Things that happened before GCSE – if something started when you were nine and you have continued it up until today then you should absolutely include it as it shows great commitment and the opportunity to develop many skills. However, if you are considering mentioning the archery you stopped four years ago, please resist the temptation. Putting something that finished a long time ago signals to the reader that you don't have much going on now – not the impression you want to be making.

Include books you haven't read – this is risky. Even if you genuinely intend to read the book, you can't make any intelligent observations about it if you haven't done so yet. In addition, you are then committed to finishing it even if you find it very dull or you risk being caught out in an interview. Stick to things you have already read. If you don't have much to say, pick some short books and journal articles and make a start today!

Starting too late – the later you begin writing, the harder you make the task. By starting early, you can do little and often, making it a much more enjoyable experience. You get more time to review, proof-read, and show it to others. And by considering your personal statement early, you have the chance to do extra things to fill in any gaps or weak areas that you spot.

Extenuating circumstances – the personal statement is to tell your story. It is not the place for extenuating circumstances. If any are applicable, this is for teachers to write in the reference. Make sure you know who is writing it and meet with them to help explain the full story.

Plagiarism – it goes without saying that you must not plagiarise, but we feel no "things to avoid" list would be complete without the most important point. Plagiarism of another personal statement is the easiest way to get yourself into big trouble. UCAS use sophisticated detection software and if any significant match shows up (not necessarily the whole statement, just a few identical sentences are enough) then the universities you apply to will be notified and are likely to blacklist your application.

Power words

These are words which can give a more proactive and engaging feel to your writing. The following list is provided for you to dip into – you will find that including just a few of these words in the correct context can help to strengthen the writing (don't overuse them!)

Absorbed	Established	Minimised	Reorganised
Accomplished	Exceeded	Modernised	Secured
Achieved	Expanded	Monitored	Spearheaded
Analysed	Explored	Moved	Streamlined
Assembled	Formulated	Obtained	Strengthened
Attended	Gained	Organised	Targeted
Authored	Improved	Overhauled	Taught
Awarded	Influenced	Participated	Trained
Broadened	Initiated	Prevented	Transformed
Collaborated	Instigated	Promoted	Underlined
Committed	Integrated	Protected	Understood
Communicated	Learned	Purchased	Undertook
Created	Led	Pursued	Updated
Customised	Listened	Qualified	Upgraded
Determined	Maximised	Ranked	Valued
Enabled	Manoeuvred	Recognised	Volunteered
Enthused	Mentored	Realised	Won

USING THE STATEMENTS IN THIS BOOK

This collection contains 100+ personal statements. Each one is an actual personal statement that was successful in getting the applicant into their chosen university.

For each statement, we've included details that show which universities it was successful in. This is included for interest and we don't suggest you over-analyse. It might be useful to take a slightly closer look at any that were successful for your top choices, but always bear in mind that the similarities between different universities are much greater than the differences, and in any case, you have to write a personal statement equally applicable to all of your choices.

All personal statements come with comments, drawing your attention to the stronger and weaker points of that personal statement. Don't look immediately at this. First, read the personal statement yourself and get a feeling for the general style of writing. Then, test yourself: decide which you think the strongest and weakest parts are. After that, look at the comments on the statement. By using the book this way, you **develop your own critical reading skills**, which you can then apply to your own personal statement, allowing you to build in improvements.

We include these personal statements for several reasons including:

- To show you different ways of showing passion for your subject
- To help you gauge what a good balance is between different sections
- To prove there are many different routes to success
- To suggest ideas of high-impact phrases to use
- To give insight into the many work experience options that exist
- To show how you can link experiences to skills and learning

- To show you that writing a successful statement is within your reach
- To help you assess when your personal statement may be nearly ready

---

IT CANNOT BE OVERSTRESSED HOW IMPORTANT IT IS THAT YOU DO NOT COPY FROM THESE PERSONAL STATEMENTS

UCAS uses anti-plagiarism software called Copycatch. This software checks your submission against all previous personal statements and any in your year of entry too. If any significant similarity is detected, then all universities you apply to will be notified. You can use the examples for inspiration and comparison, but everything you write in your own statement must be your own original work and must be completely truthful to you.

A final word of warning. We are aware there are companies and individuals who will write personal statements for you. We strongly recommend against getting anyone else to write your personal statement. In doing so, you run the risk that they are plagiarising material without you knowing; jeopardising your entire application. Even if they don't, you will be inevitably less familiar with the material at interview - how will you answer questions like "why did you write x" reliably? In addition, this will breach the declaration that the statement is your own original work. Follow our top tips, take inspiration from the examples, and put in some hard work – you'll be sure to produce an excellent personal statement.

EXAMPLE PERSONAL STATEMENTS

SCIENCES

MEDICINE

Subject: Medicine

Helping to care for children during work experience this summer at an HIV clinic in Botswana has strengthened my determination to pursue a career in medicine. It was emotionally challenging to witness children suffering, but I was inspired by the tremendous efforts of the team to help improve the lives of their patients.

→ Columbia app

My interest in medicine stems from my fascination with science and has been consolidated through work experience placements in general practice, radiology, pathology and pharmacy. One experience that has left a lasting impression was a rare opportunity of observing a newborn on ECMO whilst shadowing a Radiologist at University Hospital, Southampton. It was eye-opening to see how the pediatric intensive care team worked hard to keep the baby alive. I have gained an insight into the breadth of careers within medicine and the incredible teamwork that occurs behind the scenes during work experience with a Pathologist at Whittington Hospital. At Barnes Surgery, sitting in on GP consultations gave me an opportunity to see how building rapport and utilizing good communication skills can help in building a professional and supportive relationship, giving the patient ownership over their treatment. Attending a Medlink course enabled me to learn from the experiences of different specialists.

Skills

Learning about the complexities of the human body in Biology sparked my curiosity to learn more in Chemistry and understand the relationship between drugs and the medical conditions they are targeted to treat. To further my interest in science I took part in the 'Siemens - The Next Big Thing' national competition, which my team won with an idea of a desalination plant providing purified water and cheap electricity for less-developed countries. Another inspirational experience was being awarded a scholarship for the Honeywell Leadership Academy at the US Space Centre where I developed leadership and teamwork skills through STEM based challenges.

Motivated by my experience in Botswana, I undertook an EPQ on the prevention of HIV transmission in Africa, focusing on the latest advances in treatments and the necessity of education and social support. To research for this project, and to generally learn about advances in medicine, I have attended lectures focusing on new treatments for HIV, cancer relapses and Parkinson's disease and have read related articles in the Biological Sciences Review. All this has helped to develop my analytical and independent research skills.

Outside school, volunteering at a care home for the elderly, where I organise activities and assist with feeding, has given me a deeper understanding of the palliative care of the elderly. I have developed my ability to interact with young children from working at Kumon Maths over the past two years. I have a passion for music and have taught myself to play the piano and drums and have been a long-term member of the school choir.

At school, I have been awarded prizes in English, Maths and Science. I am also a keen sportsperson and have been awarded Borough sports prizes in netball, tennis and athletics. I have set up a school basketball team and organized professional coaching. I volunteered for a year-long National Social Enterprise competition to raise funds for the Wings of Hope children's charity and out of five hundred competing teams, my team won one of the five top prizes. Being Head of House and a member of the Head Girl Team has enhanced my time management, interpersonal and communication skills. Through a month-long expedition to Mongolia and the Gold DofE award, I have improved my problem solving, organization and teamwork skills and have learnt to work well under pressure.

My experiences have shown me that medicine is a challenging and demanding profession, however, I believe that I have the determination, intellectual curiosity and commitment to undertake the vast level of lifelong learning that medicine is going to entail.

Universities Applied to:

- University College London: Offer
- Imperial College London: Rejected
- Birmingham: Rejected
- Bristol: Interview + Rejected

Good Points:

A well-written and well-structured statement. It provides a good overview of a very diverse education career, covering a variety of medically relevant topics. The student clearly has spent a lot of time and effort gearing her education towards studying medicine. Having diverse experiences is definitely helpful as it shows determination and dedication to the subject matter.

Bad Points:

The entire statement presents essentially a list of different achievements. There is very little information on the student's original motivation for studying medicine. Whilst it starts well with the emotional side of experiences gathered during work experience in Botswana, the student fails to provide any reason for studying medicine other than her interest in science. This is a let-down as most students applying for medicine will have a scientific interest, so this student's interest doesn't signify much. In addition, simply listing achievements can easily come across as bragging. There is a very fine line between providing an insight into previous accomplishments and showing off, and it's important that you are showcasing your relevant skills and abilities in a modest way.

Overall:

The statement is strong but would have been a lot stronger if the student had managed to tie her experiences closer to the motivation for studying medicine. Whilst it is good to provide a list of achievements in a competitive course such as medicine, listing them without purpose has little effect. Most medical applicants will have a history of academic excellence and diverse medical work experience, what is going to make a difference for the application is the connection between previous achievement and the relevance for medicine.

NOTES

Subject: Medicine

"I haven't eaten all day and I don't know if I will last the night". This is one of forty similar messages left within an hour on my house answering machine and was one of the first signs of my Grandma's dementia. I began to read books on dementia as she deteriorated further which helped us cope with the challenges ahead. She has been diagnosed with Vascular Dementia and our family has been in close contact with Primary Care and the community mental health team. I was moved by their compassion and unique work ethic, which motivated me to pursue a career in Medicine.

Keen to learn more about medicine, I attended a Medical Taster Weekend at King's College London. I learned about the process of becoming a doctor and the importance of listening and history taking. Soon afterwards, I arranged work experience on the Gastroenterology Ward at Epsom General Hospital. My most memorable patient was a 70-year-old man who came in with jaundice; I accompanied doctors throughout the diagnostic process. It was detective-like; running blood tests and CT scans with the results unfortunately showing he had liver cancer. This amplified the low-points in medicine, that as a doctor you will be dealing with people at their most vulnerable moments, however seeing the doctors providing the patient individual and holistic care was uplifting. I appreciated the multidisciplinary team working together to aid his physical and emotional recovery. I have now completed 10 weeks of work experience. Having spent a week in an Endocrine Clinic I have become fascinated by Diabetes and its current and future treatments. I recently read an article about commercially available continuous glucose monitors, which soon will be used alongside artificial pancreases.

Volunteering in a government hospital in Gambia for a month affirmed my career choice in medicine. I realized the importance of empathy in Medicine as I assisted with a prolonged labor where the mother tragically died, speaking to the family afterwards was the most difficult task I have ever undertaken, but I was proud to say "Everyone tried their very best."

The whole experience was emotionally challenging as all around me patients were suffering from illnesses that could be prevented by improvements in infrastructure and education. Nevertheless, it was inspiring seeing the medical team-work assiduously to achieve the best results possible.

For the past year, I have been volunteering at a care home for adults with learning disabilities. Maintaining composure was difficult, particularly when they would throw tantrums or refuse to eat, but I have enjoyed the patient interaction and it has developed my interpersonal skills. This experience has given me the confidence to spend nine weeks in a Summer Camp in America with children who have learning disabilities.

I have been competing nationally in swimming for 5 years, and now have completed my National Pool Lifeguard Qualification, which required me to learn first aid. My first aid skills became useful on my Duke of Edinburgh Gold expedition when a team member scalded their hand with hot water. D of E has also given me the opportunity to develop team-working skills and learn British Sign Language.

In Year 13, I was awarded school prizes in Math and Chemistry, and the Pickle prize for outstanding charitable endeavors. I was also awarded the prestigious Silver UKMT Award for scoring in the top 12% of a national maths competition.

Last year, I volunteered in a national social-enterprise scheme, to raise money and awareness for the Wings of Hope Charity. Out of 500 teams, my team was invited to the House of Lords and presented with one of five prizes for raising over £3000.

Through my experiences I understand the challenges that come with a career in Medicine but my scientific curiosity, empathetic nature and sheer determination are all attributes that will help me become a great doctor.

Universities Applied to:

- Sheffield: Offer
- Liverpool: Offer
- Glasgow: Rejected
- Leeds: Offer

Good points:

Well-written and good style. Excellent personal entry into the statement. Giving insight into what motivates the student to pursue a career in medicine is centrally important. Having a concrete case to tie this motivation to is helpful as it gives the statement a human and individual touch and also provides material to discuss during the interview. The student also displays extensive work experience, which is a strength.

Bad points:

Whilst the statement gives insight into various medical experiences in the past, it only superficially ties them to new skills learned. This is important because work experiences only really have a purpose if they help to further the student's abilities. The achievements section at the end of the statement is somewhat at the wrong place. Whilst the achievements are impressive, listing them must serve a purpose that shows personal development.

Overall:

Overall, this is a good statement. The strengths definitely lie in the personal touch with the motivation to study medicine. Unfortunately, it loses strength as the student fails to tie previous experiences to lessons learned that are relevant to studying medicine. This is a pity as the student has quite extensive past experiences that certainly provided very relevant learning points.

NOTES

Subject: Medicine

Sitting in front of Mrs D, beside the Royal Marsden consultant I was shadowing, I realised that as a doctor, treating a patient's emotional concerns is just as important as treating the actual disease. A simple smile can work wonders. I also learnt how successful and worthwhile the mammography screening programme was, causing a 15% reduction in mortality rates. However, an article in the student BMJ made me think about the possible emotional, financial and physical stresses that overdiagnosis can cause. At Medlink I was excited to start developing my own practical skills by using an ophthalmoscope. I was then amazed whilst witnessing a bronchoscopy, at both the doctor's anatomical knowledge and dexterity. On my work experience on a respiratory ward at East Surrey Hospital I was struck by the seamless coordination of doctors, nurses, lab scientists and specialist teams. Doctors must be able to act as a leader within a team, so that the patients feel comfortable and secure.

At the Royal Marsden, seeing medicine as an academic pursuit as well as a practical one, cemented my passion for the field. I became inspired to read The Molecular Biology of Cancer by Lauren Pecorino and Cancer by Paul Scotting which, whilst fascinating, left me eager for more answers than they (or current research) could provide. As stem cells' infinite ability to divide is drawn from the up-regulation of telomerase - as for cancer cells - does this feature cause them to acquire so many mutations that they end up inextricably linked to tumorigenesis? Furthermore, is cancer an inevitable price we pay for life? It was then, through studying depolarisation and the cardiac cycle in biology, that I started to wonder why malignant cardiac tumours are so rare. I find the extent of current research awe inspiring but was also excited to discover that in every avenue of medicine I looked, I had so many questions that are still, as yet, unanswerable. — why I want

good shift

Medicine also requires strong interpersonal skills. Helping out at The School for Profound Education was daunting and had a steep learning curve for me, especially the challenge of communicating wholly non-verbally. However, I found that devoting my time to the care and support of these children through a range of activities from changing feed bags to wheelchair barn dancing was immensely satisfying. Helping the 'learners' to enjoy life's full potential made me realise, that despite the huge commitment, being a doctor and dedicating yourself to ensuring people get the most out of their lives would always be rewarding and worthwhile. I was also interested to learn and research further the conditions some of the children had a common example among the girls being Retts syndrome.

I have been elected as a Senior Prefect and also House Captain at my school. Finding time to relax is vital in medicine and I find playing guitar (grade VI) and piano perfect for me to do so. I have enjoyed engaging with German both in and outside of school, as an exciting opportunity to learn not just a language but also more about a foreign culture; participating in various international exchanges has enabled me to appreciate this first-hand.

I developed teamwork skills on my Gold Duke of Edinburgh expedition, and have been Club Captain of my swimming club for the last two years. Through perseverance and determination I have pushed myself to succeed in competitions and I strive to approach academic life with a similar drive. As a voluntary ASA qualified swimming teacher, and through teaching English skills at my school, I have had valuable experience of the challenges of helping, leading and interacting with young children - in particular when I had to clear the pool and improvise a session in an emergency.

I aspire to be the doctor aiding Mrs D through such tough times. When I retire I hope to be able to look back on my career and know that I have made a positive impact on society. Medicine would allow me to achieve this.

Universities applied to:

- Oxford: Offer
- Sheffield: Interview + Rejected
- Bristol: Interview + Rejected
- Edinburgh: Rejected

Good points:

The student demonstrates some good reflections on their work experience. This is very relevant as the experience only really becomes relevant for providing strength to the statement if it is put into the right context and met with adequate reflection from the student's side. The student correctly underlines the correlation of soft and academic skills in the practice of medicine. This is important as it is a commonly underestimated relationship. In addition to the clinical work experience, the student also provides a good range of non-clinical experiences that all contribute to their personal development. Particularly relevant in this context are lessons learned teaching as well as communication skills.

Bad points:

At instances, the statement lacks a clear structure and a clear message. The information provided is a little all over the place. This is a pity as the unorganised structure makes it very difficult to follow the content and learn about the student, which significantly weakens the overall expressive power of the statement. In addition, the statement remains vague and does not deliver the full extent of reflections on experiences possible. This leaves the statement superficial and falling short of the potential expressive strength.

Overall:

An average statement that is, unfortunately, let down by some stylistic and content weaknesses that make it difficult to draw the maximum amount of information about the student from the statement. With some more or less minor improvements to structure and depth of reflection, this statement could be very strong. In the form presented here, it does provide some insight into the student's character and into what they consider important, but the statement sells itself short due to lack of detail.

NOTES

Subject: Medicine

For me, medicine offers an academically and mentally challenging profession which amalgamates my fascination with the human body and my desire to work with a variety of individuals with their own individual problems on a day to day basis. It offers a chance to make a real difference to the lives of others.

69

My passion for the subject has been fuelled by additional reading, namely various books on the brain such as Greenfield's 'Guided Tour of the Brain' and Sacks' 'The Man Who Mistook his Wife for a Hat'. As well as giving me a good grounding in the current understanding of the brain it has revealed how much of it remains a tantalising mystery. I have also borrowed past A level textbooks from school that cover areas of the syllabus that have since been cut such as the anatomy and function of the human eye and I keep up to date with medical affairs using the Science and Health sections of the BBC news website.

I have explored my interest in the subject through work experience. My first placement was with a neurologist who specialised in MS. The one-on-one consultations showed me the all-important need for tact when dealing with difficult issues that needed to be addressed. It also highlighted the great potential for progress in medical research which is exciting for me.

Intro to

During my second week-long placement in a general practice I observed a GP dealing with a broad spectrum of individuals who presented cases ranging from gynaecological issues and chest infections to severe depression and even minor operations. For me, it emphasised the range of skills required to be a doctor: the knowledge of the physiological systems that underpin each illness and how specific treatments will affect these systems, knowledge that has a constant need to be replenished due to advances in medical research and technology; the vital interpersonal skills and clarity of communication required to convey what may be a complicated concept to someone with little scientific knowledge; and even the manual skills involved in thoroughly examining patients and carrying out minor operations.

⌐ going into detail

I volunteer weekly in a residential care home for severely disabled adults, most of whom have acute cerebral palsy. Feeding and brushing the teeth of the residents has taught me a lot about the value of patience and empathy in dealing with the seriously disabled. I thoroughly enjoy getting to know the habits of many of the residents and although none of them has any coherent method of communication each individual has a unique personality that I have come to appreciate over time. While challenging, finding unconventional methods of communication with the residents is very rewarding. Helping the elderly during church events has also highlighted for me the value of care and understanding for fragile individuals. Working with these people has really made me realise that I want to devote my life to using my intelligence, diligence and enthusiasm for the good of others; I think medicine is a natural career choice given this perspective. *he it back*

I believe my extracurricular activities have taught me valuable skills that will prove useful as a medic. I am part of the Nottingham Youth Orchestra and the East Midlands Youth String Orchestra. Playing as a part of these ensembles requires individual prowess as well as an ability to coordinate finely with the many other members of the orchestra. In addition, during my weekly shift at a restaurant I have the role of training new employees which highlights my ability to explain with clarity and to be friendly and welcoming.

Attending Medlink and speaking with doctors and other members of the NHS has made me appreciate how challenging a career in medicine will prove yet I am certain that this is the right choice for me as it offers personal challenge, continual development and the opportunity to make a real difference in people's lives. I hope you will give me the chance to fulfil this aspiration.

Universities applied to:

- Oxford: Offer
- Newcastle: Offer
- Birmingham: Offer
- Bristol: Rejected

Good points:

This is an excellent statement. It is well-written and well-rounded, providing a wide range of insight into the educational career of the student. It also gives a good impression of previous work experience and the student ties these experiences well into the whole picture of medicine. It makes it clear how these experiences have contributed to their choice of medicine as a subject, which is very helpful for an examiner reading this statement. The student also ties his past work experience to lessons learned that they see as relevant for medicine. This is important as work experience can only be useful if it teaches relevant lessons.

Bad points:

The paragraph addressing the interest in the scientific side of medicine is somewhat superficial. Whilst it is good to show interest in anatomy and a desire to stay up to date with current medical developments, this is also something that is expected from students aiming to study medicine. It, therefore, serves little purpose as a distinguishing feature from other applicants.

Overall:

A very good statement that ticks all relevant boxes and only has a few minor weaknesses. These weaknesses have little impact on the overall quality as the student manages to demonstrate a variety of lessons and experiences that support their choice of medicine as a career.

NOTES

Subject: Medicine

The first time I announced I wanted to be a doctor; my parents were amused but indulgent. Their reactions are understandable, considering that I was eight at the time. From a young age I have always been intrigued with the human body and it has only grown from that time. My fascination with science is one of the reasons I want to study Medicine. The continuous learning throughout my career; constant new discoveries and technologies; as well as the variety in each day are part of the attraction of Medicine.

To form a realistic image of a profession in Medicine I have undergone various work experiences which has allowed me patient contact and a chance to observe professionals. I arranged my first two-week placement at St James Hospital, where I learnt basic practice such as data confidentiality and hand hygiene which is becoming more important with the emergence of a new superbug, NDM-1. The following year, I had another two-week placement in Castlehill Hospital, where I gained knowledge of how the management and administration of a hospital operate. This is useful knowledge for understanding how much the government's demands for savings from the NHS will truly affect quality of care. My work experience has strengthened my resolve to pursue a medical career. Volunteering regularly at Harrogate Hospital over the past year has given me recurring interaction with a hospital environment.

My A level choices confirm my enthusiasm for science and demonstrate that I am able to cope with a heavy workload and rise to a challenge, which have already resulted in an achievement of an A* grade in my A-level Mathematics. I enjoy reading and keeping up to date with the latest developments in science; I am a subscriber to "Biological Science Review" and regularly read the "New Scientist". I am currently writing an EPQ on the ethics of organ donation which is self-motivated and gives me a chance to be in charge of my learning. I participated in my school's Medical Package, which enabled me to attend a Hospice Day, hospital tours and lectures and much more. I am also the creator and president of the Medical Debate Society at my school. We meet weekly to discuss common medical controversial topics.

I try to balance my interest in science with a variety of other activities. As a Senior Prefect and a School Council Member, I have excellent organisation, time management and leadership skills, along with the ability to negotiate. My communication and listening skills have developed through my engagement with the Charity Committee, debating clubs, and Netball. As a member of the Boxing club I have learnt self-discipline and determination. I am a philanthropic individual and enjoy assisting others. I am a volunteer at my Sunday school and local library. Paired tutoring is a scheme I am also involved in, where I help a younger student who has difficulty reading. Taking part in the Duke of Edinburgh scheme has shown me the importance of perseverance and motivation to succeed.

I am a focused and determined person with a fierce commitment to studying Medicine. I believe I have the academic capability and drive to succeed in a Medicine course at university. My aspiration is to become a Paediatrician and one of the top experts in my field.

Universities applied to:

- Cambridge: Offer
- Imperial: Offer
- Newcastle: Offer
- University College London: Offer

Good points:

A brilliant, well-written statement that demonstrates a varied history of academic excellence. The student provides good insight into how the early desire to be a doctor has shaped their development, both academically as well as individually. It also shows their understanding of the challenges posed by a medical career, and clear goals which they wish to pursue in that career. This demonstrates great dedication to the subject matter as well as the intellectual and motivational facilities necessary to perform well in a demanding course such as medicine. The student demonstrates good academic performance and discipline.

Bad points:

The statement is very focused on academic performance and academic detail. Personal experiences and lessons learned during patient exposure are somewhat limited, which is a pity as the student shows considerable clinical experience. It would complete and strengthen the picture of academic excellence significantly if the student had been able to add clinical and inter-person lessons learned during their time in the hospital. This includes skills such as communicating information, which is essential in medicine.

Overall:

A good statement providing decent insight into the impressive academic performance of the student. Unfortunately, the student sells themselves somewhat short by ignoring the non-academic side of medicine that is equally as important as academia. Having had the hospital exposure, it would have been easy to add this in order to achieve an even better statement.

NOTES

Subject: Medicine

In the summer of 2014, my grandfather was diagnosed with Parkinson's disease. At the tender age of 11, I was oblivious to the neurological disorder's implications. On a Saturday afternoon that summer, my father suddenly collapsed and had a seizure in the cold foods section of a Sainsburys. I have never been as terrified as I was when I watched froth come out of his mouth. Following this episode, he was diagnosed with photosensitive epilepsy, leaving me shaken and increasingly concerned about my family's health.

I view doctors as leaders in both the medical field and in society. As Head Boy of my school, I strive to do the same among my peers and in my community. I am proud to have won "Student of the Year" twice and to have represented the school varsity football team for three years. I have developed responsibility and communication skills by attending six conferences in four continents for Model United Nations, the highlight of which was leading 800 delegates as President of the General Assembly at DIAMUN, the largest conference in the Gulf region. As President of the Water for Life Club, I raised AED 75,000 (~GBP12,300) for the Aqua Initiative, a UK-based charity that provides clean water to developing nations. Inspired to do more, I embarked on an unforgettable service trip to the Sasenyi Primary School in Kenya, where I immersed myself in the local community by helping with school construction and interacting with children. Back in Dubai, I helped found the Interact Club and served as its President. We initiated frequent visits to the Senses Center, the only residential facility for special needs children in the UAE. Knowing that I can make a difference in the lives of others is something that satisfies me greatly, which further motivates me to pursue medicine.

I was also fortunate enough to attend a three-week Global Leaders Program at Cambridge University and take a fascinating online course by Brown University. From the latter, I developed a fundamental understanding of neuroscience, modern neurotechnology, neurological disorders and scientific writing. With my grandfather in my mind, I created a presentation on Parkinson's disease aimed at relatives of patients. I genuinely take pleasure in knowing that pursuing a medical career is an ongoing process of learning and reflection that will enable me to benefit individuals and society.

I have also gained direct experience in the medical field by shadowing Dr. William Murrell at the Dr. Humeira Badsha Medical Centre in Dubai. We had lengthy discussions about upcoming research papers on gold-induced cytokines, quality and compliance in biologics, platelet-rich plasma and stem cell therapy. In addition, I observed the versatile soft skills he utilized that I could relate to. For example, when working with a conservative woman from Saudi Arabia, he spent more time building trust before treatment. I then spent one insightful week at the Saudi German Hospital, where I shadowed an array of doctors with varied skill sets and specialties, thoroughly observing both real-life surgeries and clinical treatment. Though I was able to satisfy my curiosity to an extent, I am now more interested than ever in pursuing a career in medicine.

This summer, I visited my grandfather only to find out that his condition had worsened. The man who worked from dawn to dusk and still had the energy to take me around Dubai while I was growing up could now barely move across the living room without support; it is a truly heartbreaking sight. I now appreciate the importance of medical care as I understand that patients are not the only ones who suffer, entire families do. It is my dream to pursue medicine as it combines what I strive for - leadership, empathy and initiative, which are characteristics that I believe are most essential for doctors. I feel a drive inside of me, pushing me to become a person who can make a crucial impact on the health and lives of my family, my community and the world.

Universities applied to:

- King's College London: Offer
- Cambridge: Rejected
- Edinburgh: Rejected
- Queen Mary: Offer

Good points:

This is a powerful statement that demonstrates the student's hard work and drive to succeed, with a clear indication of the personal motivation to pursue medicine. Gaining insight into the emotional motivation of this student to pursue a career in medicine is a definite strong point, providing a good impression of the student's character. The student's varied experiences prior to their application all are demonstrated to serve a purpose to make them a better doctor down the line. The student manages to provide an overview of both subject academic knowledge as well as non-academic knowledge, such as communication skills and the doctor-patient relationship. This is important as these lessons are a necessity when practicing medicine.

Bad points:

A significant part of the statement is devoted to extra-curricular pursuits not directly related to medicine, and there is little academic content there, meaning that it is not clear whether the student has any academic interest in medicine - this would be a significant obstacle at any medical school which considered research to be a core component of its course. The skills they spent so much time discussing are all valuable as a doctor, but also in a range of other careers, and it would have really helped this statement to provide either direct links from these experiences to medicine, or some information about the interest and work in the medical field. It would also contribute to the quality of the statement to provide more detail relating to lessons learned from work experiences.

Overall:

A strong statement that gives an excellent impression of the student, providing good insight into their professional skills, but less insight into why they want to study medicine or what they want to do with it. It is clear though, from the considerable range of experiences they have listed, that the student is very driven and highly motivated to successfully complete a medical degree, which is an important point of interest in the personal statement.

NOTES

Subject: Medicine

I realise that medicine may not always have positive outcomes, having witnessed two deaths at a young age. However, the inevitable fallibility of the human body has driven my desire to acquire a better understanding of the complicated processes and mechanisms of our body. I am captivated by the prospect of lifelong learning; the rapid and ceaseless pace of change in medicine means that there is a vast amount of knowledge in an astonishing number of fields.

Work experience and volunteering have intensified my desire to pursue the profession; it gave me the chance to observe doctors diagnosing problems and establishing possible routes of treatment; I found the use of monoclonal antibodies in kidney transplantation fascinating. A doctor needs to be skilled, dexterous and creative. Medicine is a scientific discipline that requires a profound understanding of the physiology of the body, but the application of medicine can be an art, especially when communications between the doctor and the patient can influence the outcome of the treatment. I admire the flexibility of doctors; an inpatient needs to be approached with sensitivity and reassurance, whereas an acute admission patient would benefit more from hands-on assessments. I have been volunteering at Derriford Hospital since 2019. The most valuable part is taking time to converse with the patients to alleviate their stress and appreciate their concerns, demonstrating my understanding of the importance of listening. I appreciate that the quality of life is more important than the quantity of years, as a recent death at the ward made me realise that despite all the technological advances and our increasing understanding of the human body, there is a limit to what we can achieve.

My Nuffield Bursary project was based on finding potential medical treatments for sepsis by working on the molecular genetics of bacteria infected cells. Using theory to interpret laboratory experiments allowed me to show how an enzyme was involved in the inflammatory response mechanism.

My skills of organisation and time management were recognised by the Individual Achievement Award for my role as Finance Director in the Young Enterprise team. I used my leadership skills to assign team members to tasks to which their talents were best suited and demonstrated effective communication and teamwork to meet the deadlines. I took part in the British Mathematical Olympiad after receiving the Gold and Best in School prize for the Senior Maths Challenge last year. Regular participation in the Individual and Team Maths Challenge enhanced my lateral thinking. The numerous awards I have won such as Best Results at GCSE and Bronze in the Physics Olympiad not only show my ability in a range of subjects but also my commitment to my academic career. As a subject mentor, I developed my ability to break down problems, explaining them in a logical, analytical yet simpler way. I cherished the opportunity to work with the younger pupils; enabling them to grasp new concepts, and I believe that discussing ideas, problems or case studies with colleagues will be even more rewarding.

A keen pianist, I have been playing for 14 years. At the age of 12, I became the pianist for the Children's Amateur Theatre Society, a position I still hold. Perseverance was essential as I was learning numerous songs each week showing commitment, resilience and attention to detail, which are transferable skills applicable to medicine. Playing in front of 300 people regularly helped me to build my confidence and taught me to stay calm under pressure. Playing the piano is a hobby that I love and I will continue to pursue it to balance my academic life.

I believe I possess the ability, devotion, diligence and determination required for this course that demands a holistic understanding of both the sciences and the arts. I will relish the challenges on an academic and personal level and I look forward to following this vocation in the future.

Universities applied to:

- Cambridge: Offer
- Imperial College London: Interview + Rejected
- Cardiff: Interview + Rejected
- Bristol: Rejected

Good points:

A well-written statement that guides the reader from one point to the next, delivering good insight into personal development and the motivations to becoming a doctor. The student shows that they have a very diverse background, both academically as well as work experience. One of the strongest parts of the statements is that the student recognises the limitations of medicine and acknowledges the challenges in delivering medical care under those limitations. The student is also able to demonstrate experiences made in non-medical fields and how they contributed to their personal development. This is important as some of the skills necessary to becoming a good doctor are transferable from other professions.

Bad points:

The student provides extensive detail on awards and prizes won, but doesn't elaborate on what these demonstrate. If this was combined with an explanation of how the awards contributed to the lessons learned from work experience it could strengthen the statement considerably. Some prizes, like Bronze in an Olympiad, are not worth the space they take up in the statement, and the characters could be better used elaborating further on what they think they will enjoy about medicine and do well in (it's always worth mentioning Olympiad prizes if you won a Silver or above).

Overall:

A strong statement with a lot of information on the student's development and academic achievements. The statement succeeds at raising interest in the student and providing an overview of the individual's development. There are a few minor weaknesses that could be optimised in order to improve the overall strength of the statement even further.

NOTES

Subject: Medicine

The combination of scientific knowledge, getting actively involved in people's lives and the job satisfaction is what made me choose a career in medicine. I enjoy the reasoning behind science but the complexity of the human mind and illness intrigues me as it can defy logic.

My enthusiasm for science was sparked after learning about topics such as the DNA and nervous control. I was amazed how minute molecules control the whole system. Taking maths has built a desire to solve challenging problems which doctors face on a daily basis. I extensively read about the medical field and after 'Life at Extremes' by Frances Ashcroft I was intrigued how the body reacts to maintain homeostasis. Stirred by my placements, I researched further about Alzheimer's and to what extent it affects people. Through volunteering at a care home, I saw how dementia, a condition where medicine has limited answers, affected patients. Seeing the impact, it had, I was motivated to write an extended project on "Should Physician assisted suicide be legalised in the UK?" After researching about how other countries have implemented it and the impact it has on them I have been able to reach a conclusion of my own.

Listening to talks made by consultants in various fields, I was surprised by the diversity of medicine. In the course I saw a live knee operation through a video link. I was inspired by the precision of the surgery, the impact on the patient's life and the personal satisfaction that this could generate. To understand about the profession, I shadowed doctors and I learnt that versatility and resilience is vital when dealing with acute and chronic problems. These skills were enhanced during my voluntary work at Elhap. By working with children with learnig difficulties, I adapted to their different needs and focused on their individual interests which are crucial when working in the NHS. To help children overcome their anxieties, I tailored activities which encouraged group play and interaction. However, some had little verbal communication, which urged me to be patient and pick up non-verbal cues. Through my voluntary work I have become an attentive listener and developed as a compassionate person; qualities I believe will put me in good stead when I am a doctor.

I am the Deputy Head of School Council. This requires being reliable, liaising with senior management and work through problems with other members of school council to ensure an effective solution is reached. My team-work skills were enriched whilst working towards my Gold Duke of Edinburgh where it was important to be supportive towards other members who struggled trekking the mountains. I realised having the ability to work effectively in a team is key when I observed a multi-disciplinary team make a collaborative decision on the patient's next step regarding treatment.

I feel I maintain a good work life balance. As the leader of the orchestra, I have performed at the Barbican thus developing my teaching skills. I organise and participate in musical evenings for the residents at the care home and I encourage them to take part. Music has made me self-disciplined and effective in time management which will help me cope and prioritise work load in the future. One of the key skills I have developed from volunteering as a lifeguard is foreseeing potential problems which will be helpful as a doctor when promoting health and preventing diseases. My post certificate in LAMDA has made me more articulate and has improved my presentation skills whilst understanding the broader aspect of communication.

Contributing to a vast medical field and to its progress excites me. Although I am aware of some of the challenges that doctors face; breaking bad news, comforting patients in distress and working unsociable hours, I feel I will be privileged to be in a profession where every day is different, brings new challenges and to have the opportunity to impact positively people's lives.

Universities applied to:

- Oxford: Offer
- King's: Offer
- Imperial: Offer
- Nottingham: Offer

Good points:

This is a statement that provides insight into a diverse range of individual interests. The student lists a wide range of academic and work experience-related skills, explaining how they contributed to their desire to study medicine and strengthened their ability to be a good doctor down the line. Offering insight into other sources of learning, such as the school council, shows breadth in their experiences, which contribute to the impression of a well-rounded individual. There is also some relation to the scientific basis of medicine and the student's interest in particular areas of medical research. The student manages to draw satisfactory conclusions from their experiences which is important to achieve a complete picture.

Bad points:

There are some minor points that provide room for improvement. The most obvious one is the numerous and serious grammatical and typographical errors – you might not think that these affect one's ability to practice medicine in a meaningful way, but they suggest a lack of care, poor attention to detail, and a rushed statement, all of which sent bad signals to the admissions tutor about your work ethic. Beyond that, there is also the issue of euthanasia. Whilst it is very interesting that the student has been dealing with this issue and spent time forming an opinion, the personal statement might not be the right place to address this as there is not enough room to sufficiently address the issue in-depth. The student also thought to include mention of the challenges of practicing medicine at the very end, but it is clearly shoehorned in to the statement and reads like a list.

Overall:

A good statement with many strong points and some minor weak ones that could easily be corrected, making space for further elaboration on past experiences.

NOTES

VETERINARY SCIENCES & DENTISTRY

Subject: Veterinary Medicine

My desire to study Veterinary Science originally started due to an interest in animals and a love of science and problem solving. Visits to a local dairy farm and attendance of a Vetlink course gave me an insight into the importance of animals to human life; whether it is for food production, work or enjoyment. By understanding this importance of animals, I gained a better insight into the role of veterinary surgeons in improving animal welfare and health through education and application of science as well as their important role in human welfare and food yields. This ability to improve both animal and human welfare interested and excited me about this field of study and work.

After my initial interest I explored the subject further by spending two weeks at Quarry Veterinary Group, a small animal practice, which led to a Saturday morning job where I have worked closely with the veterinary nurses for a year. I also spent one week at both Frynwy Equine Clinics and Macpherson O'Sullivan (a farm animal practice). By spending time at a variety of practices I have developed an understanding of the day to day role of veterinary professionals in differing areas of the profession and the expanding role of veterinary nurses. I have also noticed differences in communication between the vets and customers in a number of fields of work, which seem to stem from varied: levels of knowledge, levels of emotional attachment and available finances. Completing a week each of lambing at Church Farm, milking at Home Farm and generally assisting at Twemlows stud farm has shown me a different perspective on the use and importance of animals in both food production and for leisure purposes. It has also improved my handling of these animals. Attending a three day Farm Animal Management and Production course at Harper Adams University College further improved my knowledge of the use of animals in farming.

The knowledge I have gained has furthered my interest in veterinary and I believe that I have all the necessary attributes to be successful in the field. Scientific aptitude has come naturally to me and I have developed it through hard work. I am now relating my basic science to more real life situations, such as understanding the problems with over-use of antibiotics. Furthermore, my problem solving ability is shown by high achievement in maths, where developing a fast, logical approach to problems is crucial, as in veterinary medicine. Finally, history has helped me to consider complex ethical issues from contrasting standpoints.

Through a range of non-academic activities and interests I have developed additional skills and attributes. Music has been important to me, with my achievement of grade 8 euphonium and membership of Shropshire Youth Brass Band allowing me to develop confidence through solo performance and band concerts.

I am a keen footballer, cricketer and swimmer. Having captained my junior football team, I now play at college as captain of the 2nd XI. I captained our school cricket team for 3 years. These two sports along with bronze and silver Duke of Edinburgh have improved my teamwork, organisation and leadership. Being a member of Shrewsbury Amateur Swimming Club, where I am club captain, for over ten years has developed discipline and commitment, particularly through 6:00am training sessions. It has also been rewarding with me now regularly achieving highly at county competition. In the past I have taught cricket to younger pupils at school and now work as a swimming teacher after completing my ASA/UKCC level I certificate for teaching aquatics. Overall, I believe I have a lot to offer not only to your university but also my chosen course. I feel I have all the necessary skills to succeed and achieve highly in the veterinary profession. Also I think that my wide range of interests will allow me to offer much more to the university and student life as a whole, as well as allowing me to maintain a healthy work-life balance.

Universities applied to:

- Cambridge: Offer
- Bristol: Interview + Rejected
- Royal Veterinary College: Interview + Rejected
- Nottingham: Interview + Rejected

Good points:

Well-structured. The student demonstrates a good range of practical experience spanning different veterinary specialities. Covering some of the larger specialties (equine medicine as well as farm animal medicine) is advantageous as it will provide a good range of practical insight useful for the course and also allows for the formation of contacts with veterinarians that can later be used for practical attachments. The student furthermore demonstrates that they have a wider range of other interests that provide both, a respite from academic work, as well as teaching the student valuable lessons in team-working, discipline, as well as organisational skills.

Bad points:

The student is very sure of themselves, which generally is a strength but it is also easy to shift into an overconfident representation which can come across as cocky. This should be avoided as it does not fit with the overall perception of what is relevant and acceptable in medical professionals. It would also be desirable for the student to address the relevance of financial spacers in veterinary care. The student briefly and superficially addresses the issue but does not fully address the whole complexity and relevance of the issue.

Overall:

Average statement. Strong points, but also with some weaknesses. This is unfortunate as the statement has the potential to be very good. The point related to the representation of oneself: there is a fine line between sounding cocky and representing one's strengths and achievements appropriately.

NOTES

Subject: Veterinary Medicine

Witnessing the birth of a calf was a wonderful experience and has helped to confirm my long-term ambition to be a vet. This desire has been a motivating force in all my decisions at school. Veterinary medicine is a challenging and worthwhile career that encapsulates my profound interest in animal welfare, scientific enquiry and problem solving. It will satisfy my passion to work with people and animals as well as my love of science. It requires academic rigour, is scientifically-based and provides opportunities for further research either in laboratory or clinical settings. It involves considerable practical skills and the potential for great job satisfaction with the possibility of running my own practice.

My work experience has been thoroughly enjoyable and included working with a country vet, a farrier, at a private stable, a commercial reptile centre, a dairy farm and a small animal clinic. With the country vet I observed two successful treatments on cows to correct displacement of the abomasum by external manipulation and surgery. I helped with TB testing, learning the process, its importance and the wider context. Working with the farrier opened my mind to other people who interact with the veterinary profession. Whilst involved in cleaning and feeding at the private stables I developed a great respect for horses including an awareness of the danger they can pose for humans and other animals. At the reptile centre I handled a bearded dragon, monitor lizard and snakes whilst assisting in an educational talk and at Beaver World learnt to care for guinea pigs, rabbits, beavers, pheasants and fish. During my nine-day stay on a dairy farm I took part in the daily routine of milking, and as well as observing the birth of a calf, I saw the deterioration of a cow and the eventual decision to put her down. It was apparent that working in a small animal clinic involves many routine operations like the castration and spaying of cats and dogs. I learnt that diagnosis involves history-taking, examination and investigations such as blood tests and diagnostic imaging. To gain more experience I plan to work at a city farm, participate in the delivery of lambs and carry out placements at London Zoo and the London Aquarium.

I attended VetMedlink at Nottingham University, thirty-six lectures on all aspects of veterinary care. As part of this course I voluntarily undertook my own research into potential new uses of stem cells and submitted a paper which was marked and for which I received a distinction. This is due to be published on-line sometime this year. My focus was how stem cells inserted into the brain could be used in the future to improve intelligence and treat neural problems such as Alzheimer's disease. Furthermore, I will be attending a course in November to enable me to administer aid to stranded or injured marine mammals.

As well as good examination grades, my other school achievements include prize certificates in mathematics and biology; I was especially pleased to win Gold Certificates in the UK Maths Challenge. This year I was commended for the quality of my answers in the Chemistry Challenge set by my school which required logical reasoning skills. I have a special aptitude for mathematics and attended six maths lectures at Greenwich University on themes which included matrices and types of mathematical proof.

I aim to involve myself whole-heartedly in university life, using my musical skills by playing the keyboard and perhaps playing in or starting a sports team.

I truly believe I have the ability to work effectively with people and animals. I am excited about the veterinary course since it offers the opportunity to undertake research projects, understand the scientific basis of medicine, gain in-depth knowledge of veterinary practice and develop key practical skills. I am determined to become a vet and eager to begin the formal course of training in what I know will prove to be a fascinating field of study.

Universities applied to:

- Cambridge: Offer
- London Vet School: Offer
- Nottingham: Interview + Rejected
- Bristol: Interview + Rejected

Good points:

A well-written and well-structured statement that provides good insight into the student's character and development, both academically as well as personally. The student demonstrates a good scientific foundation, achieving various degrees of academic excellence and also demonstrates a wide range of different work experience attachments that give insight into different specialties of veterinary medicine. This is particularly important due to the wide range of differences between different animal species. The broader the experience before starting the degree, the better. Furthermore, the work experience placements will provide valuable contacts for when the student will be required to conduct care attachments during his/her studies at university.

Bad points:

One of the central points of veterinary medicine not related to the academic side is the funding structure. Recognising the challenges that come with that in regard to the treatment of patients as well as the interaction with owners is an important component. Since the student experienced care in different practice settings, it is likely that he/she has come across this issue.

Overall:

A good statement that offers worthy detail about the student and his/her motivation as well as his/her individual development. It could be improved by additional reflection on the challenges of a veterinary practice, for example due to the existing funding structures.

NOTES

Subject: Veterinary Medicine

Growing up in a rural area enabled me to appreciate the whole cycle of life, and has stimulated a genuine interest in the sciences. This was recently enhanced by hatching 14 chicks, whilst a few mortalities demonstrated the reality of life and death. This inspired me to read 'Life on Earth' by David Attenborough. I especially enjoyed the chapter named 'Eggs, Pouches and Placentas', shedding light on the reproductive cycles of several species. Veterinary Medicine therefore appeals to me as it incorporates a broad base of biological science together with a practical application, suiting my passions and talents.

Undoubtedly, work experience over 10 weeks has reinforced my determination to become a vet. Time spent at small animal practices showed me the clinical role of a vet, observing the importance of teamwork and the ability to deal with owners. During a week at Newmarket Equine hospital, I learnt about routine tasks undertaken at racing yards with ambulatory vets, including endoscopic tracheal examinations. Viewing a knee arthroscopy of a mare demonstrated the rapid progress being made in the profession, of which I am eager to be part of, and made me realise the differing roles of vets in the Equine profession and that of Livestock farming. As a lambing assistant, I gained animal handling skills and of course helped with numerous deliveries, with complications such as still born and breech births. My general husbandry skills were further improved by work at an Animal Rescue centre. Staying on a robotic dairy farm allowed me to try everything from pregnancy monitoring to intramuscular injections. The absence of a traditional parlour gave more time to maintain the health of the cattle, whilst the technology enabled early warnings of problems such as mastitis.

I gained more practical experience through a placement at a zoo and helping at a livery, which taught me about a vets role in the conservation of endangered species, whilst the farrier at the livery confirmed the importance of foot care. At The Royal Veterinary College Labs, I was interested to see the necropsy of an aborted calf, which inspired me to write my Extended Project on the causes of bovine abortion. I was also fascinated to see the anatomy of cattle and sheep at an abattoir, with the slaughterman at work. Such varied experiences have both demonstrated my commitment to a future career in Veterinary Science, and fuelled my desire to do everything I can to ensure I get there.

My A level subjects have equipped me with the core skills required for my chosen degree. Of particular interest was immunology, increasing my desire to gain a better understanding of the scientific principles underlying both the health and disease of animals. Teaching younger students at a primary school science club helped pass on my enthusiasm for my subject, whilst attending a 6th form science discussion group enables me to develop my own ideas on complex ethical issues such as badger culling. Reading the Farmers Weekly has furthered my interest in this controversial debate.

Communication is a vital skill that I have developed by working as a waitress, peer mentoring younger students and being Deputy Head Girl. Despite being the only girl when I joined my village football team aged 4, my persistence and determination means that I am now a member of a Ladies Football Team. This has developed my teamwork skills, further improved by completing Gold D of E. These skills I went on to use in the Rotary supported Interact club, in which I help to organise and run Charity events, including those for our partner school in Uganda ahead of my visit there next year. Having undertaken the Community Sports Leadership Award and being a Corporal at the Air Training Corps has further developed leadership skills that will aid my future learning and career.

Being an ambitious person, I am excited by this challenging and ever-changing discipline of Veterinary Science, as my future opportunities would be limitless.

Universities applied to:

- Cambridge: Offer
- Bristol: Offer
- Leeds: Offer
- Edinburgh: Rejected
- Glasgow: Rejected

Good points:

The student demonstrates an excellent range of work experience ranging from matters of life to matters of death as well as including work with different species of animals and different degrees of hands-on experience. This results in great diversity as well as the impression that the student has gone to considerable lengths to achieve the best possible starting point for her studies. She also gives insight into some academic and non-academic characteristics she considers important in a veterinarian and demonstrates her endeavours to achieve these characteristics.

Bad points:

Some of the experiences could be described in more depth regarding lessons learned and reflections drawn, it isn't entirely clear from the statement what makes the student a good fit for veterinary medicine beyond their personal drive. Due to the wide range of experience, this is somewhat challenging but it will increase the overall quality of the piece. Additionally, the student ignores the challenges, both emotionally as well as professionally, that result from the private character of veterinary medicine where owners have to pay for the treatment of their animals, this means that the statement gives an impression of someone who has 'always wanted to be a vet' but doesn't know much about what it entails in day-to-day life, and can't show that they'd be any good at it.

Overall:

A good statement that is well-written and well-structured. There are some weaknesses, but these only reduce the strength of the statement to a limited extent due to the wide range of relevant and high-quality work experience attachments the student has demonstrated. These experiences will also provide a good basis for discussion in an interview.

NOTES

Subject: Veterinary Medicine

Veterinary medicine is dismissed by some as an unimportant offshoot of human medicine and I have even heard the term "dog plumber" used. So why study it? My work experience and common sense have led me to believe that this view is a fallacy and veterinary medicine is relevant in numerous fields and stands only to become more so.

Veterinary medicine is rooted in science and vets must have broad scientific knowledge to understand diagnoses and treatment of patients. This is an area in which I feel I excel and I hope this is communicated in other ways than high marks. For instance, I have been reading How Animals Work by Knut Schmidt-Nielsen in which he explores physiological mechanisms, from countercurrent heat exchangers in sheep scrotums to the problems encountered when scaling up LSD doses for elephants. I enjoy pursuing science beyond the syllabus in other ways such competing in science Olympiads and attending lectures at UCL and the Cambridge Physics Labs on a range of subjects, my favourite being how genes and environment interact.

I am a member of our school's biology society where we present issues to the society, my group's task being to deal with whether all species are worth saving, since their conservation can be so costly and their role in maintaining biodiversity so limited. I relish academic challenges and the opportunity for development and research in veterinary medicine can provide me with these.

But veterinary medicine is not just academic, and to better understand the practice I spent time at various establishments. Two weeks at a veterinary hospital showed me the bread and butter of small animal work (e.g castrations, vaccinations) while also being advanced enough for complex orthopedic and soft tissue surgery. I had a stint shadowing an exotics vet at another practice, giving me a peek into this weird and wonderful branch of practice, including calcium deficiency in tortoises and the use of implants to inhibit adrenal disease in ferrets. A week at a kennels was useful because I learned how they operate measures to ensure good biosecurity, namely thorough and frequent cleaning of the wards. The facility included a hydrotherapy pool, which I was able to see in use, getting a better idea of what ailments this therapy is used for and how it works.

Spending a week with a sheep farmer during lambing and two weeks on a dairy farm gave me an insight into the more traditional side of veterinary medicine. While at these farms I learned about the husbandry of sheep and dairy cattle, common health problems and when and how drugs are administered. Tasks I undertook included delivering and marking lambs, administering antibiotics, milking cows and herding animals from one field to the next. During my stay at the dairy farm I was lucky enough to be present for a visit from the local vet who got me to don a long-sleeved glove and feel around inside a cow for the fetus! I visited a sheep sale and saw the extensive measures to prevent disease transmission and the new EID tags in action.

I went down to an intensive chicken farm for a day to see how these sorts of farms were managed, taking part in some shed management and culling of sick or small birds. As unpleasant as it was, I know vets play a major role in the running of all farms and sick animals must be dealt with. All of the large animal experience helps me with my work at Stepney City farm, where I have been volunteering since 2004. This small farm allows me to follow my interest in livestock while also giving me the chance to meet and engage with new people in many different, sometimes difficult situations. This has sharpened my people skills and I feel this is a key attribute for a good vet.

During my work experience, the greatest revelation was how important the human factor is. Vets have to be reliable, clear and approachable, whether it's to the small animal owner worried about the health of their dear companion or to the farmer concerned about whether treatment for an animal is financially viable. Another side to veterinary medicine that attracts me is wide range of subjects vets are required to weigh in on, from the fate of "status" dogs to the feeding of cabbages to ram lambs, from a scientific and a practical viewpoint.

Aside from all things veterinary, I maintain an interest in Classics and am a member of our school's Classical Society which meets to ponder the merits of ancient civilizations, scholars and leaders. I play hockey for the school and have completed Duke of Edinburgh's award up to Silver level, both of which I feel have developed my abilities to work in a team. Taking part in the Senior Play helped me with confidence in speaking and performing publicly, while being Deputy Head of my house has given me some level of responsibility.

Universities applied to:

- Cambridge: Offer
- Royal Veterinary College: Offer
- Edinburgh: Rejected
- Nottingham: Rejected

Good points:

A well-written statement that addresses a wide range of core veterinary specialties. This is important in order to give the student an appropriate impression of the realities of veterinary medicine and its practical aspects, in particular, due to its often-misleading representation in popular media. Being aware of the personal as well as academic challenges of a profession in veterinary medicine is very important. The student is able to demonstrate this awareness as well as adequate exposure. It is also a strong point that the student provides specific insight into his/her reflections on their work experience rather than just letting the descriptions stand in the statement by themselves without any contextualisation.

Bad points:

The style is somewhat bizarre at some points, particularly in the beginning. It is obvious that the student intends to be original and stick out from the mass of other applicants, but the style they chose is somewhat inappropriate for this. It drags on for too long, making it a waste of valuable space that could be better used for more relevant topics such as the role of money and funding in veterinary practice. What's more, they go into some detail talking about their own convictions surrounding preserving biodiversity - this is a complex topic best disucssed at interview, and would be better dealt with here just by saying "my group's task being to address the complexities of conservation."

Overall:

A good statement with the potential to be great but is, unfortunately, let down in parts by the student's overly chatty, informal writing style. This is a pity as the student demonstrates excellent exposure and awareness to the challenges of veterinary practice and he/she succeeds in providing good insight into his/her motivations for the pursuit of a career in veterinary medicine.

NOTES

Subject: Dentistry

Everyone has the right to a good smile. A smile can have a major effect on a person's self-esteem, confidence and happiness. It would give me great satisfaction being able to have a positive effect on a patient's quality of life by being able to influence these and many more factors. Dentistry as a prospective career path has always been a very appealing profession because I am interested in caring for people and also enjoy the creativity involved with the profession.

My work experience has further fuelled my desire to study dentistry, because it has shown me how rapidly expanding the dental sector which allows continuous learning. I have worked at Smiledent Dental Practice where I shadowed the dentists and the dental nurses. This experience has highlighted the importance between the balance of leadership and teamwork required to achieve the best treatment for the patients and the efficient running of a dental practice. Furthermore, I witnessed the need to gain the trust of the patient and build a patient-dentist relationship, to allow for a smooth successful treatment.

Apart from a dental practice, I have also volunteered at Haselbury Junior School organising activities for young children at an afterschool club for three months. Working with young children taught me to adapt my communication skills, using simple vocabulary and body language. During this time, it also gave me a sense of care and responsibility towards the children. This motivated me to work with people at the opposite end of the age spectrum. I therefore volunteered at The Haven Day Centre which was a humbling yet valuable experience. I enjoyed being a pillar of support to the elderly trying to entertain them and it was a warming experience to witness their joy.

Moreover, I have regularly attended St John Ambulance Cadets for the past three years. I am now a senior member in the division teaching younger peers first aid thoroughly enjoying the additional responsibility involved in nurturing others.

In addition, I have a keen academic interest. The transmission of diseases, prevention and immunology in Biology, has emphasised to me the significance of hygiene and how rapidly diseases can spread which is vital in the field of dentistry. In Chemistry, I have particularly enjoyed learning about molecular bonding enabling me to understand why particular materials have properties that make them suitable for their job. I have thoroughly enjoyed and flourished in the practical aspects of both subjects. The experiments have allowed me to put into practice/apply the knowledge I have acquired in lessons. Studying mathematics has improved my problem solving ability acquiring practice to reach answers with a methodical yet flexible approach. In years 9 and 12, I was invited to attend lectures at the London Metropolitan University and the Royal Institution of Mathematics over a series of weekends. As a result, I had the opportunity to study branches of mathematics outside the syllabus which thoroughly challenged me. Additionally, geography has helped develop a creative aspect of academic life. In the human sector, I enjoyed the topic about smoking because it taught me the history and origins of smoking and the widespread effect it has on the body including the gums and teeth.

As part of my research, I have expanded my dental knowledge using several websites to gain extra information. I have been fascinated by crowns and root canal treatments because I am fond of the creativity involved such as choosing tooth colours, shape and material to ensure practicality for the patient and simultaneously rectify tooth damage.

Finally, from my work experience in a dental practice and I believe would thrive in such an environment.

Universities applied to:

- Birmingham: Offer
- Sheffield: Rejected
- King's: Interview + Rejected
- Leeds: Rejected
- Aston: Offer

Good points:

Clear structure and the student gives a good insight into their motivation for the study of dentistry as well as providing evidence for their personal, professional, and academic development. It becomes very clear that the student is dedicated to the subject and disciplined in the pursuit of their goals. Having a good experience from work attachments is a further strong point, demonstrating the student's enthusiasm for the subject. The student also shows a good range of other achievements and activities that contribute to the (overall) very positive impression of a dedicated and well-rounded individual.

Bad points:

There is excessive focus on work experience at the exclusion of their understanding of and suitability for the course. Also, the style of the statement is somewhat unclear. Particularly towards the end, one gets the impression that the student ran either out of space or out of ideas as the different aspects raised in the text are not discussed to their full effect, making them significantly less relevant for the overall quality of the statement. This is particularly a problem with the conclusion which makes little to no sense.

Overall:

An average statement that demonstrates some good and relevant work experience and patient exposure. Unfortunately, the statement is let down by some stylistic weaknesses that reduce the overall strength of the content, at least in some parts.

NOTES

Subject: Dentistry

There is a certain delight in being naturally curious. Yet this got me in trouble as a child, from asking too many questions to fidgeting to keep my hands busy. In an attempt to nurture my inquisitive character while suppressing my desire to dismantle furniture, I was often encouraged to visit the local museum where my fascination with the osteology of an ancient carnivore led to my discovery of the gargantuan carnassial teeth, fuelling my primitive interests in the morphology and function of teeth. As I grew older, reading texts like 'The Health Gap' fired a passion to engage in the ordeals of social justice and the issue of poor oral health within the NHS, developing my first taste of what would become a fascination with dentistry.

Witnessing the inner workings of NHS practices in areas of high dental need over a week was eye-opening. The sheer variety of cases piqued my interest; allowing me to realise that dentistry is both a stimulating and demanding vocation that is in turn, highly rewarding. The attention to detail taken while placing a filling highlighted that dentistry requires a substantial level of manual dexterity as well as precision and flair. Heading the Dental Society hones these skills, practising needlework to develop dexterity and discussing pertinent dental cases to increase exposure to the field. The fitting of a CEREC crown during a one week placement at a cosmetic practice opened my eyes to technological advancements in the field, prompting further research into possible future innovations.

Completing a Discover Dentistry course placed what I had learnt in dental practice into the wider context of public dental health issues. A culmination of these valuable experiences highlighted that both the beauty and triviality of dentistry lie in the nature of a simple smile; an often overlooked hallmark of social interaction. Shadowing dentists over two weeks during the Goodwill Ambassador Programme offered a striking contrast to previous placements, broadening the parameters of dentistry as a profession that is not only restorative or aesthetic but potentially life saving. While observing the care of a trigeminal neuralgia patient, I was truly able to value the importance of patient autonomy and trust; further affirming that dentistry truly touches lives on a massive scale.

Working as part of a multidisciplinary team in a dental hospital highlighted the level of effective communication required in the profession, urging me to draw parallels while managing the Debate Society at college. The methodical nature of the surgical team under the oral surgeon's guidance while treating a motor vehicle trauma patient was provoking. Besides the need for efficient communication, it was clear to me that leadership and management skills were vital; skills that I too, have developed through the Silver DofE Award and leading my team through Young Enterprise. Being a scholarship recipient constantly pushes the horizons of my academic abilities, nurturing my thirst for knowledge and fuelling rigorous self-motivation.

Beyond academia, I lead a local charity tutoring disadvantaged children which has given me a deep grounding in community work; stressing the significance of continued community care as well as the values of patience and trust when working with children. Being awarded Best Speaker at the Welsh Debating Championships and being invited to speak at the MDA Awards has fostered an articulate character with the ability to think quickly; making critical decisions under tremendous pressure.

Looking back, it was my curious nature towards the world around me that drove me to explore a career in such a complex and multifaceted field. Grasping every experience extended to me with the same open-minded perspective has encouraged me to constantly broaden the frontiers of my perception of dentistry; a vocation that is highly challenging yet calls to me as one that will fulfil my desire to truly make a difference in society.

Universities applied to:

- Newcastle: Offer
- Birmingham: Offer
- Queens University Belfast: Offer
- King's College London: Offer with Scholarship

Good points:

The student's opening narrative is not unpleasant to read and is instantly engaging — when done well a personal touch like this can be very effective! Throughout the personal statement the student demonstrates a clear passion for the subject with numerous examples. Moreover, this is evidenced with several accounts of clinical exposure and relevant work experience. This is clearly a very academic student with multiple references to significant extracurricular dentistry activities that demonstrate a commitment to the specialty.

Bad points:

Whilst this personal statement is filled with work experience and insight into the dentistry profession, there is little mentioned of the student's personal life. Even though in the penultimate paragraph they start 'beyond academia...', there is no mention of hobbies or relaxation. The examples are all very much academic in nature. When writing a personal statement for a course like dentistry it is essential to demonstrate an interest in a wide variety of unrelated hobbies given the high demands of such a course.

Overall:

An above average statement demonstrating significant insight and commitment within the field of dentistry, written in an engaging synoptic style. Let down, perhaps, only by the lack of an obvious logical structure and neglect of any hobbies or sports.

NOTES

BIOLOGICAL SCIENCES

Subject: Natural Sciences

When Theodore Roszak wrote that 'nature composes some of her loveliest poems for the microscope and the telescope', I feel he captured the way that science gives us greater understanding of the world in which we live. With this understanding comes opportunities to influence the lives we lead. It is my strong interest in science coupled with my inquisitive nature, thirst for knowledge and analytical thinking that compels me to read Natural Sciences. I aspire to work with others at the forefront of scientific knowledge to see how we can apply this knowledge to meet the challenges that unfold in the twenty-first century.

My A level studies have confirmed my interest in a range of scientific areas. After studying cell organelles in biology, I was captivated by reading 'Power, Sex, Suicide: Mitochondria and the Meaning of Life' by Nick Lane, delving deeper into the role of mitochondria in cellular function. Continuing to explore beyond the syllabus, reading 'Genome' by Matt Ridley and 'H2O a Biography of Water' by Philip Ball has fuelled my interest in other areas such as genetics and molecular biology. My enthusiasm for biology was recognised by being awarded the school Year 12 biology prize. In chemistry, exploring carbon nanotubes was exhilarating as I could see that they have enormous potential in diverse applications such as carrying drugs into specific body cells. It was during work experience at a local hospital I saw that scientists provide the tools for doctors and the significance of research in developing new, improved treatments. To explore further the application of science in different contexts, I attended 'Chemistry in Action' lectures at the Institute of Education, London.

I was inspired by speaking with scientists at the forefront of research whilst attending the Summer Science Exhibition at the Royal Society. Intrigued by the development of a nanocell to store clean energy using sunlight and that the cell contained porphyrin which is involved in photosynthesis, I realised that studying the structure and function of plants may provide vital information in developing new ways of storing energy. Keen to experiment, it was exciting to make and identify graphene, the first two-dimensional atomic material and to explore the potential uses of this strong, transparent and highly conductive material. It is enthralling to consider how these current scientific developments may be applied in the future. Finding great satisfaction in problem-solving and thriving on challenge, I have enjoyed studying mathematics, particularly learning new concepts such as calculus. My study of history has enhanced my analytical and essay writing skills. Moreover, it has given me a perspective on the relationship between science and society over the years.

Balancing my extra-curricular activities with my studies has required good time-management. I enjoy playing the piano and a range of sports including netball, tennis and skiing. Playing in the school netball team for the past six years has shown me the value of good teamwork. I have enjoyed volunteering weekly at Strathmore School for children with disabilities and successfully sought permission to organise an Easter Party for them which required initiative, creativity and management skills. Volunteering on the Whitgift Special Needs Activity Project has enhanced my communication and leadership skills and has made me aware of the challenges faced by those with disabilities and their families.

I believe that I have the skills, scientific curiosity and motivation required to learn from, and contribute to, this diverse and challenging course. Studying Natural Sciences will give me the flexibility to explore a wide range of scientific areas and will enable me to develop the skills to work with colleagues at the cutting edge of science.

Universities applied to:

- Cambridge: Offer
- Durham: Offer
- Birmingham: Offer
- University College London: Offer
- Nottingham: Offer

Good Points:

Very well-written with a clear introduction, main body, and conclusion. This statement begins by setting the scene as to why Natural Science, and in particular, Biology, is important to both the world and the applicant. The student clearly explains their interest in Biology and then goes on to explain their interest in the other subjects covered as part of the Natural Sciences degree. Many prospective students forget to do this, and in this statement, every point is justified with examples from the student's personal experiences which adds emphasis to the statement.

Bad Points:

At times this reads a bit like a list, and removing a few examples so that they could say more about those left would have produced a more impactful statement which would more adequately fulfil the requirements to show interest, ability, familiarity, ambition, and understanding of the course's demands.

Overall:

This is an excellent personal statement with a clear and logical structure. The student does not simply list their achievements but provides reasons for their academic interests.

NOTES

Subject: Natural Sciences (Biological)

I first became interested in biochemistry when I learnt about cellular biology. A Level biology animations show proteins, cholesterol, the phospholipid bilayer and other components of a cell, and you recognise that these molecules are the reasons why life exists. The body is a complex fabrication; the way in which we work still has much to be discovered, and that excites me. → Passion

The open-ended nature of biochemistry appeals to me, as it is the foundation for different specialisations. I would be a capable biochemist, because I challenge popular views and assumptions, I am resourceful in finding solutions to problems, and I have the creativity to explain unexpected results. For example, I thought about how the dermis is populated by blood vessels, but when you eat meat or see an animal such as a rabbit be skinned no blood vessels criss-cross from the skin to the body; the skin comes away easily. I concluded that the blood vessels in the skin must be tiny capillaries, otherwise we would see them.

My work experience at RAFT, a lab which heals damaged skin unable to repair itself due to the loss of the dermis, taught me how to do histology and other staining. I also helped with RNA extraction and completed apoptosis experiments. It made me appreciate how scientists use setbacks to progress - I thought that experiments rarely go wrong, but found that unexpected results advance thinking. I also observed how sharing ideas and research is vital in a scientific community.

After RAFT, I wrote a presentation on tissue engineering and presented it to staff and pupils at school. I was interested in looking at its potential applications, and I found out that nobody has yet grown a whole complex organ, like a liver - only tracheas and bladders have been grown. I was also interested in the use of tissue engineering to grow food, such as the £220,000 hamburger. The study of chemistry underpins the science behind these products, and I look forward to studying it at university where I can further my knowledge.

As I am interested in a field where biology and chemistry meet, I can see the applied uses of chemistry, which gives me greater enthusiasm for it in class. In my research about biochemistry, one in particular TV show caught my attention; a Horizon programme about how skin ages. It explained how glycans are cell signalling molecules which are particularly numerous in the dermal-epidermal junction. As we age, their "dialogue" fades so cells do not receive the message to produce more collagen, causing the skin to wrinkle. If we can "switch" them back on, they re-open this dialogue and re-inflate collagen, which reverses the visible effects of ageing on skin. I was particularly interested in this programme, after learning about the skin at RAFT.

As a keen climber, I have competed for the past 5 years and have always done well. Climbers depend on individual ability and performance, but compete as a team. I have learnt to be focused under pressure and keep thoughts ordered and my goals in mind, but mostly I have learnt to take pleasure in the challenge of a tough wall. I enjoy the determination required and the thrill of the height. I have been taught to keep attempting a wall until I can think my way around a problem – as a girl, I rely on technical ability, not brute strength. I have now been chair of climbing club for over a year. As a participant in the Duke of Edinburgh's scheme, CCF, the 1st XI hockey team and the school's exchange scheme, I have become an outgoing, self-motivated and diligent pupil. From being appointed Head Girl, my management and communication skills have improved, and I have proved myself as a leader.

In the future, scientists are going to become ever more important. There are problems which we will have to face up to - food and fuel shortages, global warming, over population. I am looking forward to being one to help tackle these issues, and I think I have the capability bring about real change.

Universities applied to:

- Cambridge: Offer
- York: Offer
- Exeter: Offer
- University College London: Offer
- Cardiff: Offer

Good Points:

The student's motivation to study Biochemistry is clear. The statement is written in an easy-to-read way and is immediately clear to the reader that the student is genuine. The final paragraph brings together all of the points above without repetition and demonstrates the student's confidence in a way that does not sound like bragging.

Bad Points:

Immediately, it is clear that the majority of sentences in this statement will begin with 'I'. Whilst it is important to emphasise individual accomplishment and achievements, this can go too far as the student has done in this statement. Sciences and engineering disciplines require teamwork, and the student even goes on to emphasise her individuality when playing sports. This gives the impression that the student, although very bright and capable, is best suited to work alone. This is not the message to convey when applying for a science (or engineering) discipline, and can be viewed very negatively. The student also makes no mention of the many other disciplines involved in Natural Sciences or mathematics. The statement is also very long.

Overall:

This is a very good statement, with the student's passion for the subject clear. However, the student is let down by what seems to be a clear preference to work alone. One or two examples of working as part of a team and some sentence alterations (not using 'I' so much) would make a big difference.

NOTES

Subject: Biological Sciences

Like all children, I went through the 'why' stage. But for me, it never stopped. I am fascinated by the world around me and have always been passionate about science, but Biology has always been at the forefront of my interests. This is why I would like to continue studying it at university. When I read 'The Cell', by Terrance Allen and Graham Cowling, to support my AS course, I realised that there was much more to the 'simple' cell than I realised. It was at this point that I began to explore deeper into the world of Biology and I knew then that this was my true passion. As well as books, I keep up-to-date in the world of science by reading magazines such as Focus, New Scientist and Biological Sciences Monthly.

Like most students, I had little idea of what studying a science at university was like, and any practical work I had ever done was in a classroom. Therefore, to give me a taste of university level study, I undertook work experience at the Marine Laboratory of Queen's University Belfast. During this placement, I had the opportunity to observe and take part in various experiments focusing predominantly on the behavioural biology of marine animals. Furthermore, I was able to speak to interesting and intellectual people from all sorts of backgrounds, from students working towards their PhD to retired professors with a seasoned career. This confirmed for me that studying Biology is what I really want to do.

To further expand my knowledge of Biology, I also applied for and was successful in gaining a place on Oxford University's UNIQ Summer School. Throughout this week I took part in field work, laboratory sessions and lectures on various fields within Biology. On my first day, I was set an assignment, in which I had to conduct my own research in my free time to produce an essay on sexual conflict - a topic I was totally unfamiliar with. Although it was challenging, I enjoyed working for myself and learned a great deal about something I would never have come across on my A Level course. At the end of the week I was able to discuss the essay with an Oxford tutor. For me, this was an interesting and stimulating discussion in which I was encouraged to come up with and explore new ideas in a way which is unlike the teaching I have experienced at school. I can look forward to getting another taster of university life when I attend a course in Cell Biology and Genetics run by Villiers Park in December. Although studying both Biology and Chemistry covers quite an extensive range of topics, giving me a broad insight into the biological sciences, I am particularly interested in certain topics. Consequently, I undertook a course run by the Open University in Human Genetics and Health Issues. This taught me many things, in particular the ability to study independently. There has been huge growth in interest and research in this area and I would like to delve deeper into this subject.

I consider myself to be an ambitious individual and I am involved in a range of extra-curricular activities which I am able to balance with my school work due to my strong organisational skills. I have many positions of responsibility, such as being a Corporal in my local Air Cadet Squadron, and I am a school Prefect and a member of the school Council. These positions have developed my communication skills and I believe that these will be very important in the field of science, allowing me to share my ideas and research with confidence.

I am very eager to delve deeper into the world of biology than I have ever gone before. I can think of nothing more exciting and stimulating than engaging in debate and discussion with professionals in an area that genuinely interests me so much. Though I know that this will be a challenge, it is one that with hard work and dedication I believe I will rise to.

Universities applied to:

- Oxford: Offer
- Durham: Offer
- St. Andrews: Offer
- Herriot-Watt: Offer
- Southampton: Offer

Good Points:

The student's motivation to study Biology is clear. The student has clearly gone beyond conducting simple research in order to better understand the discipline for which they are applying. All examples and experiences are clearly explained and their impacts on the student are clear. The final paragraph closes the statement in a clean way that makes the student come across as both humble and likable. You can see their interest in the course, suitability for it, academic skill, and broader character.

Bad Points:

The student relies on experiences at the UNIQ summer school, Oxford (and an upcoming experience at Villiers Park, Cambridge) too heavily. Whilst such experiences are important and can provide motivation for further study at university, such opportunities are not available to everyone. Using examples from outside the A-level syllabus and personal experiences in addition to the student's summer school experiences would have added more variety to the statement.

Overall:

This is a very good statement where the student demonstrates clear motivation. The bulk of the statement's main body is dedicated to a single experience: a one-week summer school at the University of Oxford. Whilst it is, of course, a great advantage to have had such an insight into a potential degree (and career) in Biology, it is important not to rely too heavily on any one single experience.

NOTES

Subject: Biochemistry

I have enjoyed studying Science since primary school and I have especially developed an interest in Chemistry and its importance in biological contexts. Biochemistry as a subject covers such a broad range of applications, from genetic engineering to the cure for cancer, which is what has attracted me to the subject and made me want to study it in greater detail, as I will be able to do at university. Since I want to become a science teacher in the future, studying Biochemistry will not only give me insight into Chemistry applications in Biology, but also an in-depth understanding of how the 3 sciences can be combined to answer scientific problems. The inter-disciplinary nature of the subject also fascinates me as it is becoming more apparent that scientific advances require collaboration between scientists from different fields, and I am intrigued about how this is put into practice.

In order to advance my interest in Biochemistry, I regularly read scientific magazines and journals such as 'New Scientist' in order to keep up-to-date with recent advances being made in the field. For example, recently it was discovered that ovarian cancer cells can physically push healthy cells out of the way when parts of ovarian tumours break off. As this finding sheds light on how this particular tumour can enter other organs, it may be beneficial for future cancer therapies and could be a target for treatment to prevent cancers spreading to other organs. As well as this, I am also interested in how science is presented to the general public. Reading 'The Selfish Gene' by Richard Dawkins gave me a new perspective on biological evolution, focusing on a gene's requirement to propagate, rather than that of an organism or species. In addition to popular science books, I have also looked into books targeted at undergraduates, such as 'Principles and Problems in Physical Chemistry for Biochemists'. This textbook in particular gave me more of an idea of how Biophysical Chemistry is taught in Biochemistry, which is the branch of the subject that I am most interested in studying as it combines all of the main sciences.

On top of the reading that I have done, I have also pursued many pursuits to progress my interest in science. Attending Chemistry master classes at Birmingham University gave me a taste of the style of university lectures and also taught me about specific advances made in Chemistry that have various applications, such as modifying skis for better performance in snow sports competitions. Taking part in the Chemistry Olympiad in school also gave me the opportunity to apply the knowledge I had gained in Chemistry lessons to situations that I was unfamiliar with. Needing to think 'outside the box', in order to approach the various questions, is an important skill required for higher education and receiving a Silver certificate shows that I have the capacity to tackle new problems. I have also helped out with Chemistry Club during lunchtimes, where I have demonstrated various exciting experiments to lower years and also taught students about applications of Chemistry and advances in science that go beyond the curriculum, which I have learnt about through my reading and master classes.

I have also taken part in a variety of extra-curricular activities to enhance my personal skills. Throughout secondary school I have been a council, class or charity representative, and am now a Senior Prefect for Charity and Citizenship. I undertook these roles of responsibility as I feel that it is important to voice the opinions of students to effect positive changes that benefit them, and I also enjoy organising charity events and raising awareness of various issues. I regularly attend St. John's Ambulance meetings and have also attended Badminton Club for 5 years, as I am a committed member of both. I feel that these skills have prepared me to be able to undertake a university degree to the best of my abilities, to allow me to reach my potential.

Universities applied to:

- Oxford: Offer
- Birmingham: Offer
- Leicester: Offer
- Warwick: Offer
- Nottingham: Offer

Good Points:

A well-written and structured statement. The student emphasises their teamwork skills and puts these in a scientific context. The student does not focus on one particular subject but gives attention to both Biology and Chemistry before combining these together to justify their reasoning for wanting to become a biochemist. It is clear that the student has sought opportunities outside of the core syllabus to explore their chosen subject. The student's desire to become a science teacher is used in the introduction and this establishes a high degree of motivation early on in the statement.

Bad Points:

Whilst it is important to include examples of extra-curricular work and activities, the student embarks on a list of accomplishments. This is fine to begin with, however, by the third paragraph, it is quite exhausting to read. It is important to write about good examples of personal endeavour thoroughly, but not to simply list all accomplishments and achievements in one's life.

Overall:

Overall, this is a good statement and it demonstrates the student's ambition to study Biochemistry clearly. Although the student does not come across as though they are bragging, the sheer number of achievements and accomplishments makes the statement quite exhausting to read. The student could have achieved the same impact with fewer but more thoroughly written out examples.

NOTES

Subject: Biochemistry

Going to university to study the sciences has always been my ambition, as I believe science is fundamental to the future of mankind. When I started learning the sciences at school, I was immediately intrigued. Whilst other subjects such as Latin, history and economics interested me, I became increasingly engrossed in chemistry and biology, particularly organic chemistry which is my real passion. I find it fascinating how different combinations of very similar elements can have such varied uses in industry, pharmaceuticals, and metabolic processes. My A Level choices have prepared me well for studying the sciences at university. I have not only acquired a sound theoretical knowledge of chemistry and biology, but also an understanding of the practical aspects and how this knowledge can be applied to real life and used to benefit humanity. Studying A Level maths has furthered my analytical skills as well as my reasoning abilities. I am constantly adding to my knowledge base in addition to my A Levels and, although we don't cover neurology in school, I find it really interesting and have been self-studying to further my knowledge.

To learn more about behaviour and neuroscience, I read Zero Degrees of Empathy. I found it intriguing that the size of or activity in different parts of the brain could be influenced by both genetics and early environment. I am currently basing my Extended Project Qualification around the subjects of autism, empathy and neurology, trying to discover more about how brain function differs between different people. Throughout this process I will be developing research skills and independent thinking, interviewing members of the public, contacting professionals in their fields, and reading and collating information from various sources and questioning their provenance. As part of my project I intend to design patient level literature to help educate people about autism, which I plan to distribute via doctors' surgeries and health centres.

Many experiences have contributed to my fascination with science. Whilst shadowing doctors for a week in Broomfield Hospital's Emergency Assessment Unit, I was most interested in the different medications that were administered to patients, and their effects. I have also attended many talks and conferences which I found interesting, notably Adam Rutherford on genetic engineering, synthetic species, and the future of science and technology, which showed me that now is an exciting time to be entering the world of biochemistry.

I also took part in the AD Schools' Analyst Competition at the University of Hertfordshire, and attended a Chemistry taster day at Essex University, so I have some lab experience at a university. I found both events thoroughly enjoyable. When I am not studying I relax by playing classical guitar, having achieved grade 7. I used to captain my local football team, and enjoyed the leadership opportunity; I now referee youth football. I have been a member of my school's Cadet Force since 2010, where I have learned time-management, discipline, and responsibility. I am also grateful to both my peers and teachers for electing me prefect last year, but had to turn down the role after I was offered the chance to be House Captain, where I delegate roles within my team, organise house events, and speak in front of my house fortnightly.

Three years ago I went on a French Exchange, which helped develop my communication skills and independence. I took part in the Young Enterprise Scheme in 2012, building confidence, cooperation skills, and real world initiative. I also visited Kenya last summer, staying at an orphanage and teaching in our partner school, which taught me to adapt to unfamiliar situations. I am really looking forward to continuing my studies at university. In the world of science, theories only last until a better one is created; everything is changing and research is crucial. I want to be at the forefront of the future of biochemistry.

Universities applied to:

- Oxford: Offer
- Durham: Offer
- Imperial College London: Offer
- Bath: Offer
- Exeter: Offer

Good Points:

The student explains their ambition to study Biochemistry clearly, with emphasis given to both subjects involved in the multidisciplinary subject. It is clear that the student has many talents, both academic and non-academic which gives confidence to the reader that they will not struggle when challenged at university. The student writes in a way that makes them appear confident but not over-confident, which will be looked upon well. It is clear that the student draws from personal experiences that are unique to them, rather than those shared with many others, such as summer schools etc.

Bad Points:

There are many redundant sentences throughout this statement, such as 'Studying A Level maths has furthered my analytical skills as well as my reasoning abilities'. This is surely the case for everyone who studies A-level maths, and it is not unique. Getting rid of such redundant sentences will shorten the statement and give more emphasis to the rest of the statement. The statement lacks structure as the introduction includes details of the student's A-level study and, as a paragraph, is too long. The statement would read much more easily if similar points were grouped into paragraphs, and the introduction and concluding paragraph were separated from the main body of the statement.

Overall:

This is a very good statement. The student has clearly accomplished many things. However, redundant sentences that state the obvious take away from the rest of the statement. The structure of the statement is somewhat confusing, especially at the beginning. With the removal of redundant sentences and some re-structuring, this would be an excellent statement.

NOTES

CHEMISTRY

Subject: Chemistry

When I visited my secondary school open day at the age of 11, I was fascinated by a demonstration of a colour changing liquid. At the time I knew little about the 'blue bottle' experiment but 6 years later I am using it to inspire future students at this year's event. I still get excited about discovering and understanding new chemistry, in particular the relationship betw'een chemical structures, their properties and how they interact. I am fascinated by the fact that everything around us is based on just 3 sub-atomic particles, in multiple and different combinations. I have a natural aptitude for mathematics but during my GCSEs I found that the applications of science, in particular chemistry and biology, excited me more than pure mathematics. I have continued to study double maths as I believe this will help me with scientific analysis and logical thinking and have done so on a partly self-taught basis as my A level choices were not possible within the school timetable. This has developed my independent learning skills and, I believe, prepares me well for higher education. Of all my A levels, I am inspired most by chemistry. This summer I arranged a week of work experience at Reading Scientific Services Ltd, a subsidiary of Mondelez, where I was able to be involved in real world applications of chemistry. These included using gas chromatography to check that the vitamin C content in a product matched the labelled value, and nuclear magnetic resonance spectroscopy to identify contaminants in products. It was great to see techniques I had learnt about in theory being used in practice and I concluded that I definitely want to study chemistry at degree level. I have become particularly interested in analytical chemistry as it has so many valuable applications, and I am very excited by the opportunities that I have seen in this area during my university visits.

To further my knowledge I have read 'Why Chemical Reactions Happen' by Keeler and Wothers, and I subscribe to New Scientist magazine. Keeler and Wothers has given me insight into how the world works at the atomic and molecular scale and other theories, such as how covalent bonds are formed using the model of molecular orbitals and hybrid atomic orbitals. New Scientist articles that have particularly interested me include proposed methods for controlling the building of crystalline structures one atom at a time to produce structures with desirable properties, for example as catalysts, and discussion on elements displaying properties not predicted by their place in the periodic table, leading to alternative views on how the periodic table could be organised. Spurred by my enthusiasm for both sport and chemistry, I was intrigued by news reports on how noble gases are thought to have blood doping benefits for athletes, and have read further into this. The World Anti-Doping Agency has banned their use but has yet to develop tests for them. A topic such as this as an undergraduate project would be very exciting.

Alongside my studies, I have pushed myself to undertake activities that develop me as a person. I teach beginner and advanced skiing at a dry ski slope. This requires me to observe, analyse what I see, identify underlying causes and determine solutions, which I believe this will help me in my practical chemistry. I am an academic mentor for younger pupils at school and I tutor a GCSE student in maths and sciences, through which I have learnt to see topics from different perspectives. I have been officiating as a football referee for 3 years, learning to compose my thoughts, be confident and communicate under pressure, which I believe will make a direct contribution to my development as a scientist. In conclusion, I am confident in my choice of a chemistry degree and excited by the opportunities ahead of me. I believe that I will be well prepared to get the most from the course and to make a strong contribution to my faculty and university.

Universities applied to:

- Bristol: Offer
- Warwick: Offer
- Southampton: Offer
- Oxford: Offer
- Bath: Offer

Good Points:

This is a good statement and the student is clearly motivated by their chosen subject. Although Mathematics is not a requirement for studying Chemistry at university, it is very highly regarded and emphasising mathematical ability will definitely strengthen an application. The student writes in a way that is easy to understand and expands on all experiences. The student writes things in a logical order, with academic interests/achievements first, followed by work experience and finally with extra-curricular activities. All points mentioned regarding the student's academics and extra-curricular activities are related back to an interest in Chemistry.

Bad Points:

Although the physical content is well-structured, the student has three huge paragraphs only. It is not clear where the introduction ends and the main body begins. This is also the case for the final paragraph where it is not clear where the student's closing paragraph begins. The beginning of the statement is quite abrupt, it would have been better perhaps if the student opened with an introduction to the subject of Chemistry, rather than diving straight into their personal experiences.

Overall:

This is a very good personal statement. In terms of content, the statement is excellent. However, the statement lacks basic paragraph structure. This makes it difficult to mentally separate the main points of the statement. With some basic restructuring, this would be an excellent statement.

NOTES

Subject: Chemistry

I am fascinated by chemistry and by its connections across the sciences. I relish the intellectual challenge it presents. I have a keen interest in how chemistry works closely with numerous other scientific disciplines to address the problems that the world faces both now and in the future. Studying a subject that is at the forefront of the resolution of global issues such as climate change, truly excites me. I am naturally inquisitive about the world around me, so learning about the composition and structure of matter only serves to fuel my enthusiasm further.

The understanding of how molecules are arranged in space intrigues me. Attending a lecture given by Dr Stuart Conway at Oxford University on the chirality of molecules was a fascinating experience. Subsequently, I read the relevant sections of Organic Chemistry by Clayden, Reeves, Warren & Worthers and The Foundations of Organic Chemistry Oxford primer. It was interesting to note the importance of symmetry in optical isomerism and to appreciate that even molecules that lack a stereogenic centre can be chiral. Furthermore, that enantiomers of compounds like limonene smell different due to our olfactory receptors that also contain chiral molecules and finally, that the chirality of drugs affects their action and has profound implications regarding their effects on the human body.

I particularly enjoy mathematics and its relevance to chemistry. Recently, I completed the iodine clock reaction experiment. I learnt how to use logarithms to work out the rate constant and then by using the $y = mx + c$ model, was able to deduce the order of the reaction. I enjoy the application of logic to problem solving and I look forward to further developing this skill during my degree study.

In order to improve my laboratory techniques, I have completed several first year degree level experiments. At the University of Sussex, I synthesised aspirin and in another experiment, extracted limonene from citrus fruits in order to decide which of them contained the most active, fragrant compound. I have also explored emission spectra and investigated which elements absorb specific frequencies of sunlight at the University of Reading. An experiment that I thoroughly enjoyed, whilst participating in a summer school at Oxford University, was the synthesis of indigo dye using the Baeyer-Drewson reaction and a vat-dyeing technique. I gained a detailed insight into the kinds of experiments that I will be carrying out during my degree and relish the opportunity to use sophisticated apparatus and techniques.

Next July I undertake work experience in France which will combine my passion for chemistry with my love of the French language. Working in a medical analysis laboratory will not only enable the exploration of the analytical techniques used in the industry but will also help me to learn and practice chemistry specific vocabulary in the language of the country that I aspire to live and work in.

I continually seek to challenge myself and to broaden my horizons. To this end, I have completed both my Bronze and Silver Duke of Edinburgh (D of E) Awards. By way of concurrent activity and academic demands allowing, I plan to complete my Gold D of E at an appropriate stage. I volunteer regularly in French and Chemistry classes as part of the Worldwide Volunteering scheme.

Throughout my education, I have been determined to excel. I have worked consistently hard at the subjects I am passionate about and even harder at the ones that I have found challenging. Achieving excellent examination grades based on detailed understanding of the subject matter is my main driver at this stage. I am very keen to study in a stimulating university environment alongside ambitious, dedicated and like-minded students. Louis Pasteur said, "My strength lies solely in my tenacity". I believe MY strength lies not only in my tenacity but also in my intellectual ability, curiosity and determination to study chemistry at degree level and beyond

Universities applied to:

- Oxford: Offer
- Durham: Offer
- Bristol: Offer
- York: Offer
- Bath: Offer

Good Points:

This statement is well-structured and well-written. The student starts with a general introduction into Chemistry and their passion for the subject before going onto the main body of the statement. All claims of work experience and extra-curricular activities are explained clearly. The student clearly has an abundance of additional experience regarding Chemistry, ranging from tutoring to conducting first-year university experiments. These, and their relevance to the student's reasons for applying to study Chemistry are explained clearly and the reader is in no doubt that these experiences are genuine.

Bad Points:

The student underlined the word 'receptors' and included a link to a Wikipedia page containing the meaning of the term 'sensory receptors'. This is basic knowledge, and including a link to a word's meaning risks insulting the intelligence of the academic staff who read the statement. The student also emphasises themselves in the final sentence by using capitals in 'MY'. Again, this can be taken wrongly and it would be a shame to ruin an otherwise excellent statement purely because the reader decides that the student is overconfident and condescending.

Beyond this, the second and third paragraphs talk at considerable length about particular concepts which interest them, but this isn't used to make any convincing point about why the person reading it should accept their application - focusing instead on challenges they hope to face on the course, skills they'd like to learn, or ambitions for after graduation would be valuable. On that note, they make a point that they hope to live and work in France after graduation, which will beg the question of interviewers about whether the candidate has applied to French universities as well, this can unnecessarily complicate or even harm your chances, and is best avoided.

Overall:

This is a very good statement, however, two strange cases of where the student refers the reader to the meaning of a basic term and emphasises themselves in capital letters let the student down.

NOTES

Subject: Chemistry

Few aspects of our lives remain unaffected by the fundamental subject of chemistry. Chemists have revolutionised the way we live; from the medicines we use to the water we drink, it is hard to imagine what our everyday life would be like without the help of this vast subject. I wish to be a part of the chemical discoveries of the future which is what entices me to study chemistry in greater depth at university.

My interest in chemistry has developed a great deal since starting the AS level course. Each time I learn something new, it inspires me to develop my knowledge even further. I have particularly enjoyed the organic chemistry involved in the AS course due to the practical work it entails. Laboratory work for me is enjoyable because it provides an opportunity to test out the theoretical knowledge you have gained and is also great fun! For example, I particularly enjoyed making azo dyes as it was interesting to recreate a process in the lab which is so frequently used in industry.

I have been able to develop my passion for chemistry through wider reading. I have recently enjoyed reading Molecules at an Exhibition. The range of molecules which can have profound effects on our lives surprised me and showed me again how relevant chemistry is to our lives. I have a subscription to New Scientist. An article I particularly enjoyed reading over the summer was "Rogue elements" which explores some of the unanswered questions associated with the periodic table. For example, when the elements will stop and whether superheavy elements, which exist for fractions of a second only one atom at a time, can be considered elements at all. The article also looked at the issues of where to place the elements hydrogen and helium and where the metal/non-metal divide should be. This showed me that although the periodic table is often considered to be complete, there is still much to uncover.

Reading Quantum Theory Cannot Hurt You introduced me to the concept of relativity and I was amazed to find out how this theory affects chemistry as well as physics. For example without relativity the properties of some of the heavier elements such as gold would simply not be the same. I have been developing my interest in maths and have taken up AS further maths which will be largely self-taught, I know this will complement the chemistry syllabus.

Recently I took part in a UNIQ summer school at Oxford University which allowed me to have a great insight into undergraduate chemistry. I thoroughly enjoyed my week, particularly the lecture on chirality. This was a new concept for me and I was surprised by the huge differences that can result from this form of isomerism. My subject knowledge was greatly enhanced and the skills I gained have been even more valuable. I was taught to question, develop and evaluate my knowledge at every stage and become a more independent learner.

During Year 12 I acted as a science tutor for GCSE students, helping them with exam technique. I found that explaining the subject matter to others helped to enhance and consolidate my own knowledge. My success both in and out of school was rewarded when I received Clevedon's 2014 Academic Achievement Award in chemistry.

I enjoy playing the piano and recently achieved Grade 6 during my GCSE year, developing my time management skills. My other hobbies include drama and singing and I am a member of Clevedon Light Opera Club as well as the school choir. I have taken part in several productions as well as performing in school stage shows and concerts. All of which contributed to me gaining my Gold Arts Award. I volunteer with a Rainbow group. When I started I found the prospect of running activities for a group of people quite daunting, but 2 years later I think my confidence and communication skills have improved greatly. I have developed my knowledge, skills and aptitude both in and out of school and I look forward to being able to extend these further by studying at university.

Universities applied to:

- Oxford: Offer
- Bristol: Offer
- Cardiff: Offer
- Manchester: Offer
- Leicester: Offer

Good Points:

This is a well-written and well-structured statement. The student places points in order of relevance, making the statement easy to read. All points are clearly explained and their impacts on the student are clear. There is a clear introduction, main body, and conclusion.

Bad Points:

Although the statement is written in a logical order, there are a lot of paragraphs. Whilst it is very good that student has a wide range of interests and hobbies, the student dedicates two paragraphs to these. It would have been possible to shorten the statement by removing some of the points mentioned without taking away from the quality of the statement. The student clearly has many experiences from outside of the A-level syllabus, such as the UNIQ summer school and working as a GCSE science tutor. Whilst it is, of course, important to describe individual experiences and achievements, focusing on the positives alone limits the impact that mentioning such experiences will have. It would have been nice to see what challenges the student faced through their experiences and how the student overcame these.

Overall:

This is an excellent statement. The statement is clearly written and easy to read. The length of the statement could have been reduced, however, there are no other areas in which the student needs to make significant improvements.

NOTES

PHYSICAL SCIENCES

Subject: Natural Sciences (Physics)

The more I discover about physics, the less I realise that I know, and the keener I am to further explore unfamiliar topics at university. Studying areas such as special relativity and quantum mechanics have made me question concepts I took as given, such as the nature and manipulation of time and the degree of certainty to which we can truly know anything.

My particular interest in physics was sparked when I read an article on quantum physics, and was introduced to a simple description of the fundamental constituents of matter. This led me to read further about particle physics. I particularly enjoyed Brian Greene's The Elegant Universe, which gave me a brief insight into the intricacies of string theory, and The Feynman Lectures on Physics, from which I learnt new mechanics and probability theory. I watch lectures on the MIT website, read New Scientist and am a junior member of the IoP to further my knowledge of new scientific developments. I enjoyed visiting CERN last year and learning more about the experiments conducted there. I have also competed in national challenges to develop my thinking skills further, achieving bronze in the Physics Olympiad, silver in the Cambridge Chemistry Challenge and gold in the Senior Maths Challenge. Additionally, this year I won the school leavers' physics prize.

Last summer I attended a residential Headstart physics course at the University of Leicester, and spent three days at the Debate Chamber physics school. I enjoyed performing undergraduate experiments, and was particularly interested by the lectures on recent developments in nanotechnology and the ways in which nanoparticles could be used to destroy cancerous cells in the body. I also had a tantalising glimpse of some of the complex mathematics behind General Relativity, and would love to study this intricate topic in more detail. These experiences confirmed my love of physics as well as increasing my appreciation of more complicated subjects not covered by my A Level courses. Furthermore, they helped to develop my skills in processing new information and quickly adapting to unfamiliar concepts.

I recently took part in an extended-essay competition at school, producing an independently researched piece of work on the superluminal neutrinos apparently found in 2011. I focused on the impossibility of faster-than-light travel according to special relativity, and the implications for time travel the discovery would have had if the measurements had been correct. This gave me the chance to explore further a subject I was interested in but had not studied at school. I researched my essay by reading scientific journals and textbooks, and speaking to scientists I met at physics events.

I will shortly begin a paid internship at Hildebrand Technology Ltd, where I will be using mathematical modelling of real-life situations for statistical analysis. This will be an opportunity to apply mathematical techniques I have learnt in school to more complex problems. This placement, along with self-studying university textbooks and extra further maths modules, will ensure that I maintain and expand my maths skills and scientific knowledge during my gap year.

In my final year I was captain of the school Boat Club. I have rowed in the top senior boat since I was 15, and in 2013 I won silver at National Schools and gold at Schools Head. This sport has involved intensive training, which demands self-discipline and commitment. I love music, and take part in many close harmony groups and choirs, as well as taking grades in musical theatre, singing and piano. My music and sport, along with lifeguarding and weekly volunteering at a local primary school, have allowed me to develop my time management skills and use the time I have for work efficiently and productively.

I am a hardworking and intellectually curious student and am excited by the prospect of developing my mathematical skills and studying physics at a more advanced level at university.

Universities applied to:

- Cambridge: Offer
- Durham: Offer
- Imperial College London: Offer
- St. Andrews: Offer
- Edinburgh: Offer

Good Points:

This is a very good statement. The statement is well-structured and the student's motivation to study physics is evident. All points are explained clearly, and experiences expanded on. The student uses examples beyond their A-level studies to explain their desire to study physics, which comes across very well to the reader.

Bad Points:

The student forgets to use quotation marks around the names of books etc., and also 'the' before 'New Scientist'. Whilst these are rudimentary errors, a simple proof-read would have found these. The main issue with this statement is its length. There are eight paragraphs in total. By the penultimate paragraph, it is clear enough that the student has done many physics-related extra-curricular activities. The quality of the statement will not be reduced if it is shortened. The student does not explain acronyms, e.g. 'IoP'. Some sentences can be shortened in order to save space, for example, 'I have also competed in national challenges to develop my thinking skills further, achieving bronze in the Physics Olympiad, silver in the Cambridge Chemistry Challenge and gold in the Senior Maths Challenge' can be shortened to, 'I have also competed in national challenges to develop my thinking skills further, achieving bronze, silver, and gold medals in the Physics Olympiad, Cambridge Chemistry, and Senior Maths Challenges respectively'.

Overall:

In general, this is a very good statement. It is well-written and the student's motivation to study physics at university is clear from the very beginning. Due to the length of the statement, it is quite cumbersome to read. With some shortening, this would be a compact and powerful statement.

NOTES

Subject: Natural Sciences (Physics)

I have always had a strong interest in pure science, particularly exploring how science and new technologies can be applied to deal with 21st century issues.

This summer I was selected from 3400 applicants to attend the physical science programme at the UNIQ summer school, at the University of Oxford. I enjoyed a variety of science lectures; my favourite was on nanotechnology in which a PHD student talked about his research in producing graphene. The presentation highlighted for me the importance of being able to manufacture this material as it has some useful properties, though is difficult to produce. The practical sessions which looked at the physical properties of some different alloys were also enjoyable. I related well to these as they touched on topics like the young's modulus which I have previously covered. I found all the lectures absorbing which has helped me to decide that I wish to study a very broad scientific course like Natural Sciences.

As a subscriber to The New Scientist magazine, I really enjoy reading all the articles, especially those related to materials science and nuclear physics. A recent article called 'Hidden Power' examined how materials such as paper and cement can be turned into composites that can hold a charge. I find such modifications fascinating, for example where casings for a mobile phone could actually power the phone. Currently, however, the capacity to hold charge cannot compare with the capabilities of lithium ion batteries; this is new technology and there are hopes that it will continue to improve.

After reading an article concerning the implementation of Nuclear Power, I went on to read 'Nuclear Power – A very Short Introduction,' as I consider this to be a current and relevant subject. I found forming an opinion on such a controversial issue very rewarding. This spurred me to pursue an extended project titled, 'Is thorium a nuclear fuel of the future?' I read about the nuclear fusion proposal at ITER, the needs of corrosion resistant materials, the use of fluoride salts, and the use of magnetic fields to contain the plasma.

In selecting Natural Sciences, I am choosing a course with varied possibilities for the future. At present a career in scientific journalism is appealing. I would also relish the opportunity to pursue academic experiences or employment abroad, as scientific developments occur globally.

When I am not studying, I have a part-time job at a local hotel. This experience has improved my interpersonal skills through interaction with customers. I enjoy many extra-curricular pursuits. For the past 8 years I have played rugby for a local club; taking part in a team has resulted in me working in groups, to achieve successful outcomes. It has also rewarded me with good decision making and communication skills, which are greatly required in the heat of a match for success. I have dedicated considerable time to the Duke of Edinburgh Gold Award Scheme. To relax, I read science fiction and fantasy books as I feel this stretches my mind and imagination in interesting and novel ways; the ability to think not only logically but creatively is essential for a scientist.

My proudest achievement is being selected to be head boy at my previous, highly academic, school against strong competition; this was an extremely demanding role as it required me to employ organizational, public speaking and presentational skills. I am also a student ambassador at my current college, responsible for inducting new students.

I would love to study Natural Sciences; the course modules are exceptionally diverse allowing the pursuit of scientific interests, together with the opportunity to really be at the cutting edge of science. I have a deep interest and knowledge of the sciences, showcased by an extremely successful academic record to date, and through the enjoyment of scientific publications and podcasts. I now look forward to building on these achievements as I enter my life at University.

Universities applied to:

- Cambridge: Offer
- Durham: Offer
- Birmingham: Offer
- Nottingham: Offer
- Lancaster: Offer

Good Points:

The student is clearly very motivated, and this comes across in the statement. The statement is written in a logical order and all previous experiences are well-explained and expanded upon. The student has clearly read around his chosen subject in some detail and this is evident in the statement.

Bad Points:

The student adds a great deal of self-praise to his achievements. In the first paragraph after the introduction, the student describes being individually 'selected from 3400 applicants' to attend the UNIQ summer school. Whilst this is, of course, a positive experience, it is important to remember that university admission is not decided purely on a student's acceptance on such programmes prior to their application. The student dedicates a large paragraph to their experiences during this week-long experience, which is far too much. It is important to remember that not all have such opportunities and those without cannot be discriminated against for not having taken part in such events. The student also attaches emphasis to his appointment of head boy at his 'previous highly academic school against strong competition'. Whilst again, this is a positive experience, emphasising that the student's school was highly academic makes it seem as though their experiences in school are of greater value than those of someone from a lesser academic school. This makes the student come across as overconfident, pompous, and elitist. The sentence in which the student describes his appointment as head boy is badly worded, with three commas and a semi-colon.

Overall:

Whilst this is a good personal statement, the student is let down by an abundance of self-praise. This makes the student a lot less likable to the reader.

NOTES

Subject: Physics

Understanding how things work and studying the unsolved questions of the universe are reasons why I have a continuous interest in Physics. The logic of the subject is complemented by regular use of Mathematics in all areas, which I thoroughly enjoy. Physics explains everything around us, from the fundamental particles to the stars and planets and I find this intriguing. The fact that Physics is constantly evolving, with new discoveries happening all the time - such as the finding of the tau neutrino - causes the way we think to change constantly and I am fascinated to see scientific theories grow and improve.

An appealing aspect of the Physics course is the logical way of thinking about problems, as well as the complex mathematics needed for more advanced areas of the subject. Breakthroughs in science have come in no small part due to experimentation, for example Ernest Rutherford's alpha particle scattering experiment, so I thoroughly enjoy practical work, but theoretical work is equally important, a great example being Einstein's Theory of Relativity. My father is an engineer, and as a result I always ask questions and approach problems rationally. Mathematics has always been something I enjoy, but Pure Mathematics seems to have limited use in the real world, and I believe that Physics is where Mathematics is at its most useful – helping to explain otherwise inexplicable problems. While Physics is very in-depth, it also has an extensive range, covering the most simple and the most complicated concepts, and in my opinion this gives the subject a limitless fascination.

As a result of what I have learnt I was compelled to find out about topics not covered in the A-Level course. I have read Stephen Hawking's "A Brief History of Time", Richard Feynman's "The Strange Theory of Light and Matter", Frank Close's "Antimatter" and Brian Cox's "Why Does $E=mc^2$?". These have really opened my eyes to how vast the subject is and consequently black holes and quantum electrodynamics are areas I am particularly looking forward to studying. As I learn more and more, my desire to continue to learn has grown exponentially and I feel that as the subject becomes more complex it also becomes more fascinating. The book "From Here to Infinity" by Ian Stewart gave me a great insight into modern mathematics and its applications. I am a regular reader of BBC Focus magazine and any scientific articles I come across as I try to keep abreast of current research and advancements. The particle collider at CERN in Geneva is where many of the latest advances in Physics have been made, and after university I would like to become involved in something so momentous. Ultimately I want to take my academic study of Physics as far as I can.

Playing in the school orchestra has made me realise how important teamwork is, and the need for practice and commitment to make a group project successful. Teamwork has also played a part when I was one of a group of volunteers painting an orphanage and when I was a member of a Boy Scouts troop. Being a House Prefect has made me feel a sense of responsibility for others, whilst participating in the Headmaster's Discussion Group has given me greater confidence in expressing and defending my ideas in public. A week's work experience at an offshore drilling company, while not focused on physics, gave me an insight into what the real world wants from its scientists and the need to develop applications to help with everyday problems. I have also participated in the UKMT Maths Challenge for several years, earning 5 Gold awards and a Best in School Award. With my subjects at A2 level, I can see that Physics links in with all my other subjects; with Mathematics in hundreds of ways, but also with Chemistry, such as electron spin in atoms which is very important in NMR spectroscopy and orbital arrangements. Overall, I find the infinite scope of Physics enthralling and I am eager to study it further.

Universities applied to:

- Oxford: Offer
- Lancaster: Offer
- Durham: Offer

- Warwick: Offer
- Edinburgh: Offer

Good Points:

This is a well-written and structured statement. The student is clearly highly motivated and has read extensively on their chosen subject.

Bad Points:

The student mentions family influences into pursuing a numerate discipline at university, family influence is only ever a bad thing in a personal statement, and should be avoided. The student makes a bold statement, 'but Pure Mathematics seems to have limited use in the real world'. Whilst the student's courage is taken to be a positive quality by this reader, it is important to remember that the final reader(s) of the statement will be academics and admissions tutors at universities who have a wide range of technical backgrounds. A physics tutor may have completed an undergraduate degree and possibly even a PhD in pure mathematics before moving into research which has led to them becoming physics-focused. It is important not to offend the reader. On the subject of reading, the student lists a considerable number of books which they have read, but does not elaborate on what they learned or enjoyed from most of them. It is always better to read one book and talk about it in a meaningful way, than read ten and say nothing.

Overall:

This is a very good statement. The student does not come across as arrogant or over-confident, however, makes a bold and risky claim regarding the relevance of an entire subject discipline.

Subject: Physics

"You can do anything." When people see grades like mine this is often what they say to me. But I don't want to just do anything; I need something that will challenge me and keep me constantly thinking. When you love learning as much as I do you want to learn about the big things, and what is bigger than the universe? Physics aims to study the workings of the universe from the movement of an electron into a new orbital to the periodic rotation of the greatest galaxies. What I love about physics is the way it takes this vast universe and organises it into laws, taking the apparent chaos of matter and proving there are greater forces holding it all together. I love learning about the fundamental properties of the universe that so many people don't give a second thought about and wonder why they aren't as fascinated by the miracle of light as I am. The universe is not just some distant stars to me; I am a part of it and it is a part of me. The atoms in me came from a supernova explosion and to study the physics that makes these things happen is to study myself.

I have been top of my class since primary school and learning, remembering and explaining all come quite naturally. With 10A* and an A in my GCSEs I proved to myself that I am a well-rounded pupil. But when required to think about it, I know science is where my greatest strength lies. By coming first in GCSE Biology in Northern Ireland and second in Physics and Maths it demonstrated to me that I have the ability for both explaining why and calculating how. When I come across documentaries like Brian Cox's Wonders of the Universe or read books like Paradox by Jim Al-Khalili I realise that physics is so much more fascinating than what we are taught at school. This past year I have had a real thirst for finding out more about physics, particularly astrophysics and relativity. I have found this interest has driven me in my studies and this year I received the Physics' Prize in school.

Art is also a big part of my life and I thoroughly enjoy studying it at A level. For me it is a link in my studies between learning about the world and responding to it. It teaches me indispensable skills, such as being able to analyse and think for myself, to push myself to go deeper into the meaning of a theme or object. I am constantly evaluating my thoughts, learning from mistakes and taking inspiration from those who have gone before me. These are skills that have transferred seamlessly to my more scientific work. An artist is forced to experiment and then build on their findings. The key to a good scientist is one who is not afraid to experiment and learn. Even accidents, if well observed, can lead to the greatest discoveries, like Fleming's famous penicillin find.

My Christian beliefs have not conflicted with my love of science; they make me want to delve further into the depths of how the world has been made. Reading books like "Has Science buried God?" by John Lennox confirmed to me that science and religion are entirely compatible. Professor Lennox's debates concerning this absolutely fascinated me and encouraged me to question what we believe. Although I love spending time to reflect by myself, I equally enjoy interacting and working with others. I have been a committed member of the Girl's Brigade since I was 4 and have completed Bronze, Silver and Gold Duke of Edinburgh Awards with school. I also have a passion for leading and teaching so last year I became a pupil mentor for junior science pupils which has given me a greater understanding of how to express scientific ideas. I've also led a summer camp and am deeply involved in teaching at Sunday School. This year I have been elected to be one of 6 Senior Prefects and a member of the SU Committee. I have a very enthusiastic personality and adore encouraging others to share my passions. At SU I have started a Q and A section where people are encouraged to query what they believe and seek a deeper understanding of their faith.

Music is another one of my passions; I have been playing guitar for 4 years and love composing my own songs and trying to find the perfect words for my thoughts. I've found I'm the kind of person that considers music from both perspectives; how the perfectly tuned standing waves create a longitudinal pressure wave of sound that propagates to the ear and how a couple of notes combined with the right rhythm and phrase can instantly change a mood. It is my passion for both the scientific and the creative that make me who I am and hope you appreciate this as you consider me for your course.

Universities applied to:

- Oxford: Offer
- Durham: Offer
- Bristol: Offer
- Queen's University Belfast: Offer
- Manchester: Offer

Good Points:

This is an undeniably strong and impressive statement. The student is clearly very talented at a great number of things, from academics to art and music. The introduction makes the statement stand out immediately. Reasons other than becoming interested in physics following A-level studies are abundant, clearly explained, and expanded upon. The student addresses the reader directly and closes with a point that is addressed solely to the reader. This comes across well as it means that the student recognises that the reader is an individual.

Bad Points:

This is a very strange personal statement. The student opens by explaining how others perceive her intelligence to be so great that anything is possible. Later in the statement, the student seems to brag about having 'been top of class since primary school and learning, remembering, and explaining all come quite naturally. With 10A* and an A in my GCSEs'. It is not possible from this statement to tell if the student achieved this by overcoming great adversity, or if the likelihood was low due to the poor resources of the school at which the student studied. The reader is left wondering if privilege, opportunities, and resources were abundant to the student, or if the student is a remarkable success story from an impoverished area. In either case, the student's over-confidence and pomposity is very clear and this does not come across well at all.

This reader is left in no doubt that the student is a highly intelligent and multi-talented individual, however, it's hard for admissions tutors to relate to her on account of the overconfidence with which she conveys herself. Whilst it is important to showcase individual achievements, it is important to remember that the reader is a stranger who does not know the student. Sweeping statements about oneself can be taken wrongly and out of context, and in this case, the student has failed to account for this.

Overall:

This is a very strange statement where the student makes sweeping statements about herself, which can easily be interpreted in the wrong way and taken out of context. Slight tweaks emphasising the core drivers behind her accomplishments would enhance this statement beyond its already excellent nature.

NOTES

Subject: Physics

An incessant curiosity about the laws of the cosmos has always attracted me to the study of physics. I am especially intrigued by theoretical physics and how its concepts are the foundations of all visible reactions one witnesses daily. My fascination with physics has led me to pursue my subject beyond the school curriculum and I have had a range of experiences which have confirmed my desire to study physics at university.

This summer I was selected for the Senior Physics Challenge at Cambridge University which enabled me to experience the level and pace of undergraduate classical mechanics, quantum mechanics and lab-work. In preparation for the course, I studied a quantum mechanics primer and familiarised myself with previously untaught mathematics. During the week, we tackled the Schrodinger equation, square well potential problems, Heisenberg's uncertainty principle and learnt new aspects of mathematics such as eigenstates and SHM. The course was demanding and thus highly engaging, and this encounter with higher-level physics has made me eager to extend my knowledge of quantum mechanics.

Selected to visit CERN with school on the basis of an essay competition on dark matter and dark energy, I attended lectures on particle physics and saw the LHCb experiment. The highlight of the trip being the coding activity organised by Liverpool University where, using real LHC data of a decaying kaon, we chose cuts to make in the data to improve the efficiency and purity of the signal. Gaining an insight into aspects of the research work undertaken by particle physicists was inspiring. Likewise, at a "Particle Physics Day" at Birmingham University, I had the opportunity to use computer software to identify different particles and collisions in detectors.

Last summer, I attended the "Physics Experience Week" organised by Birmingham University that combined lectures, lab-work and a rocket-building session. I was fascinated by an experiment where, collaborating in a team with pupils from different schools, we counted cosmic ray muons using a scintillation detector and took down readings together.

Having chosen to study GCSE Astronomy independently, I learnt to use the Faulkes Telescopes to take photographs of Messier objects in order to determine the ages of 3 planetary nebulae. My interest in space has been enhanced by a 2-week trip to NASA with 'Space Education Adventures', visiting the Johnson and Kennedy Space Centres. I was astounded by the immensity of the space projects and their contribution to science and history. A work experience placement in a hospital Medical Physics department demonstrated to me the application of physics in medical diagnostic imaging and the importance of physics research for advances in medicine. The Engineering Education Scheme (year 12) enabled me to work with 3 other girls to design a hypothetical football training academy with engineer mentors from ARUP. We researched and presented a business case and technical plan to a panel of engineers from other companies, gaining the Gold Crest Award in Engineering as well as valuable presentation skills.

In complete contrast, this summer I attended the Joint Association of Classical Teachers' Greek Summer School. In addition to intensive lessons, we performed Aeschylus' Agamemnon in the original text; I was cast as Cassandra. This term I am giving a talk on Ancient Greek mathematics at my school's Classical Society, having researched the topic over the summer. I enjoy performing arts: I belong to the Birmingham Young REP Theatre and I have performed in the Symphony Orchestra, a chamber music group and the Choral Society at school. Balancing academic work with other activities requires organisation and discipline. Physics is a demanding and highly rewarding field. The prospect of an unsolved problem which may not have an immediate answer is captivating. My wish to understand nature and the academic challenge this poses is the reason I aspire to study physics.

Universities applied to:

- Oxford: Offer
- Imperial College London: Offer
- Manchester: Offer

- Bristol: Offer
- University College London: Rejected

Good Points:

This is a very well-written, structured, and excellent statement. The student has a clear motivation for physics and has achieved many things through extra hard work. The statement is easy to read and the student describes their achievements yet does not brag. All points and experiences are expanded on and clearly explained. The final paragraph adds individuality to the statement, and all non-physics-related interests are kept within this paragraph which is very good.

Bad Points:

The student uses the word 'I' a lot. Whilst it is important to emphasise personal achievements, using the same words over and over again makes the statement sound repetitive. The student mentions learning mathematics beyond the A-level syllabus prior to the Senior Physics Challenge at Cambridge University, however, does not expand on what this involved. The student has missed an opportunity to describe how they gained mathematical skills independently. The student does this again by failing to describe what they learned through writing their essay on dark matter. A sentence on each of these points would have added yet more value to this excellent statement.

Overall:

This is an excellent statement. It is easy to read, well-structured, and the student comes across as a very likable individual.

NOTES

EARTH SCIENCES

Subject: Earth Science

I wonder how many people on Earth know that approximately 2, 3 billion years ago was the so-called "oxygen catastrophe" which lead to the largest extinction ever known? And if we go deeper into the earth's history we notice that life and the Universe itself are a chain of "lucky" events. This may be controversial or overwhelming, but it made me grateful for the fact that I am here to write this statement and of course, it inspired me to study earth sciences.

My fascination for nature began during my early childhood and my first family mountain trips, when I could not help asking myself "How have all these formed?" The answers started to come during secondary school when I was training with my teachers for Physics and Geography student competitions. My inclination for science was clear when I entered a Mathematics Computer Science class in high school.

My motivation grew stronger with my qualification for the International Earth Science Olympiad 2010, when I had the opportunity to approach subjects ranging from Astronomy to Oceanography both at theoretical and practical levels. My entire hard work was awarded the Bronze Medal and this gave me even more energy and enthusiasm.

Encouraged by this achievement, in 2011 I participated in the Scientific Research Project Contest for high school students where my paper won the Second National Prize for environmental Geography. My study involved the research of the evolution and impact of a local landslide to the natural landscape and villagers' life. In 2012 I participated in the same contest and I improved my cartography skills using my own GIS based maps. Later, I competed in the National Earth Science Olympiad achieving the maximum result for Geography theoretical and field test. Preparing for all there contests in the Chemistry and Physics laboratory fascinated me and made me more capable of individual study.

Although, I usually prefer to focus my energy on science I am aware of the society I live in and of the ways I can bring my contribution to improve it. For this reason, I travelled to Italy in September 2011 to be a volunteer for the International Earth Science Olympiad. The contact with highly academic technologies, the preparations of the Olympiad practical tests and the fieldtrip to the Alps gave me a taste of being an earth sciences student and convinced me to want more. Also, in 2011 and 2012 I organised the Science Week Fair in my school and I was able to cooperate with a wide variety of students, manage and integrate different ideas and to gain leadership skills.

I posses not only the relevant qualities for my course option, but during high school I also improved a lot of my transferable skills. I choose to study in a Great Britain university because I want to take advantage of the best scientific environment, modern laboratories, research possibilities and highly qualified teachers.

I am a very positive person and I am open to every scientific challenge I could meet during my studies. In my readings I have always been interested in petrology, volcanism, tectonic plates and how earth dynamic systems interact with each other to create a diverse and original environment that supports living possibilities. Therefore, I want to apply all my future knowledge and bring my contribution to the sustainable development of our planet and the understanding of the Universe at large.

Universities applied to:

- Imperial College London: Offer
- University College London: Offer
- St Andrew's: Offer
- Edinburgh: Rejected
- Oxford: Offer

Good Points:

This is a well-written and structured statement. The student is clearly very motivated and this comes across well in the statement. The student mentions several earth science disciplines, including Oceanography and Astronomy. This is very good as earth sciences is an extremely broad course, and encompasses many subjects which are degree courses in their own right. The inclusion of the student's positive character is very important as fieldwork is an important part of any earth sciences degree. This gives the reader confidence that the student will maintain a positive outlook and character when in challenging circumstances in the field, and most importantly, be able to continue working in such circumstances.

Bad Points:

The student should use 'possess' instead of 'posses' at the start of the sixth paragraph. The student has a wealth of experience from extra-curricular activities, however, does not use these to describe their teamwork skills. In earth sciences, both field and lab work involve working as part of small closely-knit teams. If the student had described their teamwork skills in addition to their leadership skills, this would have added great value to the statement.

Overall:

This is a very good statement. The student explains all experiences well, however, does not elaborate on teamwork skills. Such skills are important in any earth science degree course and are highly desirable in potential students.

NOTES

Subject: Geology

My interest in geology was initially fuelled by visiting the Natural History Museum. There, I was fascinated by the diverse range of colours and structures the rocks took, motivating me to learn about what influences the development of different rocks. I investigated rocks further by collecting them from the sea shore and breaking them open to observe the internal structure. I wondered how minerals with strikingly similar chemical compositions could be so heterogeneous in appearance. For example, the properties of carbon allow the formation of diamond or graphite allotropes, depending on the exposure to temperature and pressure over time. Some of my most interesting rocks are pieces of Agate, and whilst they are very attractive I am particularly fascinated by how they form. Through my "Mindat" account I research rocks that I find, mineralogy is a field I am particularly keen to study.

Now, as a member of the Open University Geological Society, I keep in touch with the latest geological news by attending their regular events and reading the bi-monthly newsletter. The most recent event I attended was in Warrington, where I particularly enjoyed a lecture entitled "Meteorite impact and quaternary extinctions". I was intrigued by the methods geologists had used, such as examining the carbon content in the soil layers, searching for the presence of nanodiamonds and evidence left in animal bones, to support their theories. NYC

Whilst at college I arranged a years voluntary work experience (one day a fortnight) as an Environmental Safety Officer at Bentley Motors. In one project, we raised recycling rates by redesigning the process of waste disposal. To tackle a pollution problem, I produced an information sheet on the appropriate disposal of hazardous liquids, which was posted to employees on the company intranet. Not only did I learn valuable team working skills, I also learned how important environmental responsibility is to big companies – something which will become only more important in the future.

Since leaving college, I've worked to fund lessons in both driving and Japanese language and to save towards my future education. As a night porter in a Crowne Plaza Hotel, I assist customers and take responsibility for fire safety and security. In handling difficult situations, my skills of negotiation have been developed. I also worked for Royal Mail over the Christmas period – a role which developed my skills in organisation and working under pressure.

In my spare time, I particularly enjoy hiking and hill walking, and regularly tackle the UK's highest peaks with my friends. My favourite place to walk is Snowdonia; I was fascinated to learn even more about the glacial history of the Glyderau and Ogwen Valley at a recent Open University Geological Society event. I like to train by cycling, running and playing tennis at a local club. I'm interested in Japanese culture and language and am currently learning Japanese at evening classes – something which has improved my ability to work independently.

When starting my BTEC diploma, I was undecided between my interests in medical science and geology. I decided to pursue medical sciences academically, whilst learning about the environment and geology through my work experience placement and hobbies. I feel my BTEC triple merit in medical science shows my aptitude for independent study in the sciences, but my experiences have shown me I have a greater enthusiasm for geology. Therefore my ambition is to study geology to degree level and I would be extremely grateful of the opportunity to do so.

Universities applied to:

- Keele: Offer
- Plymouth: Offer
- Derby: Offer
- Portsmouth: Offer

Good Points:

The student is obviously highly motivated and is very humble. Geology degrees involve a great deal of fieldwork and require a certain degree of fitness, so it is encouraging to see that the student enjoys hillwalking and is accustom to adverse weather conditions. This will certainly be of use when in the field whilst studying. It is clear that the student's personal interest in geology is the reasoning behind their application. This is evident from their efforts outside of their BTEC in medical science. This is very encouraging as it shows a serious commitment to wanting to pursue geology at a higher (degree) level.

Bad Points:

The statement begins quite abruptly, without an introduction. It would have been better if the student broadly introduced geology and the reasons for their interest at the beginning of the statement. Many sentences can be restructured in order to save space and to be read more easily, e.g. 'Whilst at college I arranged a years voluntary work experience (one day a fortnight) as an Environmental Safety Officer at Bentley Motors'. This could be written as, 'Whilst at college, I arranged fortnightly voluntary work experience at Bentley Motors. Here, I worked as an Environmental Safety Officer for a year....'.

Overall:

This is a good personal statement. The student comes across as honest, humble, and motivated.

NOTES

Subject: Earth Science (Geology)

Taking part in a BSES Expedition to the Arctic in the summer of 2008 and experiencing field work and mapping in the dramatic landscapes of Svalbard had motivated me to select a four-year study abroad course in Geophysics. With the grades I achieved I was offered a place on a three-year course, but I am still interested in studying abroad so I have decided to take a gap year to use the time to improve my grades and gain work experience in Geology related work. I am now applying for the study abroad Geology course as this combines my interest in Geography, Maths and Physics with my passion for the outdoors.

Studying Geography has increased my awareness of the key geographical issues facing us today. By reading Planet Earth and Geoscientist I have improved my understanding of tectonic activity and natural hazards, inspiring me to research further into prediction and mitigation of natural disasters. Maths and Physics have been challenging, but I enjoy these subjects as they have helped develop my logical thinking skills and problem-solving skills.

In 2008 I took part in an Engineering Education Scheme, which required small groups to complete a science project. My group was given an assignment by BP titled 'Investigating How Much Energy Can Be Produced by a Typical Wave and How-to Set-up a System to Recover This Energy'. In addition to credits from BP, we achieved a BA Gold Crest Award, which is based on an assessment of 100 hours of science project work. By participating in this scheme, I improved teamwork and presentation skills. In 2007, I obtained a company sponsored scholarship to attend a Presidential Classroom Programme on Science, Technology and Public Policy. This was a weeklong conference in Washington D.C. for 300 students selected from around the world with the purpose of learning about the role of government in issues related to scientific discoveries and technological advances. As well as benefiting from an interesting program, I developed leadership and communication skills through the position of Project Manager of a group of 30 students for a team presentation.

During my time at school I have held various positions of responsibility, including House Captain, Prefect, form charity representative and assistant at the Junior School, which have helped to develop my communication skills with people of all ages and strengthened my organisation and leadership skills.

Out of school I like to undertake challenges and expeditions. Taking part in the Duke of Edinburgh Award scheme has helped me become independent and self-reliant and has helped me to improve my organisational skills. I have also learnt a number of essential life skills, including map reading and First Aid. Having achieved the Bronze Award, I am now working towards the Gold Award. In the summer of 2007 I took part in a World Challenge Expedition to Namibia. Through this experience I learnt about different cultures and the importance of contributing to developing communities. I also improved on my teamwork and further developed leadership skills, as I had to lead the team on various occasions. The 2008 BSES Expedition helped to improve all the above skills, but particularly focusing on teamwork.

With my enthusiasm for Geography, Maths and Physics and the skills I have developed through the challenges and expeditions, I believe I would be a very dedicated and determined student for the Geology course and I believe I would contribute well as an individual and as a group member to the University. *Conclusion paragraph*

Universities applied to:

- University College London: Offer
- Imperial College London: Offer
- Bristol: Offer
- Leeds: Offer

Good Points:

It is clear that the student is highly motivated, to the point at which they decided to take a gap year in order to achieve the grades necessary to apply to the exact course of their choice. The student's passion for the outdoors is a highly desirable quality as all geology degrees involve fieldwork and commitment to working in challenging environments, which is of paramount importance. The statement is compact and is not too long. This is good as it makes the statement have a greater impact on the reader.

Bad Points:

The introduction comes across as quite defensive of the student's choice to spend a gap year in order to improve their grades. Whilst taking a gap year in order to improve grades is not a negative point, the statement would have read better if the student didn't come across as defensive as they do in the opening paragraph. The student has a great number of experiences outside of their college studies, and this comes across well in the statement. However, the student fails to use this as an opportunity to describe how they overcame any difficulties and challenges associated with such experiences. This would have added great value to the statement.

Overall:

This is a very good statement overall. The student has clearly thought long and hard about their choice and is committed to the subject to which they are applying.

NOTES

Subject: Geography

Geography is outward-looking, dynamic and topical. It allows me to gain insight into daily news stories on immigration and Middle Eastern conflicts for example, by highlighting their complexity and the challenge to find and evaluate solutions to these problems for the future. The diversity and vital relevance of Geography makes it an immensely valuable subject to study in depth and I would relish the opportunity to pursue further study in the field.

The area that is of particular interest to me is development geography and specifically global aid. I was introduced to the use of aid in closing the wealth divide in my A2 case studies, where bottom-up aid on a local scale was consistently depicted as a sustainable solution. I was forced to question these views, however, after reading 'Dead Aid' by Dambisa Moyo. Her critical comments on charity-based aid particularly caught my attention as they offered a stark contrast in perspective on my case studies. I found it interesting that the factors which contributed to the success of many of the case studies, including small-scale, intermediate technology and low cost solutions were the very aspects of aid that Moyo calls 'band-aid' solutions implying unsustainability. The book also touched on the controversial issue of whether aid remains a successful or even acceptable solution when the $50 billion of aid given to Africa annually is arguably not producing significant economic development or improvement. To investigate this further I read 'The End Of Poverty' by Jeffrey Sachs which explained how well managed aid can indeed offer an answer to closing the wealth divide. This led to my research into the Millenium Villages of Ghana. Here aid, coupled with local leadership, appears to have delivered a long-term solution to serious economic and social problems. This divergence in opinion over a controversial issue has excited me about exploring these issues in more detail.

To investigate these issues further, I have been prompted to take a gap year to experience the workings of an international NGO. I will be joining the work of education promoting 'Empower A Child' in Uganda for 3 months.

I hope to gain a rewarding insight into the practical relevance of Geography in the field of non-profit aid and specifically to test Sach's belief that investment into education is a viable solution to ending poverty.

My other subjects complement my understanding of economic, physical and scientific elements of development and Geography in general. Reading 'Driven to Extinction' by Richard Pearson highlighted how Biology and Geography are inextricably linked in our study of the physical world, particularly with regards to the role regulatory systems have in levels of biodiversity. Chemistry and Physics have been relevant in equipping me with the skills to devise data collection programmes and to analyse the results; skills which were necessary to my fieldwork visit to Dartmoor.

My academic background is complemented by my extra-curricular activities. I was the Organ Scholar and Choir Prefect at my school. My responsibilities included conducting and directing the Chapel Choir on a weekly basis. I was also a fully committed and dedicated member of other choirs and ensembles. I relished the challenge of arranging and conducting in the House Singing competition which required me to inspire and motivate team work within the house. I have gained 3 Grade 8's in Organ, Piano and Flute and am currently working towards my Piano Diploma. I was involved in leading the school's Christian Union through which I have catalysed fundraising for organisations such as Mary's Meals. In my gap year I am working as Organist and Choir director at St Luke's Church Grayshott before going to Uganda. These activities demonstrate leadership skills, commitment and an enthusiastic approach to challenges, all of which will equip me well for the study of Geography at university.

Universities applied to:

- Oxford: Offer
- University College London: Offer
- King's: Offer
- Exeter: Offer
- Durham: Offer

Good Points:

This is a very good personal statement and is well-written. The student is clearly interested by many aspects of geography, which is very important as geography is a multi-disciplinary subject. The student describes several areas of geography which capture their interest, demonstrating their interest and commitment to the reader. The student justifies their decision to take a gap year well, and the relevance their activities will have to the subject of geography and their interests in global aid.

Bad Points:

The student misspells the word 'millennium' in the second paragraph. The second paragraph is also very long. It is hard for the reader to stay focused when reading through long paragraphs, and it would have been better if the student had separated the second paragraph into two. The final paragraph is also very long and it is not clear where the conclusion begins. As a result, the end of the statement does not deliver the impact which the student has intended to produce. If the student separates the sentence, 'These activities demonstrate leadership skills, commitment and an enthusiastic approach to challenges, all of which will equip me well for the study of Geography at university' into a new final paragraph, this would have made the final statement much more effective.

Overall:

This is a very good statement. The student has a wealth of experiences and is clearly very motivated to study geography. Some paragraphs are very long and this reduces the impact that the statement has on the reader. With some restructuring, this could be an excellent statement.

NOTES

ENGINEERING

Subject: Engineering

All comforts of today's life are taken for granted, but who contributed towards creating them? The answer is what firstly inspired me to enter into civil engineering. Civil engineers put roofs over our heads and roads under our feet. They create bridges that minimize distances, tunnels that link countries underwater and make our world a healthier place to live in by managing efficiently the surrounding air, water and natural resources. I expect civil engineering to be challenging – as even a little mistake can be fatal – but also very self-rewarding because of its creativity and application of ideas.

The most inspiring moments of my life as an ambitious student were during my visit at CERN, the world's largest particle physics laboratory. I had the chance to be among engineers and physicists that seek answers and contribute to the understanding of the universe by studying the tiniest particles. Young researchers informed me about the existence of fundamental particles recently invented and how they link to the creation of our universe. Particularly, the Large Hadron Collider inspired me towards engineering and making a change to today's understanding. I'm currently reading, "Structures: Or Why things don't fall down" and "Remaking the world: Adventures in Engineering" and hope to read more on the subject of engineering at university.

Competitions have always been a strong point. From an early age I have participated in many competitions, receiving national awards in Mathematics, Physics and Computer Science. They provided me with the chance to challenge myself and develop a love for problem solving. Overcoming obstacles and finding solutions after hours of work gave me a sense of self accomplishment. The methods of problem solving in Maths helped me work out answers in mechanics and gain a full understanding of theoretical physics.

What's more, as part of my Computer A-Level I had to identify the problems of a civil engineering company and produce a solution by designing a computerized system. This enabled me to sharpen my analytical thinking and have a closer look at the management of such company.

Along with sciences, music is also a passion of mine. I have a grade 8 in piano and music theory and I'm currently preparing for a piano diploma in music performance. Through the preparation of it, I created an appreciation of music in a high level and enjoyed performing pieces of highly demanding technique so early in my life. In addition, I've taken place in the journalist's team of my school trying to restore the municipal park of my town. My writing and communication skills were developed as much teamwork was involved and after research and interviews we published in the local newspaper our opposition to the destruction of this green source of life. Protecting the environment is one aspect of civil engineering. I intend on practicing this profession as ecologically as possible.

Becoming a civil engineer will give me the opportunity to apply my knowledge in Sciences into making the dream reality. I am ready to face all the challenges that will come along: those of university life and those of future career, always aiming in the improvement of mankind living.

Universities applied to:

- Cambridge: Offer
- Imperial College London: Offer
- University College London: Offer
- Bath: Offer
- Sheffield: Offer

Good Points:

This is a very well-written and compact statement. The student starts by explaining their interest in a particular branch of engineering and then goes on to explain their interest in science. This may be because the student has applied for several different courses with their UCAS application, however, the statement manages to remain specific to engineering yet general enough to encompass the physical sciences.

Bad Points:

The student exclusively describes their interests in civil engineering and does not mention any other branches of engineering. Whilst this may be relevant for applications to universities offering civil engineering as a single discipline, other universities such as Cambridge offer general engineering degrees with the option of specialising available in the third year of study. To make the statement more relevant to general engineering, the student should have mentioned other engineering disciplines. Some sentences are not well-written, e.g. 'My writing and communication skills were developed as much teamwork was involved and after research and interviews we published in the local newspaper our opposition to the destruction of this green source of life'. This could be written as, 'My writing, communication, and teamwork skills were developed through the production of a published newspaper article in opposition to....'

Overall:

This is a very good statement, although is quite focused towards civil engineering. The student could have made the application more relevant to general engineering by mentioning their enthusiasm to gain a broad experience in general engineering before specialising in civil engineering.

NOTES

Subject: Engineering

As a child being driven over London's Albert Bridge I was intrigued by the sign saying somewhat cryptically 'all ranks must break step'. Years later at school next to the Millennium Bridge I wanted to understand what had caused the bridge to be closed just after it was opened and discovered the connection. The same principle applies to both situations. I observed the side to side motion of pedestrians on the reopened bridge and understood how the engineers designing it had not accounted for these lateral forces that were acting at the bridge's natural frequency, half that of the downward forces. The designers of the older and more rigid bridge had relied on written instructions to avoid the downward forces from soldiers walking in step synchronising with the bridge's natural frequency. In 2001 the unforeseen problem was resolved using dampers and stiffening against lateral deflection. These bridges and their weaknesses opened my eyes to engineering.

I take pleasure in the challenge of solving problems that require more than just knowledge of how to use an equation and instead necessitate logical thought to work out how the problem can be approached. This includes applying maths to resolve a physical situation, an area which I enjoy very much. I have spent time following up differential equation (simple harmonic motion) and mechanics questions (projectiles) which are also relevant to engineering. My coursework presentation on Kevlar instigated an interest in materials, by understanding how its chemical properties, notably the aromatic bond, combined to make such a strong, flexible and low-density material with uses in many areas of engineering from bikes to bullet proof vests.

During work experience at Halcrow Yolles I witnessed engineering in action in Structural, Mechanical and Facade engineering. In the building services department I partook in a competition for an eco-friendly building in a hot climate by researching ways to achieve HVAC efficiency by designing structures which encourage the stack effect to improve ventilation and using window film to filter out UV rays, reducing the need for air conditioning.

My findings were then discussed with my team. I relished my involvement and have since kept up my interest in environmental engineering, particularly geo-engineering, which is likely to become an important field as a last resort to counteract climate change. I would be interested to pursue this as a graduate. This placement introduced me to the analytical, mathematical and problem-solving skills involved in the processes of engineering which I feel well suited to.

Engineering at a top university will provide a challenge that I will enjoy confronting. I have a desire to gain an understanding of the principles that govern our world and how we manipulate them for our own uses as well as enjoying a balance between applied mathematics and the physical aspects of engineering. I will defer entry to university to give myself experience in both the mathematical and practical side of engineering by spending a year in industry. I am looking for a placement in the automotive industry with SEAT to enhance my Spanish. The experience will help me conceptualise the more theoretical aspects of engineering courses. I will allow time to get back up to speed with maths before university begins.

As a senior prefect who mentors Year 9s in maths and takes part in CCF and CSO I have developed my teamwork and organisational skills. Determination and focusing on my targets help me fulfill my objectives. I devised, organised, and encouraged others to train for and join in a 300 mile cycle ride from London to Paris, raising GBP 6000 for our school charity. I enjoy sports, playing football for school in my free time, but also ensure that I complete work efficiently and to a high standard.

Universities applied to:

- Cambridge: Offer
- Durham: Offer
- Warwick: Offer
- Bristol: Offer
- Bath: Offer

Good Points:

This is a very good statement. The statement is well-written and structured. The student clearly explains their motivation for wanting to pursue engineering. The statement mentions and describes the student's desire to pursue a number of different engineering disciplines, which is very good as this makes the statement relevant to applications for courses of a single engineering discipline, and to those for general engineering. The student's use of their desire to study Engineering 'at a top university' is very good as the student does not mention any one university specifically. This makes it clear that the student has taken their application to every university in their UCAS application seriously, something which is often not the case for students who are applying to Oxbridge.

Bad Points:

The student uses several acronyms which are not written out in full. This assumes that the reader will be familiar with such acronyms, which may not be the case. This reader has no idea what 'CSO' means, rendering its inclusion in the statement useless. There are commas missing in places, however, this is a minor error.

Overall:

This is a very good statement, however, the reader is left to work out what the meanings of several acronyms are for themselves. With a little more attention to the reader, this statement would be excellent.

NOTES

Subject: Design Engineering

Based on my two different spheres of interests studying Design Engineering is an obvious choice for me. Besides my fondness for drawing and photography, which has given me a particular openness to Modern Arts, I also find pleasure in problem solving hence my A Level equivalent choices of Mathematics and Physics. However, I intend to move from theories and abstract mathematical models towards their applications. My multicultural background provides me with a unique perspective that is reflected in my interest and desire to study design engineering.

At a very early age in Ecuador, my father sent me to the British School and later on gave me the possibility to obtain German system based tuition in Deutsche Schule too. So I was introduced to two different traditions and languages relatively early. Later on, when I moved to Hungary with my mother, I felt lost and rootless. But with time I realized that integrating the traditions of Europe and Latin America is also useful which I experienced at Berzsenyi Daniel, one of the top grammar schools in Hungary. My class specialized in English and German places emphasis on the historical and cultural background of both countries. I have benefited from exchange student programs as well, which were not only precious experiences, but also helped me to make new friends. In addition, my initial interest in Mathematics, Physics and drawing grew with time on account of the excellent tuition I was offered, owing to advanced Maths and drawing classes (both 6 hours per week). I was lucky to participate in a summer Maths camp, which was organized for a selected group of students. This year's theme was structured around the use of computational projective geometry for camera calibration; this was a lucky coincidence, since I take deep interest in photography. This intense learning experience showed me how to combine two different fields. Consequently, I ended up attending a preparatory course in freehand drawing using isometric projection at Budapest Technical University, the most prestigious university of engineering in Hungary. I have also audited lectures where the question was formulated in me: which is more important form or function? I think they are pieces equivalent in size of the same virtual cake.

I value team work as an important factor in every culture. This realization proved to be really beneficial both as an elected member of the Student Council and as a leading organiser of a summer freshmen camp at school. These extracurricular activities played a significant role in my life as made me focus on the fact that teamwork is the third missing piece from that virtual cake.

Many examples of the nexus between art and science can be found such as Leonardo da Vinci the famous polymaths himself and inventions of our modern age like iPod. Nowadays this connection is becoming stronger than ever in order to meet the demands of the consumers. I believe that products have to be practical, yet aesthetically pleasing. In my hobby, photography, I am trying to design a DSLR camera with a movable viewfinder in order to get new point of views when taking shots.

Design engineering represents me the most ideal way to broaden my sphere of interests, to improve my skills and to use my creativity in order to shape our future. It is not only the multicultural environment of the UK, but also the tradition of education, I came to know at the British School before, that has attracted me the most. I believe that attending this complex course at a prestigious university in the UK would be the best opportunity to combine two different fields, engineering and art.

Universities applied to:

- Glasgow: Offer
- Nottingham: Offer
- Brunel: Offer
- Aberdeen: Offer
- Dundee: Offer

Good Points:

The student's life experiences are clearly the driving force behind their choice of subject and this comes across in the statement. clearly, the student has taken the time to research their chosen subject and is enthusiastic enough about design engineering to try and design their own DSLR camera.

Bad Points:

The statement is in a back-to-front order. The student opens with a sentence: 'Based on my two different spheres of interests studying Design Engineering is an obvious choice for me', however, does not actually state what these two spheres are. The introduction is not separated from the main body of the statement which makes the entire statement hard to follow.

The statement reads more like an account of the student's life rather than a statement as to why the student wants to study design engineering specifically at university. Whilst it is, of course, important to describe important life experiences and their relevance to one's choice of degree choice, it is not necessary to give an in-depth account on one's entire life. The student goes off on a tangent early on in the statement and finally gets to the point of the statement in the final two paragraphs. The student does not make any references as to why any of the points raised in the main (second), third nor fourth paragraph are relevant to their application, making most of this statement seem irrelevant.

Overall:

Although the student has led an interesting life and is clearly very motivated by their subject, they have let themselves down. The student writes in a completely unstructured way with the majority of the statement dedicated as an autobiography. The few points explained in terms of their relevance to the student's choice of design engineering appear at the very end of the statement, whereas they should be after the introduction.

NOTES

Subject: Engineering Science

I have always considered myself creative; much of my youth was spent designing and building with my Dad in his workshop. I would read encyclopaedias on cars and watch design-related TV programmes such as BBC's Robot Wars, analysing the strengths and weaknesses of each robot and thinking about how they could be improved. This background, combined with a genuine enjoyment of mathematics and physics, has given me a desire to read engineering at university.

Reading Marcus du Sautoy's "The Music of the Primes" and Simon Singh's "Fermat's Last Theorem" has shown how individuals have dedicated their lives to solving seemingly simple problems. The main attraction of these books and mathematics more widely, is problem solving, which is also what draws me to engineering. Solving a wide variety of problems is something I really enjoy; in the most recent UKMT Senior Maths Challenge, I was awarded a gold certificate, also the best score in my year at school.

Studying physics at A-Level has helped me to understand the world, and answered questions I had as a child; why does a satellite stay in orbit? How does gravity work? Why does a clock pendulum keep in time? My favourite aspect of physics is mechanics, complemented by my maths mechanics modules. The application of physics and mechanics to engineering was obvious from the outset; it is a fundamental skill set which bridges the gap between science and invention. I also enjoy studying Further Pure Mathematics, in particular calculus, and am interested in how the solutions of second order differential equations apply to problems in mechanics.

Projects including designing and making a desk lamp, a torch and bench vice grips in GCSE Engineering gave me an initial insight into the discipline. The course gave me hands on experience with equipment typical of an engineering department. Considering the benefits of materials was important too; from an economic, aesthetic, and practical perspective. I also secured work experience at a BMW Mini Plant in the 'Whole Vehicle Analysis', section.

One project involved heating up a Mini's bonnet to address complaints from customers in hot countries that the bonnet scoop sagged. I used CNC measuring equipment and helped to write up one of a series of reports, resulting in an alloy being added to the scoop so it retained its structure. The week introduced me to engineering in the real world, the importance of quality control and precision and the cost of a company's mistakes.

Aside from my studies, I have always had a musical interest and am working towards grade 7 piano. I completed work experience at the local 'Yamaha Homeworld' music shop specialising in top range digital pianos. I am constantly impressed at how a digital piano can look, feel, and respond exactly like a real piano. I like being part of a team and am a keen rugby and cricket player. Being elected as prefect and head boy has further helped me to work well, and get on with others, as well as improving my public speaking. This has been complemented by taking Grade 8 'Speaking in Public' last year, in which I achieved a distinction. I now feel confident talking in front of large groups and being able to communicate my ideas easily. Reading Steven Johnson's "Where Good Ideas Come From" discussed the theory that "ideas are generated by crowds where connection is more important than protection" and for me this epitomises the importance of team work and communication within engineering.

Ultimately, I would like to play a role in the future of our rapidly developing world; studying engineering at university will not only give me the skills to do this, but will also stimulate my passion for mathematics and science.

Universities applied to:

- Oxford: Offer
- Imperial College London: Offer
- Bristol: Offer
- Durham: Offer
- Exeter: Offer

Good Points:

This is an excellent statement. The student begins with personal reasons as to why they are interested in engineering, and by the end of the introduction, the reader is left in no doubt that the student is absolutely sure they want to pursue engineering at a higher level. The student successfully describes a range of experiences and interests covering several engineering disciplines and keeps the application general enough to be relevant to a general engineering degree. The statement is well-structured with a clear introduction, main body, and end.

Bad Points:

Although the student mentions several experiences/interests covering several engineering disciplines, they fall short of naming a specific engineering discipline that captures their interest. Whilst this is not a requirement, naming a particular field of engineering as capturing one's interest above other fields would demonstrate a level of decisiveness to the reader. Many universities do not offer general engineering degrees, and it is possible a student who is applying for engineering at Oxford or Cambridge will also make several applications to universities for specific engineering disciplines. It is important to keep the statement general enough for applications to general engineering courses but also specific enough for applications to individual engineering disciplines. This would have been possible by stating an interest in a particular engineering discipline.

Overall:

This is an excellent statement, one that is well-written and well-structured. The student's motivation to study engineering is clear, although the student falls short of naming a specific field of engineering which capture's their interest above all others.

NOTES

Subject: Engineering

In the eyes of an eight-year-old, the Clifton suspension bridge was an amazing sight and my first exposure to the complexities of engineering. Seeing how the deck was supported by comparatively thin cables sparked my interest in the basics of material properties and the concept of tensile and compressive forces acting on various parts of structures. Encountering parabolas and catenaries in Mathematics made me aware of how apparently abstract concepts can have such an important practical role. The span and height made me appreciate some of the problems that many engineering projects face. Reading 'Structures or Why Things Don't Fall Down' by J. E. Gordon helped me understand the basic principles of structural integrity such as distributing the compressive loads on an arch through the voussoirs and to the abutments.

My previous belief that failure of the Tacoma Narrows was caused solely by vortex shedding induced resonance was questioned in the 1990 paper by K. Yusuf Bilah et al. Computer modelling of the "wobbly" Millennium Bridge in London failed to correctly predict the "positive feedback" phenomenon where the movement of the bridge, initially due to pedestrians, itself caused the people to walk instep and so compounding the resonant effect, requiring the corrective use of fluid and tuned mass dampeners. This shows that whilst engineers must attempt to consider all relevant variables and the nature of the loading whilst designing, there will always be unforeseen complications that require practical solutions.

My study of Mathematics has exposed me to concepts that have seemingly abstract uses, but when applied to engineering, they play a crucial part. Complex numbers enable us to represent cyclic systems such as oscillations, as well as being applied to principles such as the Continuity Equation. In fluid dynamics, it is interesting to see how they can be used to represent simple ocean waves using Airy Wave Theory.

Studying Physics has provided me with a practical understanding of many fundamental engineering principles as well as the limitations imposed by the actual physical properties of the materials used. Business Studies enabled me to develop the financial and project management skills necessary in successful engineering projects. Competing in both the National Maths Challenge and Physics Olympiad has given me an experience of solving challenging problems.

My work experience with GKN Aerospace and Stirling Dynamics involved working in both the design office and on the shop floor. I gained an insight into the many disciplines concerned with the designing and manufacturing of planes, as well as a grasp of many of the problems to overcome. This corrected my previous view that engineering simply applied the fundamental laws of science. Instead it uses them in a very practical way, finding solutions that, whilst always functional, often do not rule out the possibilities of creative aesthetics. Reading 'The Simple Science of Flight: From Insect to Jumbo Jets' by Henk Tennekes explained the phenomenon of wing tip vortices and helped me understand the function of the elegant vertical wing tip projections. During my GAP year, in addition to gaining maturity skills, I plan to work for an offshore oil company in Australia. This will introduce me to an international company as well as a large and complex industry sector.

The challenges of the Duke of Edinburgh Gold Award provided me with invaluable experience, strengthening my team work and leadership skills. The volunteering aspect of the award has enhanced my inter-personal skills and sense of responsibility. My many sporting and musical achievements demonstrate my drive and determination for success.

I am keen to work in the energy industry and face the challenges posed by the need for long term sustainable energy sources with managed environmental impact. My academic potential combined with my passion are but two strengths that I believe will aid me in university life.

Universities applied to:

- Oxford: Offer
- Exeter: Offer
- Southampton: Offer

- Bath: Offer
- Durham: Offer

Good Points:

This is a very good statement. The student is clearly very motivated and their reasoning to pursue engineering is clear. The student has read around their subject and evidence of this is displayed through the use of a reference to a published paper. The student clearly had skills far beyond the scope of A-level studies, and the student's ambitions are clear through their plan to take a gap year in Australia.

Bad Points:

The student plans to undertake a gap year prior to starting university, however, only subtly mentions this towards the end of the statement. Whilst there are no problems in taking gap years and making deferred applications, it is important to be absolutely clear about this. It is quite surprising to the reader to learn the student's gap year plans towards the end of the statement. The student mentions achieving a gold award for the Duke of Edinburgh Award, though, does not use this as an opportunity to describe and elaborate on how they overcame adversity and difficulties.

Overall:

This is a very good statement, however, the reader is left surprised towards the end with the student's description of gap year plans. It would have been possible to avoid this if the student had described their gap year plans (and reasons) earlier in the statement.

NOTES

Computer Sciences
Subject: Computer Science & Mathematics

My first experiences with mathematics throughout school were always enjoyable but not inspiring. While I loved working with maths, and enjoyed representing our school in both the UKMT and Hans Woyda team competitions, I felt that maths could not be the end-in-itself the school syllabus presented it as. As I progressed through secondary education, however, I began to really see it as the powerful tool to understand and structure reality that it is.

The first time I saw that my interpretation of the use of maths had some substance was during a work experience placement I organised at IMSO (International Mobile Satellite Organization). There I encountered some examples of the mathematical and computing problems involved in working with satellites: from the difference between the Euclidean geometry on a map and the Elliptical geometry on a globe, to the logistics of moving satellites around to meet demand while keeping them in orbit. These were problems that demanded much more than mere number crunching, and being exposed to this gave me a taste of what maths beyond school might involve. A second work experience spell at Siemens provided me a much more in-depth view of the important role that communication systems play in keeping a company running efficiently and effectively.

My passion for mathematics and computing was further extended while reading 'The Magical Maze' by Ian Stewart. The description of maths as the exploration of a maze of our own creation had an incredibly profound effect on my understanding of what research in mathematics involves. What interested me especially was the visual part of resolving problems, so that they did not rely completely on resolving long calculations. This was close to how I like to understand and explain my ideas in mathematics.

Douglas Hofstadter's 'Gödel, Escher, Bach' gave me a much deeper understanding of the axiomatic systems that make up maths and how parallels can be drawn between different subjects to gain a further understanding of them all. Connected by the theme of Gödel's Incompleteness Theorem, the author passes through seemingly unrelated topics, such as the problem of consciousness and the mathematics of Zen principles, to explain the theorem. Although not the focus of the book, I have also enjoyed reading the links that are presented between maths and computing; it seems to me that maths is not just related to computing – computing is the physical manifestation of mathematics.

Maths and computing are about describing mental processes in a precise, logical way. The rigour required for mathematical proof leaves little room for subjectivity: something can be proven, disproven or unproven, but this depends completely on the validity of your logic. The idea of being able to extract order from apparent chaos, working through concepts until they click is what I love about these subjects, and what has attracted me to take those as an integral part of my further education.

However passionate I am about my academic studies, I also enjoy being involved in extracurricular activities. As head of mentoring and a prefect, I have improved my organizational abilities working with staff and mentors in developing study programmes for those students requiring extra help. Completing the Duke of Edinburgh bronze award – now working on the silver award – has allowed me to practice and develop my leadership and teamwork skills.

In my spare time I enjoy playing tennis, skiing and swimming; the latter I practice at competition level. I also love travelling, as having spent my childhood in Denmark, Egypt, United Kingdom and Spain has given me a hunger for mixing with different cultures. I like to unwind by playing the piano - I find that the pleasure one derives from making a piece your own is one that few activities can match.

I am thrilled about the prospect of further study in these subjects with some of the leading professors in the fields, and look forward to participating in university life.

Universities applied to:

- Oxford: Offer
- Imperial College London: Offer
- Bristol: Offer

- Bath: Offer
- Loughborough: Offer

Good Points:

This is a well-written, structured statement. The student explains their reasons to pursue a dual honours degree and gives equal attention to both disciplines to which they are applying. The student adds personality to the statement by thoroughly explaining their own views on all of the examples of literature read around maths and computing.

Bad Points:

There are quite a lot of short paragraphs. The student could have saved space by consolidating some paragraphs into one, hence shortening the statement. The student starts three paragraphs with 'My' or 'In my'. This is quite repetitive. There are too many paragraphs; seven in total. Paragraphs five and six could be shortened and grouped into one paragraph. In the third paragraph, it appears as though the student has either forgotten to add an addition space (in order to start a new paragraph) or has incorrectly started a new line for the sentence 'Douglas Hofstadter's...'.

Overall:

This is a very good statement. The student has clearly achieved a lot and writes in a clear and easy-to-understand way. Attention is given to both maths and computer sciences, which is essential as the student is applying for a dual honours course. With some restructuring, this could be an excellent statement.

NOTES

Subject: Computer Science

I have been around computers for as long I can remember for reasons I can easily enumerate.

Playing a game, Pinball being the only interesting game that came with Windows XP, writing an essay or surfing the internet where the first things I learnt to do, from my father, who encouraged my to learn about this device. I hope that I will be able to continue learning about the computer on my future courses and extra-curricular activities at the university.

Although I loved computers from the moment, I sat in front of one, my passion for computer science emerged late, when I was in the first year of high school. I was always keen on mathematics for giving you the ability to explain different aspects of your everyday life but I have never pictured myself working in front of a computer and adore every single aspect of it. My dream field of study became clear from the very beginning, from the first pieces of code I saw and analysed.

The courses and the extra training classes I took in high school opened my mind on several areas of computer science, areas like game theory, dynamic programming or graph theory but more important, competitive programming.

I started competitive programming in my second year of high school because there was really fun to put to good use my knowledge in mathematics or physics and there were a lot of these two in the problems I solved. I started practising a lot in my spare time and especially in holidays and competed in some online contests held by websites like TopCoder, Codeforces or Codechef, contests that helped prepared me for working under pressure. I can state without any doubt that competitive programming is my favourite thing to do in my spare time because from any problem that you solve you learn something new or develop a new skill or technique, skills which I believe are essential for a good software engineer.

My passion for competitive programming keeps me informed about the recent discoveries and improvements made in the field of computer science about faster algorithms or more efficient data structures but also about the C++ standard, keeping me in touch with the development of programming languages and their applications. I also like to implement and test the algorithms that I learn in order to see if my implementation consumes less time/memory that the ones that are already used in famous libraries.

Even though computer science takes up a great deal of time, I manage to find time for my hobby, photography. I started learning photography when I entered high school by following the blogs of photographers I had heard of and by watching the tutorial on YouTube. My mother made me a huge surprise by buying me a semi-professional DSLR, which I still have, use and love. I remember the first time I went to the park with my camera, I took a photograph of basically everything, from people to fences. I continued my research and found really interesting things about photography and cameras in general, from the rule of thirds which refers to composition, to physics and how light bounces through the camera to form the image on the sensor. Besides creativity and an eye for composition, photography helped me see the beauty of nature, from extraordinary landscapes to little apparently insignificant bugs.

The knowledge I had in photography and in computer art helped me in gaining the first place in the logo design competition, organized by my high school. The same logo won the second place in the international phase of the competition, held within the European project of "Comenius Teaching Innovatively (With Focus on ICT) and its Impact On The Quality Of Education".

My prize was a trip to Mottola, Italy, where the second meeting of the project was held. There, I participated in lessons held by teachers from Bulgaria, Turkey, Czech Republic and Poland. I learnt many interesting things from those lessons and especially from the other students and saw how different subjects are taught in different countries.

I was part of the hosting team when the meeting was held in Romania, exactly one year after the Italian adventure. I saw how hard it is to organize an event like this and how careful you have to be at all the details in order to have a pleasant final result.

At university, I hope that I will learn areas that I have no formal experience of studying and, as a result, become a better competitive programmer and software engineer. I am looking forward with great anticipation to the challenges that will come and I hope will be able to bring a big contribution to the academic environment that university study will provide me with.

Universities applied to:

- Oxford: Offer
- Manchester: Offer
- University College London: Offer
- Birmingham: Offer

Good points:

This is a good statement. The student is clearly very motivated and has used personal experiences to demonstrate this. The student does not jump straight into their personal achievements but describes these after establishing their interest in computer science first. This is good as it makes the statement not sound like a list of achievements alone.

Bad Points:

The student's quality of writing is not very good in certain parts of the statement. There are numerous clumsy uses of English throughout the statement, which make it seem poorly polished and almost an afterthought. Luckily for the applicant, it was an afterthought for the admissions tutors too.

Overall:

This is a very good statement in terms of content, however, simple grammatical and type errors take away from the true value of the statement.

NOTES

Subject: Computer Science

I have a keen interest in the link between computing and the brain, an interest that was helped by the fact that I grew up in a household of scientists. This link is especially present in machine learning, even if modern machine learning is only loosely based on how the brain functions. I am fascinated by the possibility of having programs that teach other programs, and the complexity of the problems they might one day solve. Already, the Eugene Goostman chatbot, while being very controversial, suggests that machines may pass the Turing test.

The extremely logical nature of programming attracted me right away because of how universal it is. Computer logic can be applied to many different problems, and it is exciting to think that this theoretical knowledge can be extended to practical uses in inventions such as Google's self-driving cars. Making decisions in real time and in environments as complex as a street based on information from sensors seems incredible. I would like to learn how we have been able to make machines such as a self-programming computer that can establish the laws of motion simply from the way a pendulum swings with no knowledge of physics or geometry (as in Cornell's experiment).

Computer science interested me early on. With the "Lego Mindstorm" software I discovered the joy of building, from a few lines of instructions, programs that could actually move a lego robot. I also used "Gamemaker", which allowed me to build simple games. I then tried several small internet classes and learned basic Java before deciding that I wanted to go into more depth. I signed up on Coursera for the course "An Introduction to Interactive Programming in Python" offered by Rice University, and am currently taking the "Machine Learning" course by Andrew Ng. The notion of cost functions and how they can be used to derive predictions from a set of data caught my interest, and made me wonder what determines the choice of one cost function over another.

At a Cold Spring harbor summer camp on Bio coding, I recently discovered one of the many future uses of programming. We now have the tools to program DNA code and insert it into a cell in order to make it produce proteins of our choice. In the future, this technology could be used to cure sicknesses or make artificial immune systems. Combining biology and programming may further break down the barrier that exists between the real and the virtual, with technology literally becoming a bigger part of our biological lives.

Maths is important, and I have always enjoyed the type of thinking it requires. I have studied American, French and English maths, and it is interesting how they differ in their theoretical and practical approaches. I used maths in my python coursera course to create a little game with a ship - it rotated and shot asteroids. Even something this basic requires vectors to calculate the location and speed of each element, hit-boxes that use circles to calculate their positions relative to each other, and a trigonometric circle to determine the rotation of the ship. I have learned to appreciate the power of mathematical models when it comes to programming.

I also enjoy extracurricular activities such as Model UN, hosted at the International Telecommunications Union. I have developed my communication skills by working on political resolutions with others and defending them in front of an audience. In a committee about agriculture in LEDC's, I learned about the role technology could play in helping communities receive information about better farming practices. This year I am head of external communication for a conference held in 2015 that includes 386 foreign students and 33 schools.

I would like to study in Britain because it is a hub of academic activity and provides a rich and diverse environment in which I can expand my knowledge. After my studies, I would like to be in research, pushing the boundaries of computer science.

Universities applied to:

- Oxford: Offer
- Birmingham: Offer
- University College London: Offer
- Manchester: Offer

Good Points:

The statement is well-written and has a clear structure. The student is clearly very motivated by computer sciences and this comes across well. The student mentions that they come from a scientific family, however, does not give too much attention to this. This is good as it convinces the reader that the student is confident that they want to study computer sciences for reasons other than being pressured to by family.

Bad Points:

The student lists many computer science-related experiences which go beyond the A-level syllabus. Whilst this is important to do, the student would have produced more impact if they had mentioned fewer experiences but thoroughly described those which were mentioned. The student also does not talk about anything related to their subject which they did not understand/found difficult, and how they overcame this. This can be just as important as achievements, if not more, as it demonstrates to the reader the student's ability to overcome challenges and unfamiliar material. This would have added yet more value to an otherwise brilliant statement.

Overall:

This is a very good statement. The student's motivation for wanting to study computer sciences is clear. With some more expansion on the student's experiences, this statement would be excellent.

NOTES

Subject: Computer Science

I want to study computer science because I want to learn how computers work. I want to learn about the complex hardware that makes up the machine. I want to learn about how information is stored and which data structures are most efficient and useful to us. I want to learn how to code, not just more languages but the very logic that underpins them. I want to learn about the discrete mathematics that underpins the subject.

The reason I want to learn this is twofold. Firstly, computers have transformed and are transforming the world. Physics, Healthcare, Economics and many other major disciplines are being revolutionised by computing. At a local level the lives of individual people have been changed beyond recognition by the information revolution. It is my hope that a computer science degree will one day allow me to be a very, very small part of this. The second, and for me far more important, is an insatiable curiosity and a love of problem solving.

During my gap year I have been working in Technical Support Services at IBM. It has been an eye opening experience working for a company with such a pioneering computing culture and heritage. I have been working as a Client Support Manager, interacting directly with clients to provide effective and cost efficient technical support for their machines. I have learned a great deal from speaking to IBMers working in roles ranging from engineering to sales and marketing. I have gained an insight into the interplay between computer science, business and psychology required to transform a technological concept into something that can be sold to customers and clients. Of particular interest to me is the computer called Watson. It was designed to win the quiz show Jeopardy, a difficult task given that the questions are asked in natural English, understanding of which was something previously assumed to be uniquely human. Having overcome this problem and beaten the game show, IBM are now using the same technology to fight cancer. Watson is just one of a long line of developments that are increasingly blurring the lines between human and artificial intelligence, a topic I first found fascinating when reading Turing's paper on "Computing Machinery and Intelligence".

I have been reading Code by Charles Petzold. A part that interested me was the description of how Boolean logic can be applied to relays to build complex systems such as early adding machines. In addition I have been learning Python as part of the MIT Computer Science Open Course that I have been taking and have been taught the basics of C at IBM.

Throughout my gap year I have also been keeping up an interest in mathematics. I enjoyed reading the Mathematical Experience, which turned out to be just as much a journey into Mathematics as one into Philosophy and History. A chapter that I enjoyed focused on the use of computers to solve the Four Colour Conjecture in mathematics. In particular it was how the method of proof by exhaustion, now made possible on a new vast scale by computing, was questioning at a philosophical level the very certainty of mathematical proof. Furthermore I have been working to improve my own mathematical skills, by learning FP2 and by watching MIT lectures in mathematics.

Outside of work, I have spent a lot of time playing basketball, learning Spanish and salsa. I hope to use some of the money I have earned to go travelling in South America over the summer.

I think my exceptional work ethic, combined with a love of mathematics and problem solving will allow me to thrive in this degree and make the most of my time at Oxford.

Universities applied to:

- Oxford: Offer
- Manchester: Failed
- University College London: Failed
- St. Andrews: Failed
- York: Offer

Good Points:

This statement is well-written and structured. The student has a wealth of experience and does not rely on interest sparked by A-level studies alone. The student uses their experiences gained whilst working for IBM to give real-world examples of the importance of computer science. The student's motivation is clear from the first paragraph and this remains throughout the statement.

Bad Points:

The first paragraph reads more like a speech than an introduction. Whilst this may have been the intended effect, the use of the words 'I want' six times in the opening paragraph alone makes the statement sound repetitive. The student concludes the statement by referring specifically to the University of Oxford. This is very risky as the student faces possible rejection from all other universities that regard the student's clear desire to want to study at Oxford as meaning that they do not take other universities seriously. It was not necessary at all to specifically mention Oxford in the final sentence of the statement and this let the student down.

Overall:

This would have been an excellent statement if it were not for the unnecessary reference to the University of Oxford at the end. The student let themselves down and risked alienating the other universities to which they applied to.

NOTES

MATHS

Subject: Mathematics

My interest in mathematics has been closely related with competitions mostly because there were never any challenging problems in my regular classes. There were many difficult problems at my first competition which showed me that there are problems in mathematics that require both insight and talent to be solved. Afterwards I have participated in any competition I could in order to get a chance to solve as difficult problems as possible.

When I was 13 I attended my first state competition in maths and since then I have won five first places so far. At every state competition in which I participated I made new friends, had an excellent time and enjoyed solving various interesting problems. My first contact with the Olympiad problems was at the second state competition where I managed to solve one of that year's IMO qualifying questions although I have never seen any problem similar to it before. The sheer beauty of the ideas that combined to a solution of that problem demonstrated how beautiful mathematics can be and it has been like that so far.

For the last three years I have participated in many international competitions and won silver and a bronze medal at IMO 2010 and 2011, silver medal at Middle European Mathematical Olympiad 2009, silver medal at Mediterranean Competition 2009, gold medals at Mathematical Competition of Balkan Students 2009, 2010, 2011. I have also participated at few research based competitions such as International Mathematical Tournament of Towns in years 2010 and 2011 and won first prize both times. As a member of my school team I placed fifth (2010) and second (2011) at Princeton University Mathematical Competition (PUMaC).

I have twice participated in state competitions in informatics and won 4th and 8th place, four times in physics where I have won two second places one 8th and one 10th. I have been 16th in state competition in logic. At those competitions I have learned a lot about usefulness and power of mathematics in other subjects.

Every competition I attended persuaded me even more that I want to work in mathematics because it is easy to find problems with both beauty and originality of ideas and this is quite a rarity in other subjects. I have also met a lots of people at these competitions with whom I have something in common and that is love for maths. I have been training young competitors and found that I can teach quite well and I enjoy it. I've also worked with friends who have problems with maths or any related subject.

I am aware of the fact that competition mathematics is quite different from both research and college mathematics but I also discovered that beautiful ideas are common in every part of maths. On PUMaC I had a chance to work on some college mathematics subjects (linear algebra and graph theory) and I found it very interesting. On Tournament of Towns we were working on a research based project about Shappiro inequality and afterwards I wrote an article in local mathematics magazine about our results.

My other interests are table tennis and travelling. I have been playing table tennis for six years and I have won a few medals at local table tennis tournaments and I am playing 4th Croatian senior league for three years now. I believe that sport is very important and I would very much like to continue playing it as well as trying some other sport as rowing.

I have travelled a lot in last few years. Everywhere I went I met interesting new people and enjoyed myself a lot. These journeys have helped me to develop my social skills and blend in into new surroundings and I hold them vitally important for studying abroad.

I have been working in maths for the most part of my life and I would like to continue. I have a few friends studying at Cambridge and they have warmly recommended Cambridge both for educational and social quality. I like courses offered at Cambridge and research groups in which I could take part. I have chosen Trinity as my preferred college because I am interested in Combinatorics and I believe that Trinity is the best College I could choose for studying it and maths in general.

Universities applied to:

- Cambridge: Offer
- Edinburgh: Offer
- University College London: Rejected
- University of Warwick: Rejected
- University of Sheffield: Rejected

Good Points:

This is a good statement. The statement has a clear introduction, main body, and conclusion. It is clear that the student is very talented and has gone far beyond the remit of their national curriculum. The student states their achievements but does not extend into self-praise, which is usually quite common. This way, although the student clearly has many achievements, it does not sound like they are bragging or that they are over-confident.

Bad Points:

The first three entire paragraphs after the introduction are simply lists of the student's accomplishments and awards. Whilst it is, of course, important to describe individual achievements, dedicating as much space as the student has in this statement is going too far. By the end of the list of achievements, the reader is left wondering if the student believes that their achievements outside of school alone warrant a university place. It would have been better if the student listed a few of their most significant achievements and described their experiences and what they have gained from such experiences.

The student also refers specifically to the University of Cambridge at the end of the statement. This is a very risky thing to do as the student's statement will be sent to all universities which they apply to. In doing this, the student risks offending and alienating all other universities other than Cambridge, and may be rejected by all as a result.

Overall:

This is a good statement that demonstrates the student as a highly gifted and motivated individual. However, the statement reads like a CV for the first four paragraphs, and the student risks being automatically rejected by all universities except for the University of Cambridge by dedicating the final paragraph to their desire to study at Cambridge.

NOTES

Subject: Mathematics

Mathematics is a closed communication system; a way of approaching life, the backbone of all sciences and the greatest discovery of humankind. How and why I fell in love with Mathematics are currently beyond my knowledge. On the one hand the pureness of Mathematics, which is completely free from any subjective views intrigues me. On the other hand, one's ability to interpret and approach Mathematics inspires me to become an active participant in the problem solving process. The satisfaction of solving a Mathematics problem is like realising where we are after rambling in an unknown part of a city, a feeling which makes me smile when I suddenly see the trick of a new puzzle. I feel like Mathematics is the subject which engages my attention fully and the one and only subject which I will enjoy at university level.

My interest in Mathematics has expanded over the past years and I am keen to read around different topics. During my AS year a seminar on Fibonacci numbers and the golden ratio inspired me to read, Erno Lendvai's work (in the original format) on the relation of 'Fibonacci-cells' and music. The author proved how classical music is built of 'Fibonacci-cells' and how the tempo tends to change when the music approaches its golden section. I discovered how Fibonacci numbers correlate with a significant number of masterpieces, despite the location or time of composition. His work made me wonder whether it is possible to compose and model 'perfect' music by determining the right frequency, length and number of 'Fibonacci-cells' in a piece. Understanding an application of number theory on music theory has propelled my interest towards other disciplines of number theory, such as the application of Prime numbers in nature.

Last year, I had the privilege of attending a set of seminars at King's College London, called King's Factor. With the guidance of PhD students and a professor we focused on more advanced Mathematic problems. We practiced STEP, AEA and MAT questions. These sessions consolidated my A-level knowledge and guided me to approach problems in different ways. This summer I attended the Best in School Mathematics Masterclass at the Royal Institute, which has further justified my course choice. Two books I exceptionally liked were 'The Man who knew infinity' and 'From Here to Innity' have introduced me to disciplines of Mathematics which I had scarcely covered and also to the life of a brilliant Mathematician. Fractals and Chaos theory were among my favourite topics; the visualisation of different dimensions and the idea of something being deterministic but unpredictable are not among the simplest topics and I am looking forward to learning more about them.

I spent two years as an exchange student and am aware of the difficulties of language barriers, as I spoke English for the first time, when I was 15. I voluntarily translate for TED and Amnesty International Hungary, and before starting my AS year, I spent two years in London focusing on English while continuing my Hungarian studies. This was difficult as communication and the application of my knowledge had to be conveyed in a language that was not my own. Adapting to a new environment, while managing my studies at home, I became more committed to achieve my goals. I became more independent and a whole new world of opportunities opened up for me.

By funding and running the Rubik's Cubing Club (RCC) at my sixth form and tutoring younger students I am required to be responsible, precise, accurate and reliable. This teaching experience enables me to innovate simple algorithms to introduce more students to Rubik's Cubing and to other logic games. Attending debating club each week has developed my presentational skills and the organisation of a freshman camp, Sport days and being part of the student council have improved my leadership skills.

I believe my keen interest and past experiences makes me suitable for reading Mathematics at university.

Universities applied to:

- Oxford: Rejected
- York: Offer
- Edinburgh: Offer
- University College London: Rejected
- King's: Rejected

Good Points:

The student is clearly motivated by mathematics. It is clear that the student has had to overcome adversity in their life and has managed to learn English for the first time two years prior to writing this statement. The student has several experiences of mathematics beyond the A-level syllabus and these are explained well.

Bad Points:

Whilst the statement is good overall, it lacks an 'X-factor', and as a result was rejected by the Universities of Oxford, King's College London and UCL. The student relies on interests sparked from A-level studies to justify their reasons to want to pursue mathematics. If the student had engaged in activities completely outside of the A-level curriculum, this would demonstrate their desire to study mathematics and improve their ability to a far greater extent. The student only describes how 'the author proved (things) to' them, and seems to not make any judgements or critical evaluations of their own. Whilst it is, of course, valuable to carry out wider reading, that is only to add to your own understanding of the subject, which isn't demonstrated here.

Overall:

Whilst the statement is well-written, the student is let down by their lack of individuality in assessing the work of the others.

NOTES

Subject: Mathematics

Why mathematics? Although it is somewhat difficult to explain mathematicians' love of the subject without referring to the clichés, to me, mathematics in itself is the greatest construction of the human mind and contributing to it is equivalent to pushing the civilization forward.

Although I have always enjoyed mathematics, I started focusing on it only recently. My interest was sparked only a few years ago, when I read Stephen Hawking's Brief History of Time. During the period, I was just starting calculus in IGCSE Additional Mathematics and hence, while certainly finding the physics of the book fascinating, it was Hawking's mention of the mysterious 'Einstein's equations', that intrigued me the most and led me to explore the world of mathematics. Ever since, this interest has grown exponentially. There simply isn't a mathematical topic that I don't want to learn more about. Books such as Marcus Du Sautoy's Music of Primes or Simon Singh's Fermat's Last Theorem introduced me to number theory, while Stephen Hawking's God Created the Integers took me through the pages of history and introduced me to the legendary problems of Fermat, Riemann and Goldbach. Later on, Ian Stewart's Why Beauty is Truth led me to explore the fundamentals of Group Theory and Complex Analysis, while on the side I was reading Michio Kaku and introducing myself to quantum mechanics. Often, I find myself spending hours on reading starting from perhaps the biography of Euler and ending up reading on Fourier's analysis or Gödel's logic. I can positively say that I can never learn enough mathematics to satisfy my passion and that I would feel truly fortunate being able to read it in an undergraduate course.

I am an extremely quick and independent learner. I was able to skip year 10, finishing the 2 year content of 7 IGCSEs in one year and still receiving top grades. In year 12, parallel to my IB course, I completed A-level Mathematics and Further Mathematics courses on my own, as they offered some additional topics I have not yet come across. I sat all the Further Pure papers, also being the only candidate to sit FP3 in my school. Although unable to sit the examinations due to financial reasons, I also familiarised myself with the A-level Mechanics course.

Additionally, self-study of Russian textbooks gave me a much higher competence in Euclidean geometry. Moreover, throughout the year, I tutored myself with more complex problems to allow myself sit the Sixth Term Examination Paper I paper and receive a level I.

My interest in mathematics extends to my whole school life. I can even say that the main reason I enjoy my subjects is their mathematical nature. It is the world of differential equations, algebra and analysis behind Physics and Chemistry and the hidden statistical analysis and numerical methods underlining Economics that make me interested in studying these disciplines.

Outside of school, I learn programming, mainly as a tool for solving problems. For example, in the process of preparing for my Extended Essay, I wrote several pages of Python code in order to solve the otherwise tedious problem of placing 9 queens and a pawn on a chessboard so that no queens attack each other and further generalising the problem for an n by n board. My code found all the solutions for the classic board in less than a minute. Furthermore, I am currently undertaking an online undergraduate course in Python programming through the organisation called Udacity, the final product of which is a fully functioning web search engine.

I believe my Extended Essay to be my most serious mathematical treatise yet. I studied the area of finite differences and binomial transforms, proving several important facts. One of my main results was a way of expressing any integer to the power of n as a sum of at most the first n nth powers.

In choosing me you would not obtain a well-rounded student, but rather you would have a dedicated mathematician who loves this subject as much as you do.

Universities applied to:

- Cambridge: Offer
- Imperial College London: Offer
- Warwick: Offer
- Durham: Offer
- Bath: Offer

Good Points:

This is an excellent statement. Usually, for subjects like mathematics, prospective students have an extensive history of individual achievements ranging from winning competitions and awards to being top of their school in maths. However, in this statement, the student explains their recent interest in mathematics in an easy-to-read, honest, and entertaining way.

The introduction is simple, engaging, and effective. The student opens the statement using a simple question and involves the reader immediately. This makes the statement entertaining to read.

It is clear that the student has read extensively around the subject and is thoroughly committed to their chosen subject. The student's mathematical ability is proven beyond doubt by the achievement of completing two A-levels in maths and further maths in addition to their IB studies. The student cleverly relates their interest in the underlying mathematics within other subjects to explain their interest in such subjects. It is very good how the student directs the statement directly towards to the reader in the closing sentence.

Bad Points:

There are very few bad points in this statement.

Overall:

This is a truly excellent statement. The student describes their achievements without making the statement seem like a list of achievements and does not brag. The reader is directly engaged within the closing statement, making this a statement to remember.

NOTES

Subject: Mathematics

Back when I was a little child, I was always fascinated by numbers. In kindergarten I spent a lot of time solving mathematical workbooks for little children and I developed a great passion for mathematics at an early age. Throughout the primary school my interests began to spread, I got familiar with the beautiful world of mathematics and I began to compete in various disciplines – mathematics, physics, astronomy and informatics. I regularly participated in national competitions in all these subjects, winning a first place on the national mathematics competition, a third place on the national informatics competition, and a few first places in the national astronomy competitions, as well as a bronze medal on the International Olympiad on Astronomy and Astrophysics in 2013.

I have devoted my best efforts to mastering these subjects and find all of them deeply interesting, but they all have something in common – they are based on mathematics and creativity. That is why I am determined to study mathematics. I have always been impressed by the fact that mathematical knowledge is very applicable to the real world and that mathematical studies are connected with every branch of science the human race acknowledges. In order to study and make progress in one's mathematical skills one has to be committed and highly motivated – that is why I wish to study at a prestigious university. From my experience, being surrounded by brilliant people who share your interests does a lot of good, gives you an extra boost to do your best. Consequently, I am currently studying at a renowned mathematical gymnasium and I have to say that people around affect me in a most positive way, making me excel faster. I am certain that Cambridge University would exert an even more profound influence. I am also attending mathematical classes held by older university students. It made me realize that people who teach you also play an important role in your education. That is why I am keen to be a part of a successful community such as Cambridge, learn from inspiring professors and study with amazing colleagues.

In my spare time I love to read and watch TV shows – this is a great practice for my English skills. I also practice table tennis daily because I firmly believe that a healthy body is an important prerequisite for a healthy mind. Honestly speaking, I am not definitely sure what I wish to try as a profession after graduating from university but I have considered various possibilities. I am very interested in how mathematics relates to economy and banking systems. On the other hand, I would also like to teach at a university, or perhaps be a part of a research group in a science institute. Either way, I am completely certain that Cambridge would be an excellent place to begin my journey!

Universities applied to:

- Cambridge: Offer

Good Points:

In this unique case, the statement was effective because the candidate took the *extreme* risk of applying to only one university, Cambridge, and tailoring their personal statement to that one institution. If you were to submit this exact same statement in a UCAS application to four others as well, this would be a *bad* statement. With that caveat in mind, however, this is an effective piece of work. The statement is well-written and structured, and it's compactness lends it a striking impact.

It is clear that the student has overcome adversity due to the fact that English is not their first language. The student is clearly very motivated and has talent. The student describes the importance of mathematics in other subjects, such as the sciences. This is good as it shows that the student has a broad outlook and will be keen to learn about all aspects of mathematics before choosing to specialise later on in the course.

Bad Points:

At the end of the second paragraph, it seems as though there is a type error or if the student has forgotten to finish their sentence after 'Consequently'. There are many places where it is possible to shorten this statement, e.g. the first sentence, 'Back when I was a little child, I was always fascinated by numbers' can be rephrased as, 'As a child, I was fascinated by numbers'.

Overall:

This is a very good statement, provided that it is specifically aimed at the University of Cambridge. The student is clearly very motivated and does not brag about their achievements.

NOTES

Subject: Mathematics & Physics

Since childhood, I've always loved complex puzzles, logical problems and challenges. Later on I discovered mathematics and physics which offered a lot of interesting problems and I enjoyed spending time on them. I loved the fact that real-life events, such as throwing a ball, could be described by a virtual language created by humans. However the most impressive fact for me was when I discovered that mathematicians and physicists can predict events just by solving equations. That's is when I decided that maths and physics are what I want to do in life to contribute to the world.

Even though my passion in mathematics started very early, I have struggled to get to where I am now. When I got into Bratislava's best gymnasium in mathematics I found myself at a position I had never been before. That was the first time I wasn't the best in mathematics in our class, in fact I was one of the weaker students in this field. However over time I made my way to the top, but I still couldn't surpass my classmates. When I got to the 5th grade, I realized why I didn't succeed. That year we got a new mathematics teacher and she opened my eyes and showed me the beauty of maths. The most important thing that happened that year however was when I won the regional mathematics Olympiad and they invited me to KMS which is a camp for people interested in mathematics. There I realized that the school mathematics is just a fraction of the possibilities in this area. However the thing that I believe helped me in mathematics is that I started enjoying it. Rather than solving a Sudoku or crossword puzzle I was solving geometry problems. Since then I have won many prizes including bronze medals from the Middle European Mathematical Olympiad and the International Mathematical Olympiad.

Besides maths and physics I also love playing the piano and practicing Kung Fu. I have played the piano for 13 years and my personal favourites are Chopin's Nocturnes. I may not be great at it, but playing the piano helps me relax and forget about my worries for a while. I practice Kung Fu mainly for health. My favourite style is Bagua. I learned that Kung Fu is not only a martial art, but a way of living. Besides Kung Fu and the piano, I also enjoy teaching kids interesting facts or problems in mathematics. During school, I teach a mathematics club and I want to teach the kids that mathematics isn't just numbers.

Every summer I help organize a mathematics day camp for children. Mathematics may be the subject which I'm best at, but I don't want to be 'just a mathematician' in the future. Since I was little, I've always wanted to do something great like solving global issues or inventing something useful, however I realize that it is very hard to achieve this with pure mathematics. People advised me to go study economics and financial mathematics so I could have a good job and earn money, but that is not what I want to achieve in life. My goal is to shape the world and make it a better place for future generations. This is the reason I want to study physics or engineering. I started doing physics two years ago and since then I participated and won some competitions including the Regional Physics Olympiad. To be better at physics I started reading Feynman's lectures which helped me a lot, but also taught me that there is much to learn out there about the world. The reason why I want to study in the UK is because there are many opportunities compared to Slovakia. I have many friends who study there and heard from them that it's an amazing experience. The most important fact, though, is that in the UK I can study and work with people who are ambitious. I know what I want to achieve in life, and even though I don't yet know exactly how to get there or where 'there' will be, I believe that a UK university education will steer me in the right direction.

Universities applied to:

- Cambridge: Offer
- Warwick: Offer
- Imperial College London: Interview + Rejected
- Bristol: Rejected
- St. Andrews: Offer

Good Points:

This is a very good statement. The statement is well-written and structured. The student describes their life experiences without making the statement sound like a list of achievements. This is achieved because the student explains every experience described, rather than listing their life experiences with no context. It is clear that the student has many talents and achievements, and these are stated in a humble manner which does not make it seem as though the student is bragging. It is clear that the student is aware of the significance of their decision to study outside of their native homeland and the challenges that this will bring. The student explains their reasons for applying to study a dual honours course and does not neglect either discipline.

Bad Points:

The student uses the word 'gymnasium' instead of school/college. Whilst this may be the term used in Slovakia, in the UK, a 'gymnasium' is a place where people exercise and its use in this statement is somewhat confusing. The way in which the student writes about their personal experiences makes the statement sound somewhat like an autobiography.

Overall:

This is an average statement. The student clearly has personality and a high level of ability. Strange terminology is explained by a language barrier, but will never be allowed for when evaluating a statement, especially at the very best universities, which expect all candidates to be completely fluent in written English.

HUMANITIES

Subject: Law (Jurisprudence)

My academic and personal experience of law has led me to believe that it is an integral and vibrant field of study. Indeed, law is intertwined with, and embraces every aspect of our lives on Earth, extending to the very composition, occupation and history of the planet. My A level subjects have confirmed this idea for me. From History, I have seen the terrible consequences of one man taking the law into his own hands, as Hitler did through the Enabling Act (1933). In Geography, I have been angered by the injustice of trade laws, and the way they continue to hamper development in the world's least developed countries. One of the reasons I have chosen to study French is my hope that it will create possibilities to practice as a lawyer in other jurisdictions, particularly French speaking African nations.

I am most interested in International Law and because of this I have chosen to undertake an Extended Project Qualification on the subject of the legality of the Nuremburg Trials and the legal precedent they set. I also aim to incorporate research into the International Criminal Court, and how the trials led to its establishment.

To further my understanding of Law, I organised and undertook a week of work experience at Albion Chambers, Bristol in July 2010. Working with highly skilled barristers was incredibly exciting, as was the opportunity to examine CCTV evidence and sit in on interviews with clients. It was a poignant experience, as I saw how our justice system can acquit those wrongly accused, while also protecting society.

I have read a number of enlightening books such as 'The Law Machine' by Marcel Berlins and Claire Dyer and 'Invitation to Law' by A. W. B. Simpson, and have gained a greater understanding of legal basics such as the criminal process and the law of torts. Reading the book 'Eve was Framed' by Helena Kennedy has also been fascinating, as I have started to think about issues which I had never before considered – how Law might be affected by gender. Since watching two documentaries about jails in Miami, Florida, I have also become interested in the differences between the British and American legal systems.

In addition to broadening my knowledge of our legal system, I have sought to develop skills which I believe will assist me in studying and practising law. As an active member of my Sixth Form's Debating Society, I have gained the ability to analyse an argument, and also developed my confidence in terms of public speaking. Later this year, I intend to speak at a Mock United Nations Summit, in which I will help to represent one country and their interests. This has developed both my confidence in public speaking and my ability to analyse and construct arguments. During the last year, I have been undertaking a Duke of Edinburgh Gold Award at Sixth Form. This has developed the necessary organisational skills for a high pressure law degree. In fact, I have already completed one of the sections, and am well on my way to completing two more.

For the past year, I have been giving up two free lessons per fortnight to assist in a Year 11 Maths class, helping students on the C/ D grade borderline. I have learned how to explain complex concepts to pupils who struggle to understand: I believe this will aid me greatly if I achieve my ambition of becoming a barrister.

Furthermore, I am a leader of a Sunday school group at my church, where I often organise games and activities for the children. This has helped to develop my interpersonal skills crucial for practising as a Lawyer. I also attend a drama class each week at Bristol Old Vic and play for my Sixth Form's netball team.

My studies, work experience and research thus far have shown me that law presents no intellectual boundaries; it is real and relevant, continuous and alive. I am excited by the prospect of studying law and relish the opportunity to study such a dynamic subject at university.

Universities applied to:

- Oxford: Offer
- Durham: Offer
- Nottingham: Offer
- Cardiff: Offer
- Reading: Offer

Good Points:

This personal statement is very well-written and well-structured with very few grammatical errors or omissions. It clearly demonstrates that the student has made a conscious effort to engage with aspects of the subject they wish to study at university; both within their current academic study (making direct reference to their A level subjects) and in terms of their extra-curricular activities. This wide range of activities and experiences are all made to seem relevant to law and act as evidence that the course chosen is one the student has carefully considered and will enjoy. The closing two lines are particularly strong, acting as a punchy reiteration of why the student wants to study law.

Bad Points:

When talking about the wider reading or extra-curricular activities that they have undertaken, the student could have taken the statement one step further by making explicit reference to why each was chosen or what they particularly enjoyed or learned. Moreover, several references were made to the student's desire to work as a barrister and pursue a career in law. While it is good to show such ambition, it should be remembered that applicants are applying to academic institutions to study, and universities will appreciate that the student is looking forward to studying law as an academic discipline rather than a means to an end vocation.

Overall:

This is a strong personal statement overall which was clearly well-received. However, it would have benefitted from the student talking in greater depth about what they learned or enjoyed in particular when completing extra-curricular activities or wider reading. The student needed to do more than say that the activity is relevant to law; they needed to go on to explain why they thought this. Specific examples would have helped. The wider engagement with the subject is to be commended, however, being especially necessary, the subject being applied for is not one which the student currently studies in school.

NOTES

Subject: Law

I view the practice of law as an analytical debate that sees lawyers and judges treading between theoretical law and the chaotic reality of society to clarify the scope of what is right. It is this mental challenge that inspired me to a career as a public attorney with the goal of joining the judiciary.

My interest was kindled when I first undertook my IB History Extended Essay. I enjoyed developing persuasive arguments, taking into account History's investigative and systematic nature. This was a unique challenge since my topic was in an entrenched area of study and involved formulating a strong original thesis that could stand against established historians. My efforts were validated when my essay was selected for publication in the June 2013 issue of the renowned academic journal, The Concord Review. Such an adversarial mental struggle strongly appealed to me and sparked my enthusiasm for a legal career that would allow me to tackle such challenges daily.

I pursued my interest by interning at Rajah & Tann (under the Junior College Law Programme), Drew & Napier and Kim & Co, some of the most competitive and prestigious law firms in Singapore. I learnt an extensive range of practical legal skills as I drafted affidavits, submissions, researched case law and created opinions on points of law. As I became familiar with family and civil litigation law, I learned how to devise compelling arguments by contextualizing vague laws to complex situations. Once, I was involved in a correspondence with the Attorney General Chambers (AGC) appealing a charge of overstaying. This entailed researching immigration laws relevant to our client's unique circumstance. While the arresting officer was skeptical of having the charges overturned, we successfully convinced the AGC otherwise. Such experiences have given me varied perspectives of the legal world, not only of theoretical concepts but also of the practical procedures that are built upon them, laying the foundation for my foray into the legal world.

I have also kept myself updated of legal developments, notably when Singapore relaxed legislative requirements of what constitutes an arbitration agreement. I could relate to this as I took part in a noted case that involved the term 'mediation' in an arbitration clause. It was intriguing framing arguments differentiating mediation with arbitration. Through my practical experiences, I have been stimulated to critically consider the effect of dynamic legislation on legal cases. I was also fascinated by the lecture series 'Justice' by Harvard law professor Michael Sandel, in which he applies moral perspectives to perennial issues such as proportional retribution in the context of historical injustices.

I have taken the initiative of founding a start-up, 'MobForest', consisting of a team of 7 that hosts project challenges for students to tackle in return for prizes. As part of MobForest, I helped to draft contracts with companies sponsoring the challenges. I also read up on Singapore's legal environment to determine our business obligations as well as on Intellectual Property rights as a means to protect our platform. Forming MobForest gave me valuable insight into the practical legal demands of a business as well as the confidence to approach clients.

Simultaneously, my National Service duty as a Sergeant and subsequently as a Lieutenant of Singapore's firefighting force (SCDF) saw me leading a platoon of men in fire and rescue incidents. As a platoon commander, one of the obstacles to executing a task is the poor phrasing of orders. Given the chaotic nature of a fire incident, it is important that commands given successfully convey the task at hand, with each man clear of their role.

Universities applied to:

- Cambridge: Interview + Rejected
- London School of Economics: Offer
- University College London: Offer
- King's: Offer
- Nottingham: Offer

Good Points:

The personal statement is well-written, showing a clear and logical structure and having no grammatical errors. The student shows a clear commitment to law by having an impressive array of extra-curricular activities, which act as evidence of their genuine interest in the legal world. It is clear that the student follows current legal affairs and takes any opportunity they get to engage with law. The reference to the lecture by Sandel is a particularly strong inclusion to this effect as it is clearly an academic mode of engaging with legal study and academic debate.

Bad Points:

While the student has a wealth of legal experience, the focus is very much on law in a business or commercial setting. It should be remembered when applying to study subjects with clear career routes (such as law) that a university will be looking for a genuine interest in studying law as an academic discipline rather than as a means of securing a job. After all, a law degree is not a pre-requisite for a legal career; a law degree is not necessary to take the GDL or LCP, for example. Additionally, the student's more relevant activities to university study, such as the extended essay or the lecture, are given minimal attention and explanation, when in reality they would be the most beneficial aspects to emphasise.

Overall:

This is a strong personal statement but struggles with the placement of emphasis. While business and vocational activities show a strong commitment to law, their weighting in this personal statement is at the expense of more traditionally academic interests. It is these latter interests and modes of engaging with legal theory that would better impress a university. The student could undertake some wider reading in a legal area they know they will be studying should they secure a place on the course that genuinely interests them (such as one of the seven foundation subjects in law). With this, they should include more examples of textbooks, articles or legal papers in this area to emphasise their research interests.

NOTES

Subject: Law

Law is the epitome of human reason; it is the force that holds society together and the cornerstone on which great civilizations were built upon. By dictating a code of conduct which everyone had to abide by, it has created a system of accountability and allowed society to flourish. However, Law is never static. It changes with time - internalising new concepts and discarding anachronistic ones to reflect societal norms. It is this dynamic nature of the Law that I find so enthralling - that there exists a gamut of good answers but never a right one. Such idealism aside, I believe excellence in legal study and work does not come easy. It requires much passion, intellect and hard work.

At College, I offered 12 academic units (as compared to the standard 10 academic units) at the Singapore-Cambridge GCE 'A' Level Examinations. Concurrently, I represented Singapore in Swimming and was an active member of my College's Swimming and Cross-Country team, training up to six times each week and achieving numerous medals and accolades in Inter-College Competitions. Such excellence in both sports and academics demonstrates my strong self-discipline, time management skills as well as my capacity for sustained hard work.

As a student, I held numerous leadership positions such as Swimming Captain, School Prefect as well as being part of the Executive Committee of my College Freshman Orientation Camp. In addition, I undertook various community-based service projects aimed at spreading awareness on and assuaging the plight of the less-privileged in society. These experiences in positions of influence and leadership have strengthened my organisational and problem solving skills, teamwork as well as allowed me to develop effective communication skills.

For my ability to balance studies, sports and leadership roles, I was among the ten students (out of nine hundred) on my College's prestigious Principal's Honour Roll in 2011 that acknowledged distinguished academic achievement and outstanding contributions to the College. Though challenging as it might have been, I have benefited greatly from my overall College experience and would certainly look forward to continue to represent, contribute and excel in University.

During my National Service stint, I served as a Military Officer entrusted with the responsibility of leading and nurturing the next generation of soldiers. Besides leading soldiers out in the field, I had to handle soldiers from a myriad of backgrounds as well as run the general day to day administration of the battalion. I have had multiple opportunities to serve as a Defending Officer to servicemen (who were accused of various wrongdoings) in military courts as well as conduct investigations into various malpractices in my battalion. These unique and far-reaching dealings in the Army has reaffirmed my decision to pursue law, refined my ability to think critically and to work under significant constraints and duress.

I am a firm believer in the importance of reading and see it as an avenue for the pursuit of knowledge. I read on a wide range of topics including legal conundrums, science, philosophy and even military tactics as I believe sufficient breath of thought is needed to develop one's mental prowess. Through such extensive reading, I have honed my rigour of thought and widened my perspectives to a myriad of issues.

A career in law is diverse and dynamic, yet fraught with many challenges. Legal theory, evidence, clientele management and not to mention regularly navigating the bureaucratic quagmire; no other field is as challenging or multi-faceted as the field of law. Though arduous, I relish the intellectual challenges of legal study and aspire to ensure human rationale and justice continues to prevail in society. Thus, I believe I possess the necessary attributes needed for legal study and excellence in the field of law.

Universities applied to:

- Cambridge: Offer
- London School of Economics: Rejected
- University College London: Rejected

Good Points:

The personal statement is well-written with no obvious errors. The student opens with quite a conceptual statement of what law means to them and this helps to make the subject seem like a well-thought-through choice. Additionally, the student recognises that law is a difficult and challenging course but seems unafraid of the need to put the necessary effort into it. The conclusion is similar in this respect, tying back to the introductory thoughts and ending on a strong statement of why the student feels like they would be a strong candidate to study law at university. Moreover, the student gives a very capable impression by mentioning their place on the College's Honour Roll, as it suggests they can balance their extra-curricular activities with (and not to the detriment of) their academic studies.

Bad Points:

Structurally, this statement needs to be reorganised. The student's legal interests are given attention and evidence far too late with extra-curricular activities of limited relevance being introduced closer to the beginning. In a personal statement as part of a law application, law needs to be the primary focus throughout. The student's positions of responsibility also come above their academic, legal interests, when they should be given less focus and come later on in the statement. When talking about the skills they developed in relation to these activities, the student makes these developed attributes sound beneficial but does not explicitly tie them to law or why they are useful to the study of law. It takes until the penultimate paragraph for the student to talk openly about their academic interests, and even then, they do not illustrate this with any specific legal examples.

Overall:

The personal statement is good but could be easily improved. The student would benefit from reordering the structure of the content to open with legal or academic interests, and then saving less relevant extra-curricular activities till the end. Any activity or skill should be tied back to law wherever possible – giving specific examples of how they relate would also be helpful in getting across why the student is prepared to study law at university.

NOTES

Subject: Law

Law is a set of rules and guidelines imposed upon a society which reflect its moral consciousness, guided and guarded by the judiciary. I believe everyone has the right to be judged objectively by their own laws. I am fascinated by the process of examining legal arguments, by how the outcome of a case hinges on presentation of the evidence and by the law's status as the ultimate arbiter of 'justice.' It is this desire to study the analytical process and underlying principles of jurisprudence that motivates me to study law academically.

Preparing for my extended project, I studied Plato's Republic and how his analyses of different societies are relevant to modern Britain. Examining the common flaws between our own society and those depicted in Republic made me appreciate the subtlety of the law in its present-day form: many of Plato's proposed solutions to these flaws undermined what are viewed today as personal rights. This led me to reflect on how laws protect us, and also how their intricacies create a doctrine to which people adhere, both complying and incorporating it in their own morality.

Investigating Plato's ideal political system, I considered the contrast between how his laws were devised and their status in our own society. Plato's 'Guardians' (not unlike our own judiciary) were relied on both to codify and interpret the law. While their decisions were considered to be benevolent, society was expected to conform to laws dictated by a separate class. The situation in the UK is quite different: statute law, as well as case law, often reflects current popular opinion. Sarah's law (the parents' right to check the criminal record of any carer for their child) was the direct result of a popular campaign. Whether it is better to have a system of laws that evolve with society or one that is dictated by a separate body is just one example of the ethical questions behind the law that intrigue me.

Seeking experience in the area of law that first attracted me, I assisted a criminal barrister in a Bristol chambers, including client interviews for petty offences and note taking in Crown Court, where we were prosecuting an alleged serial attempted rapist. The defendant's decision to dismiss his lawyers to defend himself brought home the need for a professional intermediary to ensure fair interaction of the individual with the protocol of the law. Examining case files while shadowing a Queen's Counsel specialising in public and taxation law, I was struck by how even the most powerful individual or company is still bound to observe the law. I sought exposure to corporate and commercial law with a local solicitor, where I worked through a practical example of employment law to determine whether a client had a case. This close reading of legal documents was a rewarding and stimulating experience, confirming my commitment to study law.

Captaining rugby teams at school (now 1st XV), club and county level, I have learned how to listen and how to lead; understanding and incorporating others' opinions or feelings in my interaction was key to encouraging progress for the individual or group, to motivate them and help them achieve their own potential. I developed these skills further mentoring in French and as a Sports Ambassador for local primary schools.

Rugby is like society: there are fixed laws that define the game and how it is played, but they are constantly tested by the flair of the players. As a result, the referee must both interpret and enforce the application of those laws; in Plato's terms, he is both guardian and auxiliary. The application of the law to dynamic situations and how different outcomes might be achieved depending upon points of interpretation has fascinated me for years.

I am strongly motivated to study the law's mechanics and with this passion, combined with the necessary determination and underlying skills, I will relish the task of appreciating and mastering law as an intellectual discipline in its own right.

Universities applied to:

- Oxford: Offer
- University College London: Offer
- King's: Offer
- Bristol: Offer
- Exeter: Offer

Good Points:

This is an impressive personal statement in many regards and was clearly well-received. The student opens with a definition of law but then goes on to interpret what they understand it to mean, and by doing so, has given some insight into their personality and understanding. It is clear from the outset that the student's interest is an academic one, and this will gain them favour from top academic institutions if sustained. The discussion of the student's extended project is given a clear legal dimension and the student competently makes cross-links, which display their strong grasp of sources of UK law - having a current example to underline this point. In this instance, the discussion of work experience complements the academic interests well because of the way the statement is structured – by saving work experience till later, the student made clear that their primary focus is academic and intellectual, but they do have a commitment to engaging with the subject at a practical level.

Bad Points:

Having two paragraphs about rugby probably gives the sport more attention than is necessary. Moreover, while the student has endeavoured to present all their skills as relevant to law, the links can read as somewhat tenuous, particularly in the sporting examples. Replacing one of these paragraphs with one about some wider reading in a purely legal area of interest (as opposed to reading as part of the extended project) would have been a more beneficial addition.

Overall:

This is an extremely strong personal statement. The student clearly gets across their interest in studying law, but more than this, it is unquestionable that their interest is in studying law as an academic discipline rather than practicing law as a career once they have graduated. Structurally, the statement flows well and covers sufficient facets of the student's activities and interests to explain why they want to study law and why they would be successful in doing so. The only real improvement to be made would be to add discussion of a time the student engaged in academic reading or research into a legal topic beyond what is required of them in their studies.

NOTES

Subject: Law (with French Law)

The way in which the British legal system both reflects and sculpts our constantly changing society fascinates me. Most recently, Tony Nicklinson's fight for the right to die, the pivotal precedent his case set and the legal challenge presented to ethical views exemplified why I want to read and, ultimately, practise law.

The role of the media in extradition cases such as Julian Assange and Abu Qatada, and Helena Kennedy's 'Just Law', made me aware of how extradition can infringe people's rights. The European Arrest Warrant has the ability seriously to undermine the right to freedom, allowing extradition without evidence previously examined in court, as in the case of retired judge Colin Dines, who was extradited to Italy and spent 18 months in jail before coming to trial.

Work placements have widened my interest; a case of suspected fraud at Dickins Hopgood Chidley LLP Solicitors (in which the law was used legitimately) demonstrated the law's ability to restrict a morally correct outcome. This prompted my exploration of jurisprudence, the philosophy of law and varying theories on the link between law and morality. Dworkin's 'Law's Empire' offered particular insight; moral values already exist within the law as unwritten 'principles' and 'policies', but it is judges who ultimately reveal the values to which our legal system is committed. In a recent critical essay discussing the extent to which British moral values are included in our laws, I combined research - such as Finnis' distinctive theory derived from the question of what constitutes a worthwhile, desirable life - with my own evaluations on how morality enters legal decisions, one possibility being the jury.

Observing court procedures and the complexities of different cases (for example, cases of appeal at the Royal Courts of Justice) offered me a first-hand understanding of Dworkin's theory of law as integrity. The intricacies peculiar to each case (such as a case of Count 2 rape re-classified by the Judge as Count 1) the tiers of argument and the clarity of reasoning behind each judgment re-ignited my enthusiasm to pursue a legal career. A Bristol Crown Court trial proved similarly interesting when one defendant changed his plea to guilty, radically affecting the other defendant (pleading not guilty)and requiring one barrister significantly to change his argument. Watching techniques in practice I had learnt during a mock trial at a 'Debate Chamber' master class confirmed how challenging, unpredictable and immediate law can be. It also motivated me to improve vital skills in creating a spontaneous argument without losing the importance of precision and research.

My love for the French language has grown immensely over the past year whilst reading both classical and more modern French novels, particularly enjoying Sagan's 'Bonjour Tristesse' and Claudel's 'La Petite Fille de Monsier Linh'. Work experience at Hill Hofstetter Ltd (with European business links) illustrated how valuable a second language and international awareness is to a law firm; this prompted my search for the opportunity to spend a year in France as part of my degree.

Cross-disciplinary A levels and various co-curricular interests have helped me hone transferable skills well-suited to a law degree. Maths has developed problem-solving and logical aptitudes; analysis of historical sources has advanced my ability to formulate a structured argument, and my knowledge of the genesis of English law. Cicero's 'In Verrem' has heightened my appreciation of the origins of our current legal system, and was made more exciting by comparing ancient techniques to those I witnessed in court, with many (such as speaking directly to the jury) still relevant.

My motivation has always been to maintain top grades alongside involvement in a wide range of activities: I now want to push this academic focus to a higher level and merge all areas of interest into one solid field of specialism and expertise.

Universities applied to:

- Oxford: Offer
- Durham: Offer
- Warwick: Offer
- Bristol: Offer
- Exeter: Offer

Good Points:

The personal statement opens with a topical example, giving the impression that the student takes interest in legal issues from the outset. Importantly, the introduction is conscious to mention the student's desire to read and practice law – setting up an academic interest from the beginning. The student continues to mention specific legal examples throughout, emphasising this genuine interest. When talking about their legal work experience, the student shows how this progressed back into fostering a specific academic interest in jurisprudence, before then giving what they learned from this study practical application. Such interplay between work experience and academics is highly impressive. The student's current subjects of study are given clear links to law and the punchy ending is effective both stylistically and in emphasising the student's strong personal attributes.

Bad Points:

The only area in which slight improvement could be made is the discussion of the student's French interests. The application is being made to study Law and French Law, and so adding a legal discussion in the paragraph concerning their French interests would have been beneficial.

Overall:

This personal statement is highly impressive. The student capably links everything back to the study or application of law, and this is precisely what will impress academic institutions. The student includes aspects of current legal affairs, specific topics of legal interest, and examples of engaging with law at every available opportunity. It is unsurprising that this personal statement was well-received.

NOTES

CLASSICS

Subject: Classics

'Sunt lacrimae rerum et mentem mortalia tangunt,' (Aen. I) epitomises for me the connection between Latin's beauty and the ingenuity of its grammatical principles. The precision each word gains through its affix renders word-order and superfluous lexis unnecessary, whilst also intensifying its meaning. Virgil exploits this by using balancing phrases that invest his language with extraordinary resonance. In a single line, he acknowledges both the tragedy of the Trojans' fate and the harsh reality of human existence, producing an expression so rich in meaning, it is almost untranslatable into English. I am fascinated by the relationship between the language and the eloquence of its literature; the linguistic subtleties revealed by Ovid in the closing passage of Daedalus and Icarus (Met. VIII) captivate me. The present participle 'clamantia' reflects Icarus' lingering hope as he calls out to his father, yet the subsequent severity of the passive verb 'excipiuntur' in the historic present emphasizes his helplessness. The poignancy culminates in the violent perfect tense 'traxit,' indicating a sense of finality as the 'caerulea...aqua' permanently robs Icarus of his identity.

Whilst I have enjoyed reading The Aeneid, The Odyssey and The Iliad in translation, I feel that their depth of meaning can only be fully uncovered with analysis of the original text. Anderson's profound observations in 'The Art of the Aeneid' developed my understanding of the intricacies within Virgil's language. His opening nouns 'arma virumque,' present Homeric allusions to the Iliad's martial theme and the Odyssey's focus on a central character; however, in their inevitable interaction, he highlights that his poem will take on a deeper dimension by examining how war affects the individual. Writing after a century of political turmoil, Virgil was conscious of war's destruction, and therefore, unlike Homer, does not portray the 'kleos' to be achieved in battle, instead presenting conflict as an undesirable requirement.

Homer's heroic accounts are consummate in pace and narrative drive, but I was struck by Virgil's realism and political awareness. Though he echoes the optimism of the 'Golden Age' in his praise of Augustus, he presents a genuine understanding of the burden of responsibility. Aeneas is not a self-seeking hero like Odysseus, but rather a 'pius' figure with a very public fate. As Anderson argues, in the end Aeneas is almost dehumanized by his duty; in killing Turnus, he defeats the final obstacle in his cause for Italian peace, yet Virgil's choice of the manic 'fervidus' to describe him indicates that, as an individual, he is destroyed for his descendants' future.

This concept of political duty captures my interest. Virgil's reflection of the hope for the new Principate in his analogy between the journey from Troy to Rome and Rome's political transition is supported by the power struggles illustrated in Harris' 'Lustrum' and 'Imperium,' which reveal the precariousness of the Republic. However, as Graves shows in 'I Claudius,' the Roman Empire itself was soon to become inherently corrupt. He suggests that effective government lies in a delicate balance between the stability of centralized rule, and the liberty of a Republic. Contrastingly, in his Republic, Plato advocates a rigidly hierarchical society headed by his reluctant 'philosopher-kings,' thus implying that it is not power itself that corrupts, but the desire for power. Yet, perhaps ambition is innate to human nature, making such a society unachievable. Such diverse issues are testament to Classics' infinitely broad spectrum.

I participate in a drama youth group, and have achieved Distinction in my Grade 8 LAMDA exam. I have been keen to link this interest to Classics by seeing productions of Electra and Orestes, and a modern interpretation of Orpheus and Eurydice. I seek to share my enthusiasm for studying languages and history with younger students by running a weekly language club, and through my role as a History Prefect. Above all, it is my love for language as the foundation of a culture that has fostered my interest in the Greco-Roman world, and I am eager to pursue this at a degree level.

Universities applied to:

- Oxford: Offer
- Durham: Offer
- Bristol: Offer
- King's: Offer
- University College London: Rejected

Good Points:

The student opens their personal statement with a quotation – while this can come across as cliché, the student engages in such a deep analysis that its inclusion is justified. The student's knowledge of a range of literature comes across well, with several cited examples being offered via analysed quotations. The student has a clear appreciation of both the language and societal aspects of the course they are applying for, suggesting they are a suitable candidate for study.

Bad Points:

It takes half a paragraph for the student to make reference to their own personal interest in Classics. All discussion to this point, while intelligent, is phrased very much abstractly rather than offering an example of personal excitement or engagement with the material. The use of key terms is similarly attempting to serve the purpose of displaying the student's knowledge of Classics concepts, but the phrases are used with little context or explanation. This means that it reads to an admissions tutor like the candidate is using words they don't know the meaning of. Terms should be included when relevant, not for the sake of inclusion alone. Structurally, there is a fair bit of jumping between texts; and, while this is clearly for the purpose of comparison, this creates a disruption to the natural flow of the statement.

Overall:

The statement shows a clear engagement with the subject but needs refining. The student should aim to answer one of two questions with every point they include: why they wish to study classics, or why they would excel in doing so. Currently, the former question is not given sufficient weight, though the second is implicit in the student's constant engagement with the subject.

NOTES

Subject: Classics

Listening to operas like Handel's Acis and Galatea, or looking at paintings like Raphael's exquisite Triumph of Galatea, I am always reminded of Ovid's brilliant manipulation of sources in producing stories now well ingrained in our culture - in this case transplanting the terrifying Cyclops of Odyssey 9 into a comic love triangle from Theocritus. In the Iliad, by contrast, Homer tells a deeply profound story of the cost of war, in which the humanity and inhumanity of war, presented through the sympathetic voice of the poet and the scope of the action respectively, are drawn together throughout the poem, culminating in the meeting of two tragic figures, Achilles and Priam, in Book 24. For me, however, the most moving part of the Iliad is Hector's speech to Andromache in Book 6 when he imagines her being enslaved, because it combines the shame-driven bravery of the heroic code with an acute sense of conflicting duties, alien to most of the other characters in the poem. It is this variety in Classical literature, especially in the rich traditions of epic and mythology, that most appeals to me about Classics. In reading Classics at university I am particularly looking forward to studying more Greek tragedy, since I so enjoyed reading King Lear and Endgame at English AS-Level and the Antigone at Bryanston.

The infectious curiosity of Herodotus, the witty cynicism of Tacitus: Ancient History offers the whole range of authorial perspectives, but what struck me the most last year when I studied Ancient History for the first time was the fact that one need look no further than Plutarch's Lives to find the whole range of personalities still found in today's politics. An idea particularly resonant in modern politics, from Neil Kinnock to Joe Biden, is that of the 'novus homo', and my interest in Cicero, through studying his works at AS-Level, led me to write an article for Omnibus in which I argued that Cicero intended to publish not only the seventy-nine epistulae commendaticiae of ad Familiares 13, as suggested by Ludwig Gurlitt, but also some of the letters to Atticus.

In my Extended Project dissertation I investigated the issues surrounding the UK's euthanasia legislation. In researching this subject I studied the views of Immanuel Kant and Jeremy Bentham, but also the opinions of more recent philosophers such as Peter Singer. I was especially impressed by Joseph Fletcher's essay, The Cognitive Criterion of Personhood, because his clear and logical argument for defining a 'person', especially the criterion of one's sense of the future, was the foundation for my argument concerning the value and sanctity of human life.

Outside the classroom I like to be involved in a lot of music, mostly singing - in which my favourite genre is Baroque oratorio - cello, and harpsichord. I recently performed in Mendelssohn's Octet at the Cadogan Hall, and having won first prize in London's Spring Grove Chamber Music Festival with my string quartet we are spending the money on making a CD of some of our recent repertoire. My other pursuits include some amateur journalism and representing my school in public speaking, while at home I particularly enjoy reading the books of P. G. Wodehouse and watching the 1950s films of Federico Fellini and Ingmar Bergman.

Universities applied to:

- Oxford: Offer
- Edinburgh: Offer
- Exeter: Offer
- Manchester: Offer
- Kent: Offer

Good Points:

The student clearly engages with the subject and is eager to demonstrate the knowledge they have already built in their studies. Importantly, attention is given to both classical literature and ancient history, showing that the student has well-rounded interests within their chosen subject. The student is able to talk competently about a number of classical sources and figures, but can also link this to current affairs. Mentioning the article was a strong inclusion because it shows the student took initiative and undertook an academic-style activity, moving beyond what is required of them in their studies.

Bad Points:

The student takes some time to begin discussing their own personal interests in Classics. The phrasing for the first half of the introductory paragraph is for the most part quite abstract and factual. Writing in this way can present difficulties in getting your personality across. The paragraph about the student's extra-curricular activities would be better if the activities given attention linked to classics in some way. While a wealth of extra-curricular activities may demonstrate that the student is capable of balancing their interests and their studies, it would be more impressive to show a commitment to Classics, in this instance, through these activities. Wider reading in a particular area of Classics that the student finds interesting would be more relevant than what they enjoy reading or the types of film they enjoy.

Overall:

This personal statement is well-written and demonstrates the student's wealth of knowledge about Classics from the outset. At times, it sadly lacks in personality. The student talks happily about facts and concepts but does not sustain a noticeable passion throughout - resulting in a personal statement that seems, at times, overly factual. While by no means a bad personal statement, it would benefit from getting across at every opportunity the view that the student has a real passion for this subject and engages with it at every opportunity. The student should be the focus, not the subject.

NOTES

Subject: Classics

I first became intrigued by the classical world whilst learning about the Romans in primary school. Since then an inspirational Latin teacher, trips to classical sites and the writings of Homer have cemented my fascination with this subject. Having studied Latin GCSE and AS level, as well as AS Classical Civilisation, I have come to appreciate the rich cultural depth of the ancient world and its profound influence upon society today as the origin of so many of the fundamental aspects of our daily lives, from democracy and English language through to the justice system. It is for these reasons that I wish to study Classics at degree level.

As part of my Latin AS course I found the structure of Latin and its legacy in terms of modern European languages fascinating. This led me to research the derivations of the English language as part of my Academic Research Course project with a specific focus on Latin and Greek influences and I found that Latin influence on English especially is huge both in terms of vocabulary and idiom. Studying The Iliad in translation for the AS Classical Civilisation course has stimulated my interest in ancient literature, quickly appreciating its striking sophistication and lucidity, prompting me to read The Odyssey. This epic, for me, particularly raised the question of the nature of morality in ancient Greece as the portrayal of Odysseus is as a pious and kind man, yet his indiscriminate slaughter of the suitors and servants at the end would seem to conflict with this. Having seen certain short passages in the original Greek I have come to further appreciate the subtle word play of Homer such as the section in which Odysseus outmanoeuvres the Cyclops by saying that his name is 'nobody' which is yet more impressive when seen in the Greek as the translation cannot fully convey the use of double meaning.

In addition to my AS subjects I have attended a weekly Ancient Greek class and completed the Bryanston Greek summer school course. I feel this has given me a good grounding in ancient Greek that I can build on this year in preparation for a Classics degree. I am also involved with running the college Classics society which is helping to develop my organisational and presentation skills.

Having taken trips to Pompeii and Greece I found the opportunity to see parts of the ancient world in the flesh, such as the Parthenon, awe inspiring. It was an experience which made the ancient world seem far more real to me and gave me a sense of the scale and significance of the ancient sites which cannot be gained from photographs or drawings so I hope to visit more in the future.

I also found the AS Philosophy course most absorbing and through this have gained a detailed understanding of some ancient philosophy, such as Plato, which is an area of classics I am keen to study further. This led me to read Aristotle's Nicomachean Ethics, which I found to be strikingly convincing and relevant to the modern world considering its age. I particularly found the concept of virtues and the 'Golden mean' a compelling argument for how we should make moral decisions as the idea of moderating our behaviour between two extremes is an intuitive one. The Maths AS course has developed my skills of logical thought, a discipline which is proving useful in other subjects when analysis is required for essays or translation.

Music is also a great interest of mine and over the course of the last year I have taught myself to play the guitar proficiently and I am also a very competent drummer, having taken lessons for several years. Both these pursuits, but in particular teaching myself the guitar, have developed skills of perseverance and self-motivation, which are of great use to any academic study.

I relish the opportunity to study Classics at the highest level and especially look forward to working with both experts in the field and other students who share my passionate interest.

Universities applied to:

- Cambridge: Offer
- Durham: Offer
- Bristol: Offer
- Exeter: Offer
- Manchester: Offer

Good Points:

The personal statement is very strong with no obvious errors. The student's strength, in particular, is their ability to make Classics relevant in all of their listed academic interests. This is done notably well in the paragraph about A Level Philosophy, which the student used as a springboard to undergo their own research. Indeed, the Academic Research Project was another well-chosen inclusion as independent research work is more closely in line with the style of working at university, and the student seems comfortable working in this way. The ending lines work well in underlining that the student is eager and excited to begin this course.

Bad Points:

The opening line is somewhat of a personal statement cliché. Talk of developing these interests fully at such a young age is, more often than not, unconvincing. Structurally, the balance of the statement seems to be weighted towards language or literature aspects, with societal dimensions coming later. Ensuring that all aspects of the course are covered from the outset, or as soon as is practical, will help to give the impression the student is a good fit for the course as a whole, rather than only being interested in smaller aspects. In terms of engagement with ancient texts, The Odyssey (as with The Iliad and The Aeneid) is fairly standard and usually on the Classics A Level Syllabus. Given that the majority of students applying to study Classics at university will be studying it at A Level, going off syllabus to more niche texts might set the student apart from the crowd.

Overall:

This personal statement is strong stylistically but there is room for potential improvement. The content may come across as fairly standard, particularly in terms of the ancient literature the student has read (at least up until the section on Philosophy). The current content is all unproblematic, but to stand out from the crowd, the student should talk about more independent work they have done beyond what is required of them in school.

NOTES

Subject: Classics & French

The fresh perspectives afforded by different ages and separate cultures can only add to the study of literature and be of benefit in meeting the linguistic challenges of language-learning. This is my belief and why I find the prospect of combining Classics and French so attractive.

I have always loved languages. Balancing two modern languages with Latin was perhaps the highlight of my academic experience at prep school, and led to the top scholarship at my senior school, with a discussion of the origins of the Germanic language-family forming the major part of my interview. More recently I have enjoyed the intricacies and complexities of language through classical prose composition. I earned second place out of 275 in the Phaedrus Latin Contest this year, submitting an original fable in Latin. Preparations have started for next year's entry, which is to be in the iambic trimeter Phaedrus used, and this is something I would love to pursue a little at university.

I benefited greatly from attending summer schools in Durham and Bryanston. The opportunity to read more widely among other keen minds gave me an exciting sample of what life studying for a classics degree might be like. Additionally, I have explored the classical perspective on violence, using ancient literature, philosophy and culture as a lens through which to evaluate the potential dangers of excessive violence in contemporary cinema. The essay I produced on this subject won me first prize in the Postgate section of The University of Liverpool's Postgate & Walbank Essay Competition.

My work over the course of last summer reinforced my conviction to apply for this Joint Honours course. I read Euripides' Hippolytus in conjunction with Racine's Phèdre, analysing the former's influence on the latter. A comparison particularly of the character, values and actions of Phaidra and Phèdre formed an interesting focus in reading the plays, and I intend to give a talk on this subject to a group of sixth-form linguists at my school. I feel there is much overlap between the studies of Classics and French, and the connections (in tragedy in particular) are ones I would be keen to follow up at university.

In French, oral and written fluency is an exciting element of the course. My competence in French has already allowed me to engage with non-English speakers – most memorably over a fortnight at a language school in Cannes, with a group of Italians; I have subsequently visited one of them in Italy, where we spoke exclusively French. The study of vocabulary, grammar and syntax appeals to me intellectually, but I look forward to its fruition, namely the chance to interact with a new range of people as a stronger speaker of French.

Furthermore, I enjoy the academic challenges which come with the study of French literature. I read L'Etranger in my lower 6th year, where I was struck by Meursault's intriguing character and existentialist outlook, and was duly infuriated by his refusal to draw judgements or create any real meaning in his irreligious existence. Since then I have met Flaubert, in the form of Madame Bovary, where the ultimate corruption and downfall of the main character felt to me like witnessing the ruin of a Greek tragic heroine, such was the force of her passions and disappointments; Julian Barnes' Flaubert's Parrot was an excellent companion in this reading. I like to engage with French culture in as many other ways as possible, whether through watching films, listening to music, or reading the Analyse du jeu des échecs of 18th century chess-player Philidor.

Alongside my studies, I have kept myself active as a cross country/half-marathon runner, competitive chess-player, debater and cricketer. I have enjoyed representing my school on two cricket tours, as well as completing the Ten Tors challenge. At university, I hope to sustain as many of these activities as possible without detracting from my central ambition of achieving a top degree in Classics and French.

Universities applied to:

- Oxford: Offer
- Durham: Offer
- Edinburgh: Offer
- Exeter: Offer
- Newcastle: Offer

Good Points:

This is an impressive personal statement. The student comes across as extremely well-read with each of the texts they chose to speak about being highly relevant to the course they are applying for, but also acting as very individual choices which will set them apart from other potential candidates. The student clearly has a strong passion for the two subjects and is able to show what they have done outside of the classroom to engage with this passion, which is highly commendable. A balance is struck between highlighting their strong academic achievement through the mention of prizes and awards, and activities they have chosen to undertake simply because they have this strong personal interest in the subjects.

Bad Points:

The personal statement is very language-centric. While this might be acceptable given that the student is applying for a combined Classics and French course, extra focus on the historical or societal aspects of the Classics half would not go amiss, if only to ensure all bases are covered. Stylistically, the student should not be afraid to use shorter, simple sentences to get their point across. The student often uses commas to link several clauses together to create longer, complex sentences; and this is unnecessary and, at times, to the detriment of flow and clarity. The student also makes several references to things they would like to continue looking into at university and so should be careful to first check that these are topics covered in the course at each university they apply to, even if only to ensure none of the institutions are being alienated. Their extra-curricular activities are dealt with swiftly at the end of the statement, but their inclusion may be questioned, given that they are of limited relevance to Classics or French and the student has not attempted to draw attention to any transferable skills.

Overall:

This is a very strong personal statement and was met with much success. The student should remember to proof-read (ensuring that capital letters are used for all references to Classics or French subjects), but the content is undeniably strong. It is clear that the student has a genuine interest in the subjects they are applying for, both individually and in combination, and this works to make them come across as a highly capable candidate.

NOTES

ORIENTAL STUDIES

Subject: Chinese Studies

If there is one issue that towers above others in importance in our world today, it is the rise of China as a political and economic power. Chinese Studies excites me, however, not only because of its indisputable relevance, but also because of its academic challenge, both linguistic and cultural. I love the way the subject continually leads the student out into other fields of knowledge: language and literature, geography, history, politics, economics and international relations. For example, Jung Chang's shocking portrayal of life through three generations of her family in 'Wild Swans' opened my eyes to some of the horrors the Chinese had to go through during the Chinese and Cultural Revolutions. This biographical work in turn led me to read Chevrier's 'Mao and the Chinese Revolution', an introductory history of C20th China.

Not only will Chinese Studies lead out into new fields of knowledge, but I have also been surprised how some of my long-cherished interests feed back into it. Take Music and Geography, for instance. While exploring the style of the Beijing Opera I discovered how closely Chinese music is bound to its social, historical and political context. Watching a modern version of the opera 'Journey to the West' led me to read the translation of the classical novel on which the show was based, which introduced me to Chinese literature and also to traditional Chinese mythology, religions and values. In IB Geography, I have enjoyed opportunities to develop my appreciation of China's exceptional population change, its booming economy and regional diversity. I was stimulated by J. Watts' analysis of the scale and speed of China's carbon-fuelled industrial revolution in 'When a Billion Chinese Jump', while a project on the Three Gorges Dam helped me understand the great potential danger China's surging development could bring not only to itself, but to the whole planet.

My appetite for language study has been stimulated by being brought up bilingually. A German, I have lived in the UK since I was a baby. Growing up in this way, as well as learning French for five years and taking IB Higher Spanish, has made me realise how crucial linguistic competence is to enable full access to, and appreciation of, a culture and a people's way of thinking. Having made a small start on Mandarin when I was younger, I can also appreciate the difference between learning a European and an Oriental language; it is, however, the extraordinary features and considerable challenges of Mandarin that attract me.

I have a proven record of time management, balancing my academic work with a wide range of co-curricular activities. A music scholar, I sing in two school choirs, play the piano and perform at recitals, concerts and competitions. Recently, I played the lead role in a production of 'South Pacific'. I also love physical exercise: football, volleyball and swimming. Taking part in Gold D of E expeditions and living in a boarding house community have made me aware of the importance of bringing my strengths to a group and being open-minded to other opinions. I have used my competence in languages to teach German and Spanish to younger students and I am an elected member of the school's 'Wheeler-Bennett Society', where I enjoy discussing current cultural and political issues with my peers.

Standing in the middle of Tiananmen Square this summer, walking along the skyline of the Shanghai Bund and living with a Chinese family confirmed my desire to read Chinese Studies. These experiences highlighted to me the gulf between the Chinese political system and the desires of the young generation, the clash between the explosive modernisation of China's cities and the country's rich heritage and the contrast between frantic consumerism and traditional values. I cannot wait to study a course that will equip me with an extraordinary language and will unlock doors into a rich culture and society, which at present I have but only glimpsed.

Universities applied to:

- Cambridge: Offer
- Durham: Offer
- SOAS: Offer
- Leeds: Offer
- Sheffield: Offer

Good Points:

This candidate is able to clearly articulate the relevance of their previous experiences — both academic and extra-curricular — to their chosen area of study. They can demonstrate a wide range of influences that tie together their interest in Chinese Studies, including influences that they have independently identified and pursued. Through their discussions of both linguistic and cultural areas of interest, they are able to demonstrate their potential ability for a wide-ranging and challenging course. This candidate has thought far beyond the bounds of their classroom and is able to allude to a variety of areas in which they have thought independently, and can see their personal pursuits intersecting with their undergraduate study.

Bad Points:

While this statement is impressive in a number of ways, as an overall piece, it does present some potential areas for improvement. Though the list of extra-curricular activities undertaken by this student is impressive, this candidate has not always convincingly emphasised how these pursuits are relevant to their studies. This statement would have also been given further weight by the substitution for highly personal and subjective experiences in favour of more academically considered thought. This candidate could also further develop their overall tone, which varies somewhat over the course of the statement between areas of academic clarity, areas of near-patronising tone, and areas of more informal anecdotal discussion. As such, a more thorough overview of this candidate would have been achieved by a more cohesive, persuasive, and academic tone of discussion.

Overall:

This candidate very consistently and engagingly demonstrates their interest in their chosen area and provides evidence, both academic and personal, for their continued involvement in this area. While the statement covers a wide and rich variety of subject matter and personal pursuits, it lacks a certain overall thrust of argument and cohesion of tone. The statement, while impressive as an overall piece, could have been developed further with greater consideration of academic areas that are likely to appear on their chosen undergraduate courses — particularly literature.

NOTES

Subject: Classics & Oriental Studies

One can better understand the whole of Western civilization through close study of Greco-Roman culture, as I have noticed while reading many modern texts. No literature or civilization exists in a vacuum; as a bicultural person living between the Arab and the Western world, I have a heightened perception of this. Therefore I believe that it is necessary not only to study single civilizations in depth, but also to observe how they influence one another, in order to comprehend our global culture. One way to achieve this is through the study of language- directly and indirectly an expression of the social and individual human- and especially of the most beautiful use of language, that of literature. For this reason I wish to apply for a joint degree in Classics and Oriental Studies.

I have studied Latin, Italian and English literature at high school and I found intimate connections between them. For example, the idea of poetic immortality is present among the Romans in Horace and Lucan, in Italian literature from Dante and Petrarch to Foscolo, and in the English one in Shakespeare and Spenser's sonnets. I have found Vergil in Dante, and Dante in Eliot. Further, more nuanced connections can be found, and links exist between a wider variety of cultures. It would be particularly interesting, through the tensions of the political world, to grasp the links between the Western civilization and what lies outside it.

Through my study of the sciences at Liceo Scientifico level, with a focus on Maths, I have developed the precision necessary for detailed philological work.

My love of knowledge has been fed by the Greek philosopher Plato, whose Theaetetus taught me the importance of thinking critically and interrogating my perceptions. I have also realized that socially, humans face the same problems: Ovid did not hesitate to blame rape on the victim rather than the perpetrator, a way of thinking against which we still battle today. Similarly, the great sentiments persist through the ages, Catullus' "Vivamus, mea Lesbia" still resounds vital as ever, Lucretius' "O miseras hominum mentes" maintains intact its desperate strength.

Such timeless sentiments are also present in the literature of Ancient Near East, such as Enheduanna's Nin-me-sara, which captures the pain of exile and the relationship of the individual with God.

I have given short talks on Enheduanna during my school's Cultural Week, while distributing copies of her poetry. I have often dedicated my free time to ancient literature, participating in the Certamen Ovidianum, writing and producing a play based on Pascoli's Latin poetry, which I have recited metrically, and helping organize my displaced school library.

I have also cultivated modern languages. I have independently gained reading knowledge of Spanish and French. To improve my Icelandic, I spent a summer in Iceland. I am also fluent in Arabic, which I used during my two-year stay in Kuwait, where I attended a Cambridge English School.

I am interested in the Arts, and enjoy spending my weekends in museums and churches. Living near Rome, I have the privilege of admiring the Pantheon and the Colosseum and how they influence the modern landscape, as the civilization they belong to influences the modern mind. I better grasped Ovid when I saw him in Bernini, or in Correggio's 'Danae'. I have tried to communicate this beauty to the children I have tutored, an experience that made me bring out from the ancient world what was relevant to the various contexts in which they live. I hope to continue spreading this beauty through research and teaching.

Universities applied to:

- Oxford: Offer

Good Points:

Throughout this statement, this candidate is able to illustrate their wide range of academic reading and their subsequent independent thought on these topics. This student can clearly articulate how they have thought about their academic work within a broad global context. In particular, this student's breadth of reading in a number of different languages and across a variety of diverse eras illustrates their ability to tackle a wide range of literary issues — in a way that is far above and beyond the demands of school-level study. Their cogent and apposite use of more complex academic terms concisely supports their profound and developed interest in their chosen area of study.

Bad Points:

While this candidate's academic pursuits are impressive, the dogged attention to detail around their reading creates a statement which is somewhat airless. Although the candidate does allude briefly to personal and extra-curricular pursuits, it would have given a more thorough sense of the person as a whole if there was an additional sentence or two of relevant but personal detail. This applicant is also at risk of fashioning themselves as a pompous individual due to their tone — this statement would have benefited from some relaxation of the general conversation register, as it reads as rather overbearing. While this position does give the applicant greater room to explore their academic credentials, it is indicative of a haughty and outmoded essay style, which could be a mild cause for concern for potential tutors.

Overall:

The success of this statement rests on the fluidity and comprehensive nature of this student's literary discussions. They are able to call upon a wide and substantial range of works and demonstrate their engagement with them at a high level. It would have been a welcome addition to have seen greater personal engagement beyond their reading and to understand further about the applicant's interest in a non-curriculum area for undergraduate study. The candidate would also benefit from adopting a register that better suits their academic interests, rather than a tone that is suggestive of superiority.

NOTES

PSYCHOLOGY

Subject: Experimental Psychology

The boundaries of the brain are confined only to the limitations of the inquisitor. The understanding we can acquire from our behaviour is endless and fuels my determination to study Psychology. I participated in the College Debate on whether the concept of Gender should be abolished. At first glance, this idea seemed impossible. However, our subsequent research revealed that my initial reaction was evidence of my own limitations and society. I relish the opportunities that Psychology offers to challenge and expand my ideas.

Taking part in a Youth Philanthropy Initiative allowed me to form relations with Send Family Link, a charity that helps children whose mothers are in prison. After reading studies about these children, I was left wondering whether they could share similar, perhaps psychopathological, traits with their parents due to their genetics. This offered a cross-curricular link to my Philosophy studies on evil, and I completed an extended essay on the roots of evil. This linked Philosophy, Psychology and Neuroscience, and also two of the main debates in Psychology: Nature/Nurture and Free Will and Determinism. Zimbardo explains his theories on this subject in his book 'The Lucifer Effect: Why Good People Turn Evil', which I enjoyed. Hearing him speak about this in person at a student lecture I attended was fascinating, as was the opportunity to meet him.

Social Psychology intrigues me, as it reveals much about the way people interact with each other in everyday situations. I explored this further by studying why people obey and conform. With a keen interest in History, I related this to real-life topics, such as the Holocaust and why the Nazis obeyed Hitler's orders to complete such inhumane actions. I am surprised by the extent to which individual and group responses are influenced by the people and culture surrounding us, whether or not we are aware of it.

At A Level I chose to do a broad spectrum of subjects to provide a sound foundation for a Psychology degree. Maths and Statistics develop my analytical and research skills, whilst Philosophy highlights ethical and moral issues and develops my essay writing and argument skills. French offers an insight to the linguistics and language skills studied in Psychology. In addition studying French has provided me with the opportunity to work with children in France and participate in a course at the French Institute of Fashion, both of which add to my understanding of different cultures. As a Psychology mentor, I help AS students improve through tutoring. I am a keen singer and am completing the Contemporary Music Practitioners Award at College and enjoy working with the diverse group of people I encounter with these different subjects.

Last summer I completed a 6 week volunteering program in America, where I trained and worked as a counsellor in a YMCA children's summer camp. The challenges of working with children from all different countries and social groups reinforced the importance of social norms and cross-cultural differences in society. Back home, being Netball Team Captain and working as a Netball Coach allowed me to explore ideas of motivation and communication.

My knowledge has been expanded by reading in and around the subject. 'The Brain That Changes Itself' by Norman Doige raised my awareness of the developing discipline of 'neuroplasticity' and the advances in understanding brain function as a whole. This book was a stepping stone to my growing interest in this field. Novels such as 'A Beautiful Mind', 'The Room' and 'Before I Go To Sleep' took real psychological disorders, issues and scientific facts and portrayed them from a first-person perspective; enabling me to see how actual sufferers are affected.

I am a motivated, enthusiastic student who is genuinely excited by the ever-expanding horizons of Psychology and I am determined to contribute to the academic and real-life applications of this extraordinary Science.

Universities applied to:

- Oxford: Offer
- Bristol: Offer
- Exeter: Offer
- Durham: Offer
- University College London: Rejected

Good Points:

This candidate is able to eloquently engage with a wide variety of academic and contemporary issues surrounding their topic, which demonstrates their awareness of the subject not just as an area of closed study but as a growing, morphing, and complex material. Their continued inclusion of extra-curricular activities is always linked very well to their chosen area of study, which gives the overall effect of presenting the candidate as someone with a hotly-pursued interest in their area — but with a consistent, personal slant. Through the inclusion of analytical literary discussion, the candidate also demonstrates their ability to take on complex academic tasks in a slightly removed area, which is suggestive of general academic curiosity and well-rounded academic interrogation skills.

Bad Points:

While this candidate is very impressive in their ability to call upon a huge breadth of interest areas, they are running the risk of giving snapshots of a variety of areas rather than demonstrating their ability to engage deeply with any one of them in particular. Although much of this breadth is understandable, given the wide reach of their chosen undergraduate study area, it would have been beneficial to include further, focused thought on areas within their degree that they might particularly like to pursue, and the reading that they have done to date in order to bolster that particular standpoint.

Overall:

What is most impressive about this statement is its demonstration of an enormous range of academic and extra-curricular pursuits — and their consistent relevance. The range of material within this statement contributes to an overall impression of the candidate as an able, curious, and tenacious student. They could streamline their discussions somewhat in order to also demonstrate their ability to construct and present an academic argument, but their current structure does not detract from their credentials as a highly capable candidate.

NOTES

Subject: Experimental Psychology

How does the mind work? The mind is a mystery housed within the most complex mechanism known to man: the human brain. My innate curiosity compels me to find out more about such a mystery through the study of Psychology.

I have long been interested in how our minds differ: for example, why have I always been a strong mathematician while my brother finds it challenging? Being a musician, I found Kathryn Vaughn's research supporting a correlation between musical and mathematical abilities particularly thought provoking, while I have also wondered whether my childhood obsession with jigsaws helped me develop problem-solving skills, which are particularly relevant in Geometry: the area with the biggest rift in our abilities. Ann Dowker's argument, in 'Individual Differences', that educational methods influence such differences was also particularly compelling. Therefore, in my gap year, whilst helping struggling learners in KS3 Mathematics at a local school, and, when I help educate children in Tanzania as an International Citizen Service volunteer with the VSO charity, I will evaluate the success of different educational methods.

251

This will give me experience of carrying out my own research, and, will develop skills such as empathy, which is important in the more sensitive areas of Psychology. Furthermore, I recently assisted a University of Oxford researcher conducting follow-up assessments with children in local primary schools. These measured reading-age, language comprehension and numeracy level, and are used to gauge and refine the Catch-Up charity's numeracy intervention programme. As some of the children being assessed were from a control group, my involvement also enlightened me to ethical aspects of research.

Differences that occur in the criminal mind are also of great interest to me. As an elected Student Ambassador for the Holocaust Educational Trust, I visited Auschwitz-Birkenau earlier this year, where I learnt about Rudolf Hoess. Hoess exterminated thousands of families, yet lived with his own family just outside the camp. This ignited an interest in complex behaviour; therefore I read Stanley Milgram's research into whether 'the Germans are different', and learnt about his Theory of Obedience. This developed an interest in Forensic Psychology, and I subsequently attended a Forensics course at Nottingham University, where I learnt about a Forensic Psychologist's role, during Mental Health tribunals, for example.

Deterioration of the mind, and methods to counteract this, also interest me. Reading the Psychologist has given me an insight into how the effectiveness of such methods could be analysed using a high-resolution 3D brain atlas; while a presentation from Claire Rytina enlightened me to useful cognitive treatment designed to rebuild and retrieve memory following her Viral Encephalitis. I have also voluntarily worked at a Nursing Home with some Dementia sufferers, and noticed that many sufferers enjoyed me playing music from their past, and sometimes, this triggered some of their memories.

This made me wonder whether the music stimulated neurones which had lain dormant for years, similarly to when neurones are used for the first time, as Hubel and Weisel's nature/nurture research has shown. Studying this in A level Biology gave me an interest in neuroscience, while Biology also stressed the importance of controls and fair tests, which are invaluable during Psychology experiments too. My mathematical skills in statistics will also be beneficial when analysing empirical evidence; and, the deep level of analysis and evaluation used for varying sources in A level History will be useful when studying case studies, while my essay techniques will help me when writing reports, and when considering issues from different perspectives.

Overall, I feel that my broad interests and skills will enable me to thrive as a Psychology student at a demanding University, where I would also make a positive contribution to University life.

Universities applied to:

- Oxford: Offer
- Warwick: Offer
- St. Andrews: Offer
- Durham: Offer
- Exeter: Offer

Good Points:

This statement is powered by a broad range of academic interests — all of which the candidate has explored to a deep and commendable level. They are able to articulate how these interests came about, why they are important, and how they intersect. In so doing, the candidate clearly demonstrates their ability to think independently, to undertake independent projects, and to foster a wide-ranging curiosity. Furthermore, they clearly illustrate how their academic interests have had a bearing on their actions outside of the classroom; activities which require a substantial amount of initiative and endeavour.

Bad Points:

While the consideration of a range of different areas of psychology is illustrative of a consistently curious individual, this statement would have benefited from greater cohesion as an overall piece. The candidate could have also found a less rhetorical way of opening their statement; their tone at this point is not a mode of speech that they return to elsewhere, and as such, it seems somewhat like a non-sequitur. Their prose thereafter is much more engaging, and it seems unfulfilling and irrelevant to include such mystifying text at the start.

Overall:

This candidate maturely presents their academic interests and particular areas of personal pursuit. As a result of this, they are able to demonstrate moments at which they have taken impressive amounts of initiative, and have really gone out of their way in order to experience their academic interests outside of the classroom. They are thereby able to fashion themselves as a curious, energetic, academic individual, who is able to think independently and develop their own work. There are potential areas for stylistic improvement within the statement but they do not hinder the overall impression given of a capable and committed candidate.

NOTES

Subject: Experimental Psychology

When I first became aware of the crimes that took place in Abu Ghraib I was shocked. I couldn't understand why anybody would behave in such a way for no obvious reason – I wanted to know what was going through the soldiers minds at the time. This led me to read the Stanford Prison experiment which critics argue explains why people might act so abusively. At first I was absorbed by the astounding results and satisfied that it explained the crimes, however, having contemplated the experimental design and read criticisms of the experiment I realised that perhaps these results should have been expected. After all, when a group of young men are given power they are unlikely to sit around chatting, especially when research has shown that experimental participants actively try to do what they believe the researchers want them to do.

I am particularly interested in our awareness and perception of the world. In a recent finding Mohamad Koubeissi has claimed to have found a location in the brain where all brain activity is packaged and relayed to produce conscious experience – the claustrum - he hopes that stimulating this region could stop epileptic seizures. Reading "Phantoms In The Brain" by V.S. Ramachandran taught me a lot about how the brain is structured. What I realised when reading this was that there is so much about the brain that we don't understand and this is partly because we are restricted to our conscious mind only. We never experience the other processes occurring in our brain so it is much harder to study them. You could even suggest that our consciousness is simply an aid to ensure that we survive and our genes are carried forward to the next generation. Biologically this makes sense as our advanced awareness evolved from the first organisms with the most basic view of the world, in order for us to make better decisions for our survival.

Neurology is also an area that interests me – I was lucky enough to hear Prof Guy Tear speak about his work at Kings College. He is currently working with a team that is trying to replicate chemical signals that the body produces, to direct neurones to their correct position in the body. Their hope is that if they are successful they will be able to stimulate growth of neurones in people with paralysis and to restore function of the affected muscles which would be an incredible breakthrough.

Gaining a work placement at Econic Technologies, a research group based in Imperial College, was extremely valuable to me. Although it is not concerned in an area of psychology it taught me how scientific research, such as Prof Guy Tear's, is carried out and demonstrated what it might be like to enter a research profession – I saw the rigour with which they carried out experiments and it seemed like very rewarding work, especially when advances are made towards the goal. While I was there I helped collect data for a paper which they were working on and gave a presentation about where I thought their research could be used commercially.

I would like to take part in or coordinate my own psychological research while at university and I think I have developed a foundation of the necessary skills to do so. I gained my level 2 award in Community Sports Leadership which developed my leadership, communication and planning skills by coaching children various sports who may not otherwise have this opportunity. I was not just teaching these children, I was also responsible for their health and safety. I gained my Gold Duke of Edinburgh award which further built on my teamwork skills and organisation. We had to provide for ourselves and navigate independently for 4 days and nights.

Outside my studies I have many interests with tennis being my favourite sport. I am also a keen golfer, rugby player and cricketer. I find endurance events to be a good test of my self-will so I often compete in biathlons and ran a 20 mile race for charity.

Universities applied to:

- Oxford: Offer
- Bath: Offer
- Birmingham: Offer
- Durham: Offer
- Bristol: Offer

Good Points:

Through consideration of both more micro-scale individual problems and high-level concerns, this candidate is able to demonstrate their ability to think in complex and wide-ranging ways. They are able to situate their subject within its broader context and can illustrate articulately why it matters as an area of study. Within that, they can also illustrate areas in which they have identified and pursued particular interests. As a result of these various layers of thought, this candidate demonstrates their ability to undertake independent academic projects and to work from their own initiative — rather than within the bounds of their school-level academic demands.

Bad Points:

This candidate loses eloquence when they begin discussions of their extra-curricular activities. While this does not impede the academic credentials of the statement as a whole, it does seem deflating after careful and rigorous prose about their more academic interests. As such, their aim to tie their extra-curricular activities to their chosen area of undergraduate study falls slightly shy of the mark. The candidate would also benefit from thoroughly structuring their statement in order to persuasively build an argument and a cohesive tone, rather than writing a statement in granular sections of individual interest.

Overall:

This statement has a good balance of personal information and considered academic thought, but would benefit from matching that balance of content with balance of tone. At present, the statement lacks clarity and persuasion in its discussion of extra-curricular pursuits, whereas its more academic sections are focused in their aims. What is particularly impressive about this statement is its ability to consider the subject from a variety of standpoints and to discuss problematic issues on a very minor and broader level, and moreover, at levels that may or may not be possible to comprehend.

NOTES

Subject: Psychology

The study of merely the physical world was never quite enough for me. I strive to look beneath the surface, into the mind and soul's continuous quest, where there are likely to be more questions than answers. Moving from Europe to the Middle East, I gradually realised the underlying presence of Psychology, as I found myself not only looking at people, but thoroughly into them. Natural empathy drove a keen observation of emotion, behaviour and relationships, marking the beginnings of a fascination that I wish to pursue professionally.

As a Finnish international student, I have spent 11 years in Frankfurt, Germany, and two and a half years in Bahrain. My exposure to a variety of ethnicities, religions and languages has allowed me to gain a level of maturity through diverse international perspectives; through life in the metropolitan central European banking capital, and on a miniscule island state in the Arab world. Since the age of 5, I have been taught in English, and so for the majority of my life, English has even been the language that I think in.

Higher level Biology has introduced me to the topics of neurology, the brain and behavioural ecology, while practical Biology has developed my skills in obtaining accurate, objective results in experiments such as the Elisa test. Furthermore, language subjects have refined my literary analysis skills, and allowed me to look into social and interpersonal issues in literature. Reading 'Psychology: A very short introduction', by Butler and McManus, and 'Phobias: Fighting the Fear' by Helen Saul, with research into mental illness, modern therapy developments such as CBT and the debatable role of genetics, empiricism, cognition and neurophysiology among others in the foundations of the human psyche have fuelled my interest in the branches of clinical and abnormal psychology.

In morning shifts at a Finnish hospital's surgical department, I tended and talked to people with not only physical impairment but also mental conditions such as Alzheimer's and Anxiety Disorder. I found patient contact to be something so natural, so effortless, as several of them confided their life stories to me. I learned to regard the delicate hospital environment as an inexpressibly rewarding experience. I undertook voluntary work in an old people's dementia home, and a kindergarten that included children with learning difficulties and Down's Syndrome. Once again, I was struck by the ease with which I could establish a connection with strangers, and found something so profoundly similar in the youngest and oldest generations: the circle of life being completed. My interactions with different age groups were genuinely moving and a valuable introduction to both child- and geropsychology. In addition to these experiences, I have tutored a younger girl in science subjects, and consequently learnt to focus on the academic needs of an individual. My hobbies mainly include skiing, running and swimming, through which the skills of perseverance and motivation have been strongly highlighted for me. More recently I have started a highly enjoyable Ballroom and Latin dance course. Travelling has been a passion for quite some time, as I find myself fully intoxicated by languages, cultures and sights. On trips and at home alike, creative photography is a developing interest, and has helped me to view the world from various angles.

Psychology continues to intrigue me academically, but also within the trivial experiences of everyday life. The natural aptitude that I seem to have for analysing social phenomena underlines my passion for Psychology; as an amateur psychologist I can imagine no greater satisfaction than embarking on a journey that will ultimately lead me towards the professional field.

Universities applied to:

- Cambridge: Offer
- Warwick: Offer
- Bath: Offer
- Durham: Offer
- St. Andrews: Rejected

Good Points:

This candidate is able to demonstrate a rich range of practical experience in their chosen field, which energises their statement. They are able to clearly articulate how their subject interacts with their personal experiences, which strengthens the force of their argument through its demonstration of their passion for the field. They have tied together a variety of experiences — personal, practical, academic — in favour of their statement, by isolating how each of them contributes to their interests in psychology. This mode of thought and discussion is illustrative of an analytical way of thinking, which in turn, presents the statement as the work of an academically-able student.

Bad Points:

While the candidate quite naturally aims to shine through in their statement, they are running the risk of developing a haughty tone of discussion. As a result, this statement would have benefitted from a relaxation or a focusing of register. Further contributing to this sense of haughtiness is the large amount of personal detail. Although this personal detail does need to be laid as a foundation for discussion more relevant to the topic, the candidate could have streamlined these more anecdotal passages in order to leave room for greater academic consideration. In particular, this candidate could have referenced and utilised a greater range of literary or academic material, since they have ably discussed their more practical experience with their chosen subject area.

Overall:

While this statement very successfully highlights relevant practical experience, it could be strengthened further by greater academic discussion of written material and independent thought. Nonetheless, it is still demonstrative of an analytical mode of thought and an ability to construct an argument from seemingly disparate pieces. The candidate has clearly thought about the relevance of their subject matter both within their own personal context and within a much broader context, which further bolsters their work as that of a capable and curious thinker.

NOTES

Subject: Psychological and Behavioural Sciences

"Such a shame she will not study medicine!" I heard several times as my interests finally steered into a university degree. Having grown up with my mum – a psychologist, from primary school I constantly questioned human behaviour. And although parents from small towns dream of their children becoming doctors, phenomena that I saw in my surroundings, like eating disorders or extreme shyness, relentlessly attracted my attention. I knew I needed to pursue an intense educational path to gain the depth of knowledge I desired.

My exceptional curiosity led me to follow the IBO program. Thanks to its curriculum, I relished the opportunity to extend my private research and put it into academic framework. While working independently on my Extended Essay "Should introversion be treated?" I discovered Susan Cain and her book "Quiet: The Power of Introverts". My puzzle of introversion developed into educated distinction for introversion, social anxiety disorder and behavioural inhibitions. In addition, the EE helped me understand the role of biology, encouraging me to start an online course "Introduction to psychology" taught by the University of Toronto. My curiosity still reaches far beyond these introductions and I am looking forward to studying details of brain lobes during biological modules of the course. Moreover, since the subject of eating disorders is too sensitive to be researched in high school, I cannot wait to approach it at an academic level and discuss it with world class experts.

My in-depth, intense processing applies not only to theory, but I also appreciate the material world we live in. Hence, to step out of my comfort zone and into reality, I attended a Business Week program organised by Washington City in Gdansk. My initial function as Vice-President for a business simulation left me with a deep aspiration for a better performance. Therefore, I followed-up Business Week program with an advanced option and became the CEO of my team. Right then I started to appreciate the contribution of every member. I took real pleasure in guiding my team through the processes of marketing, pricing, R&D, production and the construction of a business plan, all of which I understood quickly and precisely thanks to analytical thinking skills I developed during a demanding Maths HL course.

My commitment and eagerness to learn may also be seen by the title of a finalist in the French Language Olympiad, meaning that I reached an advanced level in just two years. Furthermore, I participated in two exchange projects with a Provencal theatre to check my linguistic competencies with native speakers. Although both exchanges were awarded with European Language Label, what counted most was my exceptional chance to explore the French culture inside out. My other interests include French literature, contemporary dancing, horse riding and behavioural economics. The latter led me to the online course organised by the University of Queensland, Australia. The course outlined concepts from Daniel Kahneman's "Thinking Fast and Slow", of which planning fallacy and confirmation bias I consider of greatest importance. Moreover, thanks to good time management I constantly look for other initiatives, such as a charity campaign or volunteering in teaching English or organising TriMUN as Deputy Secretary General. During TriMUN I explained to participants how to follow all the diplomatic procedures - those activities made me wonder about different approaches I had to take in order to teach.

I no longer want psychology to remain only an interest of mine; instead, I need dependable academic tools to understand the research already done. As psychology is a relatively new field of science, early starting form Wundt in 1879, there is still space for much more to be done. I believe that a strong scientific background is crucial for building a career involving communicating with people efficiently and helping them function optimally in our complex material world.

Universities applied to:

- Cambridge: Offer
- Edinburgh: Offer
- University College London: Offer
- St. Andrews: Offer
- Glasgow: Offer

Good Points:

This candidate is able to identify a range of ways in which they have developed their interest in their subject area beyond the demands of their current courses of school-level study. They are also able to demonstrate that they have thought clearly and carefully about what kinds of material they might encounter at the undergraduate level, and how that intersects with both their current interests and their potential areas of interest in the future. In order to have arrived at these opinions, the candidate has read a range of texts and is able to utilise their thoughts on these texts in their statement. As such, they draw together various aspects of their academic pursuits in order to fully paint the picture of themselves as a motivated and tenacious academic student.

Bad Points:

While the candidate is generally able to express themselves clearly, there are moments where the syntax and exact choices of vocabulary seem slightly stilted, suggesting perhaps a non-native speaker or an unedited statement. This slight lapse in language skill does present areas where the communication level is affected, and therefore, puts pressure on the content of the statement as a whole. The statement also relies heavily on anecdotal evidence and does include some slightly uncomfortable generalities. In addition, the candidate would benefit from perhaps adjusting the tone of their moments of personal reflection; the statement has the potential to be read in a way that suggests the writer is arrogant or pompous, and it may well be that this is solely down to word choice rather than intention.

Overall:

Although this statement illustrates the candidate's academic fervour, it does also show areas for potential improvement. It would have been beneficial for the statement as a whole had the candidate maintained a clear and developed level of academic prose throughout, and they could have more clearly linked some of their extra-curricular activities to their chosen course of study. In addition, while the candidate ably discusses texts that they have read in preparation for undergraduate study, these discussions could have taken prominence in the statement, over and above the inclusion of more personal or anecdotal material.

NOTES

MUSIC

Subject: Music

Music means something different to everyone. For me, music is an all consuming passion, evoking emotion and providing intellectual challenge; a highly influential art form which will always remain a constant source of enjoyment and fascination.

Since beginning the violin aged 6, my enthusiasm has continued to grow and after receiving a music bursary on entry to secondary school, I took up the saxophone. Having achieved two grade 8 distinctions, I look forward to the challenge of my grade 8 piano exam in December. Learning such a variety of instruments has not only made me efficient in managing time, but has provided superb opportunities to play in many musical styles. I particularly enjoy playing chamber music and on winning the school's Mary Gough scholarship, funded my attendance of the Pro Corda International Chamber Music Academy, enabling me to play in a range of ensembles guided by inspirational coaches.

An academic and, to me, stimulating aspect of music relates to its history and the influence of certain composers. Recently, I attended a talk on impressionist art and music and was interested to learn how both art forms have developed side by side. I liked exploring how composers created impressions through harmony, rhythm, and tone colour. For instance, Debussy's frequent use of whole tone scales. Attending work experience in the Creative Arts Department at the National Centre for Young People with Epilepsy opened my eyes to yet another facet of music. Here, music therapy is used; it was astonishing and encouraging to see some of the more severely disabled students clap in time. To pursue my interest in music psychology I read 'This is Your Brain on Music' by Daniel Levitin, which drew upon my scientific knowledge. It amazes me that a sound's frequency or timbre has so great an impact on our responses to music. The analytical and investigative skills developed by taking scientific A Levels has also aided my approach to harmonic analysis and I find it useful to take a mathematical slant when harmonising Bach Chorales.

At school, I sing in the Senior and Chamber Choirs and co-lead the Senior and Chamber Orchestras. I am also a member of the Concert Band, Saxophone Quartet and Gospel Choir – which I will be running this year. Being so involved has improved my sight reading and has led to my exposure to a large and varied repertoire; this term I am excited to be performing 'Mozart's 3rd Violin Concerto' with the Orchestra. In preparation, I watched Mozart's opera; 'The Marriage of Figaro'. I look forward to the chance to learn more about opera, particularly after watching an engaging interview with conductor Antonio Pappano. It made me think about the relationship between music and drama and the role of music in influencing the emotions of an audience in scenes which may otherwise be ambiguous.

Aside from music, community work at a local care home and Oxfam shop has developed my interpersonal skills and demonstrating team work was key to our company's success in the Young Enterprise Scheme. As a school prefect, high levels of responsibility are expected. In addition to school work, I took an Open University module entitled 'Life in the Oceans', for which I had to work independently and write essay based answers; skills I know will be useful in further education. I also attend Stagecoach Theatre Arts weekly, successfully auditioning for the national showcase productions of 'Unsinkable' in 2009 and 'My Fair Lady' in 2010. I was intrigued to watch the work of a professional musical director as he arranged, taught and conducted the music and am keen to develop skills in these areas in the future.

I am excited by the prospect of a studying music in higher education as I seek to answer some of the many questions I have whilst furthering my practical ability. I feel prepared for the challenges of university life and am a highly motivated student who will endeavour to carry out all work to the best of my ability.

Universities applied to:

- Cambridge: Offer
- Manchester: Offer
- Bristol: Offer
- Royal Holloway: Offer
- King's: Offer

Good Points:

The strength of this application is in its clear articulation of thorough engagement with its subject. The applicant is able to clearly demonstrate how their subject intersects with their personal life at various junctures and ties their extra-curricular activities to their academic application well. The applicant alludes to specific musical achievements, but more impressively, is able to demonstrate how these achievements make them a suitable candidate for university study; they do not rely on the strength of the achievements alone to speak for themselves. In addition to their practical achievements, the candidate references works that they have pursued beyond the bounds of their course. In particular, the initiative taken by the candidate in being both a member and a leader of groups is illustrative of their commitment.

Bad Points:

While this candidate is able to clearly demonstrate their dedication to practical musicianship, their consideration of academic music study is slimmer in content. It would have strengthened their application to allude in greater detail to areas of interest in a more academic/research context. The applicant could also be slightly warier of using quite personal/informal ways of articulating their experience and thoughts. Their use of technical vocabulary is also relatively sparse and remains quite general. Greater specificity and consideration in their use of terminology would have given greater indication of their seriousness about academic study.

Overall:

While this application illustrates the writer's longstanding engagement with music on a practical level, it could do with greater in-depth analysis of particular works or reference to independent academic study or thought. The applicant demonstrates how they have pursued their subject beyond the expectations of A Level, and is successful in tying together their personal projects and academic interests. The applicant writes in a consistently clear and articulate style, which could be further embellished with academic inflection.

NOTES

Subject: Music

I have enjoyed music for as long as I can remember. As I have grown up, my enjoyment has become a deep fascination. The more I learn about music the more the subject impresses and excites me. I find myself thinking, talking and reading about music more and more. I have come to realise that music will always be a major part of my life and my hope is I will be able to make it the focus of my career. I can therefore think of no better way of spending the next three years than by deepening my understanding and appreciation of music.

Performing with clarinet, piano and voice first drew me to music and continues to give me great pleasure; but it is the breadth of music as a subject which has driven my growing enthusiasm for it. On reading 'Music: A Very Short Introduction' by Nicholas Cook I was struck by the idea that all descriptions of music involve metaphor. The crux of this idea; that we approach music as if it were a kind of shape-shifting object; helped me to understand the satisfaction I get from studying it. This was reinforced by thinking about music in the context of my other A level subjects: Maths, English and History.

Music can be approached as a mathematical problem which is resolved through identifying patterns of harmony and form. It can be analysed like literature in terms of the effect of its 'patterns' upon those experiencing it, such as intended meaning, emotional impact and mood. Or it can be looked at in a historical context; the influences upon it and its affects, as one would understand a historical artefact. All of this enhances the immediate appreciation of music through performance or listening, as well as the pleasure of composition. I believe it is the diversity of ways in which music is experienced and understood that interests me most.

As well as enlightening me on many of the key moments that led our music to sound as it does today, the book 'Big Bangs' by Howard Goodall, impressed me with the notion that, in regards to music, we are standing on the 'tip' of something that has been continuously present throughout human history. I increasingly seem to experience this as a tangible feeling when practising and performing, especially in ensembles. I think this why I so enjoy being part of school groups: Jazz Band, Wind Band, Clarinet Group, Orchestra and Choir, and county groups: North Bedfordshire Youth Chamber Orchestra and Bedfordshire Youth Orchestra. At the recent Eton Choral Course I attended, I became more familiar with choral repertoire and consort singing. Again, I enjoyed experiencing the development of music through performing choral works from Monteverdi to Rose. Attending the premiere of James Macmillan's choral work 'Credo' at the 2012 BBC Proms made me feel that I was witnessing the very 'tip' of musical development advancing. I look forward to continuing my involvement in ensembles at university, both as part of wider university life and as part of the course.

Aside from taking part in ensembles, I have pursued my interest in music by taking ABRSM practical exams, achieving grade 8 Distinction in clarinet, grade 7 Distinction in piano and grade 7 Merit in singing. I am now looking forward to taking the ABRSM diploma on clarinet. I am also working on an EPQ in music, for which I am composing a new score for the silent film 'The Cabinet of Dr Caligari'. This is allowing me to explore composition in more depth than at A level and to research German art music as an influence. Through my musical activities and others, I have also aimed to develop organisational skills, initiative and leadership abilities. This includes managing the staging and performance of my EPQ, undertaking my Duke of Edinburgh Gold Award, work experience in a school music department and weekend work in a local supermarket. I believe such personal skills will help me practically channel my love of music so that I can achieve my full musical potential at university and beyond.

Universities applied to:

- Oxford: Offer
- Manchester: Offer
- Birmingham: Offer
- York: Offer
- Durham: Offer

Good Points:

This candidate is able to clearly articulate their dedication to practical music-making, and can further bolster this interest with instances of academic pursuit of the topic. Discussing their EPQ helps to demonstrate how their practical and academic interests are already relating to each other, and it indicates how it might continue to do so at university level. By combining instances of personal enjoyment (such as concert attendance) with references to specific texts, this candidate helps themselves to stand out as a student that both applies themselves academically and goes out of their way to incorporate their academic interests in their everyday life. They are able to discuss the potential impacts of their subject on both a micro level (its impact on them personally), and on a macro level (where it is situated in broader contexts of academic thought).

Bad Points:

While the candidate does discuss academic lines of thought and research in their area, these elements are somewhat sparser than their instances of practical experience. It could be a potential area of development to redistribute the weight of their material; the courses they are **applying** for are geared to a more academic focus, and are not solely courses in practical musicianship. The candidate should also take care over using too many instances of subjective experience — although it is important for them to underline the subject's impact on them personally, there is room in this statement for a more focused line of argument about their academic pursuits, and that would have potentially added more value than an insight into their broader, hypothetical hopes for the future.

Overall:

This statement is strong in its ability to demonstrate a range of interests and a variety of instances in which their interest have been practically exercised. However, it could be developed further by more rigorously using it to demonstrate their academic lines of interest. Though the candidate has expressed their interest in areas of academic research, and they are able to discuss how their interests connect across different disciplines, these areas of discussion could be further explored in order to best demonstrate their ability as a candidate preparing to undertake a theoretical music degree.

NOTES

Subject: Music

I cannot remember a time when music was not the most important aspect of my life. Whether through playing piano from the age of 5, or through 6 years of study at the Royal Academy of Music's Junior Department, music has never ceased to be my passion. I have developed a keen interest in the analytical and historical side of musical study in my composition lessons at JRAM. It has been fascinating to explore developments in musical harmony, tonality and style, such as Bach's fugal expositions and the Serialist techniques of Schoenberg and Webern and to subsequently incorporate such ideas into my wider understanding of musical theory. Exploring my creativity through freer styles of composition set for a range of ensembles, including a rondo for string quartet and a tone poem for choir with orchestra, has broadened my perception of harmony. Additionally, I have refined my skills as a performing pianist and flautist through my appointment as principle flute in the Buckinghamshire County Youth Orchestra, and more recently through winning the prestigious Chamber Prize at JRAM in a piano trio. I have also enjoyed the exciting and motivating atmosphere at the Academy, where Supporting Musicianship lessons have provided an insight into the vast history of Western music. I have built upon this foundation through wider reading of books such as Cook's 'Music: A Very Short Introduction' and, more specifically to my interests, Taruskin's 'On Russian Music'.

Throughout my education I have proved to be a diligent and capable student, with the ability to manage a large and demanding workload. Whilst maintaining a 6-day working week with my Saturday's spent at JRAM I have attained two grade 8 distinctions, as well as excelling in my academic work. My competitive nature allows me to thrive in a challenging atmosphere and I am often praised for my ability to contribute regularly and thoughtfully in lessons. I have committed to playing organ for my local church weekly and to teaching piano and theory to a number of students. I play an active role in the musical life of the school and wider community, not only involved in my own school's ensembles and choirs, but also accompanying the choir of a school for disabled students, which I have found incredibly rewarding.

After performing Tchaikovsky's 4th Symphony with the BCYO, I realised my budding interest in late-Romantic Russian music, and have since developed my knowledge of this era in my reading. My studies led me to consider the changes in Russian ballet music that can be seen in the work of the subsequent generation of composers, focusing most closely on the legacies of Stravinsky's 'Rite of Spring' in comparison to the more traditionally Romantic ballet music of Tchaikovsky's 'Swan Lake'. By examining these scores, and studying some of the scholarly discourse surrounding them, I have developed my ability to listen to and analyse music, which has deepened my desire to continue my studies to degree level. Although I have long-suspected that music would be my chosen subject at university, I have maintained a keen interest in my other studies. I am an able linguist, studying French at A-Level as well as having taken Italian lessons out of school, which combined with English Literature has broadened my ability to analyse and write in a cohesive way. By taking Mathematics, I have struck a balance between creativity and practicality in my studies, which will enable me to thrive on the varied challenges presented by a music degree.

For me, music is about much more than just performance. Although I enjoy playing the piano, my real passion is for developing my understanding of the wider meaning and significance of music and examining the techniques employed by composers to communicate with their audiences. I would relish the opportunity to immerse myself in the study of music and know that I have the potential to bring as much to the course as I would want to take from it.

Universities applied to:

- Cambridge: Offer
- Manchester: Offer
- King's: Offer
- Bristol: Offer
- Southampton: Offer

Good Points:

Through the inclusion of a wide range of examples, the applicant is able to show how music has impacted their life beyond their course and can keenly demonstrate their commitment to their subject. They are able to present themselves as a well-rounded individual with a great deal to offer. They allude to instances where they have considered music from a profound, critical standpoint, and are able to reference material that they are particularly interested in. Throughout the statement, the applicant articulates themselves concisely and intelligently, drawing upon academic vocabulary where appropriate. They are able to give concrete examples of their achievements and can refer to how this contributes to their general strength as an applicant.

Bad Points:

While the applicant's academic potential is clear, their use of overly confident language and self-presentation has the potential to represent them as slightly arrogant. As such, given they are clearly a capable applicant, their tone seems to do them a disservice. This statement would benefit from going beyond the use of facts or bald statements, and instead, embellishing these or developing them into a more useful part of their statement - either by justifying them with evidence or by using them as a springboard to furthering their statement.

As a general rule throughout the statement, the applicant is most persuasive at moments where they use clear evidence and examples to express their thoughts and are least persuasive at points where they fail to fully articulate themselves through anecdotal or subjective discussion. While the applicant references works beyond the remit of their A Level, their examples remain relatively mainstream and could be more reflective of a significant and actioned interest in reading/listening around their subject.

Overall:

This application seems to represent the work of an able practical musician, but by comparison, offers less information about academic interests. While the statement is authoritative and confident in tone, it runs the risk of conveying an arrogance to the reader. The applicant could draw on a greater range of academic interests and could demonstrate this more clearly through a wider variety of explored works and independent thought. This statement is powered by the applicant's enthusiasm, which remains clear throughout the writing. The applicant is able to indicate how they involve their interest in their subject elsewhere in their life - and in turn, they demonstrate how these examples contribute to their suitability as an applicant more broadly.

NOTES

ENGLISH

Subject: English

Everyday life as a subject and ordinary people as protagonists are integral to the nature of literature. Wordsworth stepped away from the "gaudiness and inane phraseology of...modern writers" towards "situations from common life"- allying accessible poetry with a moral centre. This is a progression from the works of Shakespeare (plays for common men), despite heroes like King Lear fitting Aristotle's tragic archetype of "an imitation of persons... above the common level". Becoming no better than 'Tom O'Bedlam', Lear's fall from the "bias of nature" evokes the intended tragic effect through his loss of position and sanity. However, I agree that the common man and ordinary life may be as appropriate subjects for both tragedy and literature. McCrum's notion that motifs "drawn from ordinary life... (enthral)" echoes Arthur Miller's 'Tragedy and the Common Man'. Feste's declaration in 'Twelfth Night' that "A sentence is/ but a cheveril glove to a good wit: how quickly the/ wrong side may be turned outward!" epitomises major themes through an everyday object; both glove and world are turned inside out, as though the traditional Lord of Misrule is present within the plot.

My EPQ has further explored the ambitions of Wordsworth and Shelley in their poetry, relative to what poetry should achieve and the poet's role. 'To A Skylark' exemplifies Shelley's desire to enable the observer to experience beauty, with illustrations of clear celestial images of the "unbodied joy", a parallel to his desire as a poet; to provide delight, yet remain aloof. In contrast, Wordsworth's didactic purpose is evident in 'Simon Lee', in his subject choice of common humanity, instructing the reader to consider such acts of compassion as unremarkable.

A similar 'exemplum' of moral ideals is achieved in Chaucer's 'Franklin's Tale', scrutinising the existence of providence and the necessity of 'trouthe' through both his 'Breton lai' fairytale itself, and the narrator not of noble birth. The Prologue uses the idiosyncrasies of the main character to generate concerns of 'gentillesse', striving to render himself 'gentil' through imparting his knowledge of classical poetry to the more socially elevated of his company. Thus the text stands as a component in illustrating, through 'The Canterbury Tales', a cross-section of characters from medieval England, and their desires in relation to their places in society.

Virginia Woolf's exploration of the reflections of her characters in her 'Mrs Dalloway' achieves a multi-faceted examination of a patriarchal and pious section of English society and the oppression it inflicts upon each character. An echo of Joyce's use of the internal monologue, 'Mrs Dalloway' serves as a successful integration of several individuals' musings on one day. The disparity between the often mundane thoughts of the protagonists and the singular, outstanding event of Septimus' suicide appears to mirror Clarissa's own struggle to balance her internal perspective with the external world.

Work experience with a Channel 4 drama provided me with an insight into the problems of adapting text to screen, while emphasising the importance of collaboration and time management. These skills translate naturally into continual participation in school drama and my role as Chair of the Yearbook Committee, while demonstrating my creative passion that also surfaces through artwork and Grade 8 piano. My early years in Botswana and a charity trip to Romania have made me aware not only of another culture, but the nature of life in developing societies.

T S Eliot states that "a perception, not only of the pastness of the past, but of its presence" is imperative for a full comprehension of a text, relative to the "simultaneous order" of other literature. I aim to develop this awareness of intertextuality both in close and comparative reading, as well as the element of my own interpretation that is essential for not only University but a lifelong appreciation of literature.

Universities applied to:

- Oxford: Offer
- Bristol: Offer
- Durham: Rejected
- Leeds: Offer
- Royal Holloway: Offer

Good Points:

Through quotation and reference, this statement clearly and efficiently demonstrates a dedication to reading a wide variety of text. The applicant has also managed to embed these quotations/allusions in segments of their own thought, thereby illustrating their ability not just to absorb texts but also their ability to apply their own critical approach. The statement consistently and accurately uses terminology which is specific to critical theory, which further bolsters the applicant's statement as one which reflects their interest in literary studies. The more personal information that the applicant provides is well-tied to their subject area — and they also allude to their EPQ research in a way that is helpful to the statement; they do not simply state that they have done an EPQ, but they are able to discuss why their work is useful and what it has revealed to them.

Bad Points:

Though the range of quotations is impressive, the statement does read as a relatively fragmented survey of their reading; each paragraph seems watertight, but an overall argument is unclear. The applicant, therefore, runs the risk of peacocking their reading habits rather than cohesively structuring their statement towards an overall goal. In addition, this concentration of literary references also makes the statement appear slightly airless — the most personal information at the end is useful in counterbalancing this, but the statement is perhaps toeing the line of not giving away a great deal about the applicant as a well-rounded student.

Overall:

This statement confidently and impressively discusses a number of relevant areas of interest within their chosen subject. It combines the use of literary sources with careful independent thought and demonstrates a commitment to going above and beyond the classroom demands imposed on them for A Level (or equivalent). The applicant shows a clear and focused commitment to their subject and incorporates more personal details to produce a statement that gives a good indication of their overall character and calibre.

NOTES

Subject: English

Growing up in a house where books have replaced wallpaper, acquiring a love of literature was inevitable. I love the way in which writers explore, question, and critique aspects of human nature through the presentation of their worlds and characters. My favourite pieces of writing are ones such as Levi's 'Order on the Cheap', Gogol's 'The Overcoat' or Hartley's 'The Go Between', where a particular human tendency is both beautifully presented and meticulously analysed. In his short story, Levi explores curiosity by invoking that of his audience: readers become distracted by the narrator's descriptions of his experiments and overlook their morally problematic side. Hartley employs an opposite technique, allowing the reader to be often sharply aware of the innocence and naivety of the protagonist. Gogol manipulates the reader even more, invoking a painful sense of pathos around the main character whilst at the same time daring us to find Akaky's concerns a little ridiculous.

I have to admit, however, that I am drawn to Levi's short story not only because of its literary merits, but also because I sympathise with its main character: a man driven by his fascination with the process of creation. My favourite parts of my Chemistry A level were the 'practicals'; I derived great excitement from the process of taking a simple substance, subjecting it to particular conditions, and thereby creating a completely different, and often much more complex, chemical. In 'The Monkey's Wrench' Levi seems to emulate the same process in his development of the character of Tino. Starting from a simple first picture Tino is slowly developed, snippet by snippet, as the stories progress, until a fully evolved character finally emerges.

I find it fascinating how unexpected links can suddenly emerge between works: reading around a set text, Murakami's 'Blind Willow Sleeping Woman', I read his 'Kafka on the Shore', which led me to read some of Kafka's short stories, including 'The Penal Colony' and 'A Country Doctor'. Whilst the works of the two writers are in many ways extremely different, I noticed some stylistic similarities. Both present protagonists whose apparently unexceptional lives are suddenly interrupted by a series of unexplained fantastical events. These events are often a metaphor for a wider-reaching process in the life of the narrator.

But without a doubt, poetry has always been my favourite form of literature: I like listening to poems or reading them aloud, appreciating their rhythm and sound, before going back and analysing them. Some of my favourite poems are those in which the sound is almost as important as the words themselves, for example, Lawrence's 'Ship of Death' or Frost's 'After Apple Picking'. In this vein, I have a YouTube channel on which I post my readings of various poems, and have also earned at least several pence through poetry busking in the streets of Waterloo.

Eagleton's 'Literary Theory: an Introduction' gave me another way in which to approach texts. As well as my visceral response and the various meanings extracted through analysis, the texts might exemplify the literary or political beliefs of a particular period. Further, members of different literary movements might approach them in very different ways - I enjoyed trying to put on the 'mask' of one movement or another and read a poem through it. Similarly, whilst studying 'Othello' I was interested by the hugely varying approaches of different critics, from Bradley who focused chiefly on character but seemed to forget the literary context, to Empson who concentrated almost solely on the changing meaning of the word 'honest' throughout time. Perhaps most significantly, Eagleton and the other critics reinforced the idea that engaging with a text is itself a creative process.

However, Eagleton's book is just 'an Introduction': what draws me most to the study of English literature is not only that I love it, but that I want so much to learn more about it.

Universities applied to:

- Cambridge: Offer
- Durham: Offer
- Sussex: Offer
- University College London: Offer
- King's: Offer

Good Points:

The candidate clearly demonstrates a keen and actioned interest in their chosen subject through the presentation of their reading and subsequent thoughts. They can articulate their present interests in their subject as well as the sources of these interests and their potential directions for further development. They indicate their ability to think laterally and creatively through their cohesive discussions of seemingly disparate texts, and are self-aware in their strengths and weaknesses as a reader. Their statement is fuelled by their evident personal enthusiasm for their subject, which makes it an engaging and urgent read.

Bad Points:

The candidate has acquired a relatively personal tone, which veers into the casual or confessional at times; their point might have been made more clearly or precisely had they adopted more strictly academic modes of communicating. Their consideration of various works is quite itemised, insofar as their statement reads as a series of 'nuggets' of information rather than a clearly-focused piece with argument and direction. The candidate does reference another subject they study for A Level, but beyond that, they have not included much information beyond their academic reading and interests. While this could certainly be justified as an approach, it does leave the statement suggesting that the writer is not particularly engaged in questions or activities beyond specific areas of literature.

Overall:

The statement is at times quite chaotic in style due to its familiar tone and slightly haphazard structure. However, it more than compensates for this since its familiarity is clearly a result of the candidate's sheer enthusiasm for the subject. In addition, the range of material that they consider is very impressive — it includes both primary texts (of various forms) and secondary reading. The candidate has, moreover, articulated their own ideas on these works, and even if their exact communication of these is not particularly precise, the level of thought and consideration is still strong.

NOTES

Subject: English Language & Literature

George Eliot's metaphor for imagination- 'inward light which is the last refinement of Energy ... bathing even the ethereal atoms in its ideally illuminated space'- is beautiful. The powerful image supported by the underlying liquid consonants skilfully leads to the action it describes, but it is also the suggestion of particle physics and mass-energy equivalence that interests me about this quotation. In this way, I have gained more from reading 'Middlemarch' as I appreciate Eliot's constant links between science and fiction, and I believe scientific study has generally sharpened my abilities of analysis and concise expression.

I have loved working as a steward at the Globe Theatre; I had the opportunity to see many plays, including a production of Marlowe's 'Dr Faustus'. I read Dante's 'Inferno' and several books of Milton's 'Paradise Lost' for a different portrayal of hell and sin to that depicted in 'Dr Faustus'. I found the torment and suffering described by Dante graphic, whilst the first person narrative drew me closer to the pathos fear and disgust expressed. Milton's depiction of a mental state is much more powerful in my opinion, and has interesting parallels to Faustus' state of damnation. I also saw Shakespeare's 'As You Like It', 'All's Well that Ends Well' and 'Much Ado About Nothing' whilst stewarding. 'Much Ado About Nothing' reminded me of the surprising similarity between Shakespeare's comedies and tragedies. Claudio and Hero's troubled love and Don John's self-proclaimed villainy seem to mirror the actions of Othello, Desdemona and Iago. Viewing comedy as a structure, 'Much Ado' contains the potential tragedy of 'Othello', but an added last act resolves all tensions and ends so happily and neatly that it seems to me rather unrealistic.

I enjoyed Dickens' 'Our Mutual Friend' for its satirical portrayal of superficial London society. His depiction of characters and scenes make the novel humorous and therefore very different to 'A Tale of Two Cities'. Here, the powerful characterisation emphasises the terrible human suffering and moral corruption, for example his effective personification of 'La Vengeance', who encourages the cries of bloodlust from Parisians. I found it easier to empathise with Jude in Hardy's 'Jude the Obscure' than with Dickens' creations however, since his actions appear futile against the fate which continually works against him. There seems to be no hope in the novel, unlike the eventual triumph of love over death in 'A Tale of Two Cities'. Just as in 'Tess of the d'Urbervilles' and 'A Pair of Blue Eyes', love and happiness seem only like a prelude to grief and sorrow linked with the relentless passing of time. I find Donne's approaches to this theme interesting too: in both his love poems and the Holy Sonnets, Donne uses form to counter and control the passing of time and the prospect of change.

I have participated in many music groups and ensembles at school, having achieved Grade 8 with distinction in both Flute and French Horn. I have worked for two years in my local Cancer Research shop as part of the Gold Duke of Edinburgh award, and also spent a residential week with a charity called Activenture, looking after children of different ages and abilities, for which I received the Young Carer of the Year award. During my gap year, I plan to join my local orchestra and travel for three months around South America, but ultimately I am most excited about the time I will have to read and further explore English literature.

Universities applied to:

- Oxford: Offer
- Durham: Rejected
- St. Andrews: Offer
- Exeter: Offer
- Bath: Offer

Good Points:

The candidate's wide range of personal interests are clearly demonstrated, and — for the most part — are well-linked to their subject application, giving it further strength. They are able to use independent thought to illustrate how various bits of reading they have done are linked. The list of works they discuss range from poetry to plays to Victorian novels; a strong variety of works. They evaluate these across genres and are able to apply critical thought and analysis to them. Throughout their discussions of various texts, the applicant clearly illustrates their enthusiasm for the subject; their writing is energised by positivity and personal engagement with the material.

Bad Points:

The candidate could have worked even harder to connect their extra-curricular activities to their application (though their relevance was clear in most instances). The effect of the applicant's use of independent thought and personal experience was often slightly dulled by their use of highly personal and personalising terms such as 'beautiful', or simply 'I enjoyed'. Though there is perhaps nothing wrong with these evaluations as an initial starting point, the candidate could have pushed further with their readings to interrogate these works further. Although the applicant demonstrates a wide literary foundation, their commentary did at times lapse into plot summary, which is less interesting than their own thought.

Overall:

This candidate's application reads as both impressive in its depth of knowledge and personal in its illustration of thought and enthusiasm. As such, it reads as a statement that is well-balanced and well-judged; the reader is able to get a good sense of this applicant's interests on both a personal and academic level. The statement could have made greater use of critical language and could have included fewer instances of value judgements; small alterations which would have given the candidate's discussions greater academic depth.

NOTES

Subject: English Language & Literature

Losing my hearing to meningitis aged four, I quickly found books to be the most accessible entertainment available to me. My disability did not impair my ability to engage with and enjoy literature, evoking an interest that refused to diminish, with reading remaining my favourite pastime today.

A significant part of my reading has focused on fantasy works, read to capture my imagination, such as Brent Weeks' 'Night Angel' trilogy. Often, I found that the worlds created within demonstrate the power of literature to intoxicate readers. It seemed logical to me, therefore, to root my Extended Project within this genre, examining which attributes of fantasy novels give them their unique appeal to readers of all ages. After attending an open day for English applicants last February, I was encouraged to challenge myself further in my reading, with more classical and thought provoking works. Reading Bram Stoker's 'Dracula', I noticed the dark, gothic themes dominate the usual Victorian setting, and I enjoyed comparing the original characters to those found in the numerous adaptations available today. Iain Banks' 'The Wasp Factory' allowed me to compare the gothic horror ideals in a modern perspective. In particular, the focus of the novel was much more on the warped cognitive processes of the protagonist, which instilled a grim foreboding as the novel progressed, with the characters remaining mysterious and unpredictable.

Visiting the Thiepval memorial on the Somme battlefield in France, and reciting Laurence Binyon's 'For the Fallen' to a gathering inspired me greatly. Seeing the multitude of graves helped me visualise the scale of The Great War. This in turn assisted my understanding of the renowned 'Birdsong' by Sebastian Faulks, as well as touching me personally. Experiencing the location first-hand provided me with a chance to appreciate how horrific battles played out but also gave me a more understanding voice when writing about such texts. I then decided to read Seamus Heaney's modern translation of 'Beowulf', to discover how ancient tales of battle were presented and found both the pace and action in the poem unrelenting.

Some of the archaic phrases, such as 'ring-giver' for king, also added beauty to the poet's voice, making it an even more captivating read. I recently saw a performance of Shakespeare's 'The Taming of the Shrew' at the Globe Theatre, where the audience participation and beautiful language made for a memorable afternoon, as well as boosting my confidence when studying the play in class.

Being fortunate enough for my performance to feature captions enhanced my experience further, as I was able to concentrate less on listening, and more fully on the action onstage. The modernisation of the opening scene showed me how adaptable Shakespeare is to all audiences, with the portrayal of Christophero Sly as a football hooligan swiftly engaging the crowd.

Being a mentor to two other hearing impaired pupils, at different stages of their education, has helped me show empathy to others, by helping them adapt to get the most of their schooling experience. My role as a one to one mentor was complemented by participation in a Pyramid Club scheme in which I assisted children with low self-esteem at a local primary school. I manage the rest of my free time working in a pharmacy, where I communicate with the public, manage money and work within a team. Currently, I am also studying to pass my MCA (medicine counter assistant) course, so I can legally take a more active role in the pharmacy.

I believe I have the right attitude to study English at university as I am passionate about reading and always challenge myself in my work. My determination would also assist me in my studies, while helping me overcome any difficulties faced. Above all, the chance to read great literature, under professional guidance, presents itself as an experience I am eager to approach with commitment and enthusiasm.

Universities applied to:

- Oxford: Offer
- Durham: Offer
- Newcastle: Offer
- York: Offer
- Warwick: Offer

Good Points:

As a result of both the content and the writing style, this statement reads as the work of an applicant that has devoted a significant amount of time to literature. They are able to reference and effectively call upon a range of texts and can furthermore articulate their thoughts using language in an elevated, precise, and academic register. This language is used accurately throughout the statement, and on both a large and more micro scale — in close-reading and more structurally analytical contexts. Beyond their purely academic focus, the applicant is also able to communicate a range of more personal facts that contribute to the overall image of this statement as one written by a well-rounded and engaged student.

Bad Points:

The statement, at times, felt oddly weighted; the applicant dwells for relatively long amounts of time on quite diminutive moments or events, but yet also strides through quite broad considerations of dense texts. As such, the statement could be made to be more cohesive and flowing if it were to be slightly restructured. The applicant seems quite guided by ideas of the canon and reputation, and there are instances where they supplicate to popular view rather than going into their own thoughts — it would have been an even more critically urgent statement had the applicant consistently called upon their own independent thinking. At points, the statement felt structurally guided by the applicant's route through their own memory; it would have given the statement more directional focus if it had instead been energised by an argument or goal, rather than using a more anecdotal mode of communication.

Overall:

Through eloquent discussion of a range of material, this statement effectively communicates the applicant's profound engagement with their chosen subject. This particular applicant deals maturely, concisely, and usefully with their own unique set of personal circumstances, which is to be commended. While the statement clearly indicates the applicant's capacity for engaging and complex thinking, it is nevertheless written in a rather sprawling structure that would benefit from some streamlining or re-balancing.

NOTES

MODERN LANGUAGES

Subject: French

France has developed a literature of unequalled richness and variety. Europeans in any age have had few thoughts, desires, or fantasies that a French writer somewhere has not expressed - it has given the Western mind an image of itself. In this sense, French literature serves as a pool in which many cultures meet. Therefore, in particular, it is French literature's universality which interests me.

Nevertheless, I enjoy how literature provides a window into an author's contemporary society. For example, 'Madame Bovary' draws us into Flaubert's disgust for the bourgeois existence of the 19th century; Zola's 'Thérèse Raquin' invites us into the leprous lower-depths of Paris. I am interested in how both these writers, unparalleled in their psychological clarity and narrative muscle, provide such a brutal and relentless account of their chosen subject matter: for Flaubert, the indulgent decadence of the bourgeoisie, exemplified by Emma Bovary; for Zola, the moral dankness of the murderous lovers. In addition, I have watched Kassovitz's 'La Haine' and Truffaut's 'Les quatre cents coups', both similar to Zola and Flaubert in their rigorous exploration of character. Focusing on social outcasts, these films act as an exposition of societal problems. 'La Haine' sheds light on the all-encompassing violence and cultural exclusion of the suburbs of Paris, while 'Les quatre cent coups' reveals the shocking injustices in the treatment of juvenile offenders. Thus, such French cinema serves to illuminate the neglected – I relish this narrative potential in the discovery of truth.

Besides these more realistic works, both my English and French A Levels have introduced me to Absurdism. I have appreciated the works of Beckett ('Fin de partie', 'En attendant Godot') and Ionesco ('La Cantatrice Chauve', 'Rhinocéros'). These tragicomedies simultaneously entertain and provoke – the reason why I found them so enjoyable and yet so powerful. To pursue this interest in Absurdism, I read Voltaire's absurd 'contes philosophiques', 'Candide' and 'Micromegas'. Fiction, I found, proved to be the perfect medium of expression for Voltaire's empiricism and scepticism. Therefore, like the tragicomedies of the 20th century, I thought Voltaire's work succeeded both as entertainment and as an accessible manifesto of his philosophical beliefs. Furthermore, I decided to follow up this interest in such 'contes philosophiques' by undertaking an Edexcel Extended Project, entitled 'Ancient Influence on French Existentialist Literature', for which I was awarded an A*. Here, I focused on why Camus, in 'Le Mythe de Sisyphe', Sartre, in 'Les Mouches', and Anouilh, in 'Antigone', chose to use classical themes and motifs to communicate their own particular perception of Existentialism. Despite its challenges, the more I worked at this project, the more certain I was that this is what and how I would like to study.

Moreover, I have taken an interest in symbolist French poetry. Having studied some poetry by Baudelaire ('Les Fleurs du Mal') and Verlaine ('Romances sans paroles'), I have become fascinated by the crippling and contrasting emotions communicated in these poems. I now admire how the very sound of the French language can control the register of a poem and, thus, highlight its true meaning even amongst the most abstract, intangible imagery, employed by Baudelaire and Verlaine. I am intrigued by the French language in part due to this precision.

Finally, I contributed regularly to my school's Modern Languages magazine, 'Babel', and have competed in 'Les Joutes Oratoires', a national French debating competition in which I reached the final. Through these experiences, I have begun to thoroughly enjoy communicating in French. I believe an extra language extends one's range. It releases you from the inertia of one cultural gear – a change of perspective that I find truly enlightening and enjoyable. I will be working in Paris from January to March.

Universities applied to:

- Oxford: Offer
- Durham: Offer
- Edinburgh: Offer
- Exeter: Offer
- Newcastle: Offer

Good Points:

Throughout this statement, the applicant engages consistently with a range of French texts at a very advanced level. The applicant is able to demonstrate not only an awareness of a huge tranche of French literature but also how specific works intersect. This comparative criticism is carried out by the applicant across several different forms in a manner that is lucid and impressive. The applicant has mentioned their personal research and is able to indicate why it is interesting and relevant. They are also able to indicate how their personal pursuits are reciprocally and beneficially related to their academic studies.

Bad Points:

At particular moments, this applicant veers from an academic register into an overtly formal one; a stylistic turn which, while remaining clear in meaning, is a little jarring. More personal information would have been a welcome addition to this statement, especially since its academic calibre is so relentlessly clear throughout; the statement has the potential to be slightly breathless in its rapid consideration of big swathes of literature. The statement could, therefore, have happily absorbed more personal information without diluting its clear academic potential. In addition, the candidate could have taken slightly more care over their phrasing, which occasionally takes a tone bordering on reductive or patronising; a risk which is perhaps not worth taking in this context.

Overall:

The candidate effectively and efficiently communicates a level of cultural awareness which goes far above and beyond the demands of their curriculum. They are able to demonstrate how they practically carry forward their interests in extra-curricular and academic activities. Throughout the statement, the applicant engages a muscular, academically-considered tone which is clear and authoritative. There was room in the statement for greater personal depth and warmth, and for greater justification for some of the strong academic arguments being posed.

NOTES

Subject: French & German

Living in an interconnected world makes studying languages fundamental, as they enable us to interact with a wide array of people and develop the attributes of empathy and cultural awareness. My ardour for French led me to complete three language summer schools this year at: UCL, University of Cambridge and Lancaster University. I attended numerous lectures exploring enthralling topics I had not previously considered, including: surrealism, language diglossia and dialectology. A lecture from Dr M.Griffin at Cambridge on Medieval French Literature was particularly engaging. We studied de France's lais 'Bisclarvet' and compared its themes with those of the contemporary novel 'Truismes.' The lecture inspired me to begin reading a broader assemblage of French literature from across the literary époques. At Lancaster University, I obtained the academic award for languages due to my participation in seminars, research into minority languages and concluding presentation, demonstrating my capability to work at university level. The research I carried out at Lancaster encouraged me to commence an EPQ based on sociolinguistics and the argument surrounding language and identity. Taking ab-initio language lessons at UCL has impelled me to begin an AS course in German this year.

My curiosity for French and German literature and cinema has incentivised me to keep a film and reading journal, analysing the works that I encounter. Alongside this, I research the historical, philosophical and political contexts behind these pieces, which is pivotal to appreciate the themes and ideas presented. Watching the German film 'Nosferatu', I found that its themes and visual presentation were atypical of other German films I had see, leading me to research German Expressionism. I discovered that the arts of this period are analogous to one another and I believe they reflect Germany's political, social and economic situation at the time. French literature from the classical, enlightenment and romantic époques is of particular interest to me.

Across these literary periods, I noticed disparities in tone and style; the conventions governing the way the playwrights Racine and Molière wrote are a stark contrast with the freedom in the works of Hugo and Chateaubriand. Reading Pascal's 'Pensées' and Voltaire's 'Candide' furthers my understanding of the philosophical ideas during those periods, whilst Price's 'A Concise History of France' introduces the historical events in France at the time. I also appreciate modern French literature and find it fascinating to compare these texts with those I read for my A-Level English Literature course. Gide's 'L'Immoraliste', Joffo's 'Un Sac de Billes' and Sartre's 'La Nausée' are decidedly compelling novels as each diversely questions the human condition. For October, I have arranged work experience in France and will stay with a host family, providing an opportunity to develop my oral and aural skills and gain an insight into French life.

As the French Ambassador in my Sixth Form, I offer support to fellow A-Level students. Additionally, I mentor GCSE language students, assist in lower-school lessons, promote languages at open events and have achieved the Foreign Language Leader Award. Through these activities I can share my ardour for languages and develop communication and leadership skills. As a member of Erasmus+, last year I collaborated with students from across Europe to tackle racism. Each country involved presented its ideas at an inspirational meeting in Spain. I now identify myself as more than a British Citizen; I am a Global Citizen. I regularly carry out exchanges with other Erasmus+ students, thus developing my cultural awareness.

My avidity for language learning and cultural appreciation has assured me that languages are the ideal degree for me. I greatly anticipate university study and having the possibility to refine my linguistic skills and develop international awareness.

Universities applied to:

- Oxford: Offer
- St. Andrews: Offer
- University College London: Offer
- Warwick: Offer
- University of London Institute in Paris: Offer

Good Points:

By engaging with a range of French texts and by calling on anecdotal evidence of strong academic engagement outside of the classroom, this candidate is able to efficiently demonstrate their continued and widely-applied enthusiasm for their subject. They are able to assemble information that presents them as highly-skilled and, generally, very impressive. In expressing this information, they consistently use reflect upon what they have learned from their reading. The candidate is, moreover, able to explain how their reading intersects with other areas of study, and can navigate across interests in various different subjects (while at all times demonstrating that their key focus is on French literature).

Bad Points:

This statement relies more heavily on relaying personal achievements than it does on the literary discussion, and it seems that there could have been room to more greatly delve into literary criticism. Though the applicant's use of university-level terminology is at times impressive, the statement reads as though the writing style is fuelled by a conspicuous need to engage with complex phrasing, and it would have benefitted from a more relaxed approach at times, just to prevent the style from becoming stilted. The one thing the candidate was guaranteed to communicate was that they *thought* that they were very clever. This will seldom go down well with admissions tutors. The applicant also runs the risk of presenting themselves as slightly overbearing in their intellectual self-belief and would have nullified that risk by slightly adjusting their tone.

Overall:

Through the use of strong examples, the candidate very clearly demonstrates their academic track record. However, anecdotal evidence of participation and enthusiasm is given significant weight in this statement, resulting in the compression of any literary discussion within the statement. While the range of activities that the applicant calls upon is highly impressive, the statement has room for further illustration of their ability to think creatively around literary issues. In addition, though the applicant's dedication to spoken skills is also laudable, the nature of Oxbridge language degrees as primarily literature-based means that any discussion they can include of literary or cultural works has potentially more value word-for-word than discussion of oral work.

NOTES

Subject: Spanish & German

The ability to speak a foreign language fluently is not only immensely satisfying but also infinitely useful, and I believe that a university degree is the best way of beginning to achieve this skill. I strongly value he ability to speak foreign languages because it enables a much deeper understanding of the local societies. The highly informative book, 'Through the Language Glass' by Guy Deutscher strengthened my belief that people are best understood in their mother tongue, as he explained the concept of untranslatable phrases and key variations in languages. This has led me to see the study of foreign languages as a vital part of my education and future.

Having grown up in a bilingual household, the fantastic opportunities presented by the ability to speak German never went unnoticed. For this reason I spent a year acting as a UK-German Youth Ambassador, encouraging the learning of languages, particularly German, amongst younger children. I organised activities such as the weekly German club, which was successful in raising the profile of the language in school. German fiction has featured throughout my school career, with the pinnacle being 'Der Vorleser', an informative novel, addressing the thought-provoking theme of illiteracy. I was introduced to German poetry at the age of twelve whilst on a five week study placement there, where I read 'Der Erlkönig', a poem I have recently gone on to study further.

My curiosity for languages later extended to Spanish, enhanced by my interest of the culture. Most recently I have become fascinated by South America after my visit to Peru, where I lived with a Peruvian family and volunteered for two weeks. A further two weeks spent discovering the colourful culture prompted me to read 'La Casa de Espíritus' as it gave an insight into the issues faced by a Latin American family of that era. I found that Isabelle Allende's decision to omit any specific location or time period added to the sense of magical realism, and I have begun to explore this genre further by reading Garcia Marquez's 'Cien Años de Soledad'. 'La Casa de Bernarda Alba' by Lorca has introduced me to attitudes towards women in 20th century Spain. One performance I saw was set in the Middle East, supporting my view that these issues still have relevance today. Having also organised a Spanish exchange, I am looking forward to the chance to fully immerse myself in the Spanish culture and language.

My Geography and Economics A levels have complemented my language studies, particularly due to Germany's ongoing economic success led by Angela Merkel, which I have read about in 'Der Spiegel'. Together with BBC Mundo, I have learned from international newspapers about the issues facing EU citizens. My AS level in English Literature has also enabled me to appreciate the subtler meanings of literary techniques as my awareness of popular symbols and imagery has increased. Additionally GSCE Latin has allowed me to comprehend the foundation of words in my chosen languages.

I have also developed attributes useful for university through activities such as music and drama. Persevering with Lamda lessons to gold medal standard has improved my confidence and communication skills, aided by part-time waitressing, where I work in a team. Juggling employment and a demanding amount of schoolwork has encouraged me to manage my time effectively. I have risen to the challenge of being Deputy Head Girl; delivering speeches to prospective pupils. Sharing responsibility for maintaining the welfare of my peers has required a problem-solving approach and leadership skills.

After university I hope to pursue a career in journalism; as a foreign correspondent I could use languages frequently and travel widely. A university degree would help me to develop a multitude of skills for my career aspirations, as well as being an invaluable opportunity to dedicate my time to the study of subjects I find fascinating.

Universities applied to:

- Oxford: Offer
- Durham: Offer
- Bristol: Offer
- Cardiff: Offer
- Edinburgh: Rejected

Good Points:

By citing a variety of information sources, this applicant demonstrates their ability to think creatively; they have accessed material and furthered their skills through a variety of different channels. This is reflective of an applicant that is engaged in their subject across various different aspects of their life.

The applicant is able to draw together how their academic interests are actioned in their personal pursuits, and can combine all this information to convincingly argue for their engagement with languages. Furthermore, they are able to articulate where they hope to go with languages, as well as why they think that university study is the best pathway into learning languages.

Bad Points:

While this candidates' breadth of interest is impressive, this statement is quite sparse on literary engagement. Though it references a range of works, the applicant's criticism is relatively light and does not indicate as in-depth a knowledge of literary approaches as it perhaps could. The statement alludes quite casually to literary movements (e.g. "magic realism"), but the applicant could develop their arguments and considerations further in order to more clearly illustrate their potential as a student of foreign literature. It would have been very persuasive to have seen the applicant move from value judgements or superficial readings of texts and onto more evaluative, in-depth analyses based on their own approach.

Overall:

By binding together personal interests and academic curiosity, this applicant is able to demonstrate their continued interest in their subject and how they have managed to practically put their interests into action. However, this statement could do with greater academic grounding in its consideration of literature. It could also, perhaps, do with greater focus overall. Though it cites a range of sources of influence, which demonstrates commitment and engagement, it also lends the statement an air of being unclear in its precise interest.

NOTES

Subject: Spanish & Portuguese

I would like to study Latin and Spanish at degree level because my interests lie in looking at how foreign cultures, ancient and modern, function in comparison to our own. I have developed an aptitude in analysing literature and interpreting and translating Spanish and Latin and I have a growing knowledge of syntax, the history of both cultures and diversity within the societies as we know them today.

Latin is the subject which incorporates my strongest skills: analysing literature and interpreting foreign language. Having studied text by Virgil, Ovid and Tacitus, I have developed an interest in comparing styles of writing among Latin authors but also comparing ancient and modern attitudes to integral social issues including religion, politics and relationships. I am looking forward to approaching new texts at university, going much deeper into their meaning and relevance in a modern context. I expect to improve my ability to read and appreciate them in their original form and enhance the way I analyse the Latin passages. I am currently mentoring a Latin GCSE student. We have weekly tutorial sessions and as well as seeing an improvement in her grades, the mentoring has been extremely valuable for my own studies of Latin.

My fundamental interest in learning Spanish is for the purpose of communicating with others in their own language, opening opportunities for employment and travel for myself. I am excited about the prospect of a year spent abroad, deepening my knowledge of language and awareness of culture. When I began learning Spanish I was initially attracted to the form, structure and sound of the language. Since studying it at A Level I now appreciate the essence of Spain itself having studied its history, politics, traditions, laws and environment. Also we have begun to study life in South America.

For my independent coursework topic I chose to analyse the benefits of Castro's rule on the society in Cuba and I anticipate going deeper into various aspects of life in Latin America and Spain. I enjoyed studying García Lorca's "La casa de Bernada Alba" and it has enthused my interest for examining a greater range of original Spanish literature and growing to appreciate the culture through the perspective of the authors.

I was elected head girl at my school, a post which stretches my organisation, communication skills and leadership abilities. I and the three deputies have made several speeches to a variety of audiences, at year twelve and year six open evenings and at the school's annual foundation day; we have planned and delivered numerous assemblies in school and provided weekly contact between the sixth form and the senior management team.

At university I hope to be involved in various activities outside of my studies. At present, I co-run the school's weekly Christian Union as well as attending and assisting at Girls Brigade through my church. Both of these are voluntary and require regular preparation and delivery as well as giving me a chance to interact with people of assorted ages. I love ballet and modern dance and have recently achieved grade 5 in ballet and grade 4 in modern and hope to join a dance group at university. I worked as a sales assistant in WH Smiths for one year and I am currently a waitress at a conference centre/ hotel. Working with members of the public, growing up in the church and maintaining my posts of responsibility have consolidated my confidence and people skills which I feel will be of great value in learning a foreign language as well as putting me in good stead for university life and a working environment later on.

I am prepared for the transition I will face in my life over the next few years and feel mature and responsible enough to handle the adjustment to university life. I intend to embrace the experience with motivation for my course and a keen interest in extra-curricular activities.

Universities applied to:

- Bristol: Offer
- St. Andrews: Offer
- Leeds: Offer
- Manchester: Offer
- Nottingham: Offer

Good Points:

Through their targeted use of examples from their extra-curricular activities, the applicant is able to effectively communicate why they are a strong candidate for university, and in particular, why they are a suitable candidate for this particular field of study. The statement is clearly written throughout and includes a balanced amount of information in both personal and more academic areas. This includes being able to identify personal strengths and demonstrate convincingly where they fall within the subject's remit. As such, the strength of this statement is in the candidate's self-awareness in their abilities and their presentation of those abilities in secure and well-communicated examples.

Bad Points:

This statement regularly comes back to "I" clauses and deals with the applicant's desires and thoughts at a relatively surface level. There is room here for greater depth of intrigue and interest rather than exposition — the applicant does not, for example, need to state what it is they are expecting to study at university (as it is hoped that they will know what is on the course that they are applying for). While all evidence of passion for their subject is helpful, this statement does favour anecdotal and more tenuous connections to their subject rather than an in-depth engagement with literature or other cultural areas.

Overall:

While this statement demonstrates the candidate's interest and ability across both academic and practical settings, it is written in quite sparse prose. The effect of this is to remind the reader that it is a student writing about themselves, rather than having the effect of formulating and communicating urgent literary arguments. This is significant since, during the introduction of this statement, the applicant draws attention to their "aptitude in analysing literature". As such, it would have made for a more wholly satisfying statement had the applicant been able to provide evidence for this claim. While it would have been very persuasive to have seen critical engagement with texts, it would even have been useful to have seen a statement written in a way that incorporated critical, theoretical, analytical or academic language.

NOTES

Subject: Modern & Medieval Languages, French, Spanish with Dutch

My love of languages started at a young age. I always tried to speak French on camping holidays, playing with French children. At High School I went beyond taught lessons by reading French children's literature, and during GCSEs and A Levels I read novels such as 'Therese Raquin', and works by Sartre and Camus which introduced me to a wider range of language, aspects of French literary style and existentialism. After my GCSEs I travelled to France to stay with family friends for two weeks, before going to Carcassonne to work with a church, as part of their outreach into the immigrant community. I used French constantly at work and amongst the people I was staying with.

I completed the AS and A2 French in my first year of college, independently researching the AS topics, and embracing the challenge of an increased workload and new aspects of grammar. I now maintain my French skills by listening to French radio, reading French literature, newspapers and work with a French language club in primary schools. I will be writing my EPQ on the influence of World War 2 in French literature and film.

When learning Spanish in Year Eight, I immediately fell in love with the language and culture. To learn more I watched 'Aguila Roja', a Spanish TV drama, which, although fictitious, taught me Spanish history and culture during the reign of Felipe IV. Differences and similarities to 17th century English culture and continued prevalence of certain aspects in Spain interested me. I have also read books such as 'Cien años de soledad,' and was interested by the magic realism genre. It introduced me to the history of Colombia, events such as the Thousand Days War, and the myths and legends of the country, as well as a new literary style. This summer, the seven weeks I spent working in an orphanage in Peru, teaching and looking after children, transformed my life. I was immersed in the life and culture of a Spanish-speaking nation, and improved my language skills greatly. I attended the Villiers Park course for Spanish, learning a great deal about Hispanic history, and enhancing my deep interest in aspects of Spanish literature, influences of the Spanish Civil War and the 'Microrrelato'.

I studied AS German ab initio last year, working in a mixed class of post-GCSE and ab initio students, making rapid progress, proving my ability to learn new languages quickly. I used websites such as memrise.com to learn new vocabulary, listened to German radio and read articles on Deutsche Welle. I quickly worked up to the level of the post-GCSE students and achieved the highest AS grade in the group. By the end of the year I was reading books such as 'Der Schimmelreiter', and 'Die Verwandlung.' When studying post-war Germany, I was fascinated by the idea of 'Vergangenheitsbewältigung' and how such concepts apply to British culture, and other countries.

Due to the similarities between music and languages, and the acute hearing that learning music brings, musicians are often good at foreign languages and developing an authentic accent. I completed a Piano diploma, and I teach two pupils. Competitions, attending Chethams Piano Summer School and a Pianoman Scholarship with Richard Meyrick have given me confidence in performance. For five years I have been a church pianist, showing commitment, teamwork and ability to listen and cooperate with others. I will be taking Grade Eight cello examination shortly, and have taught myself guitar and accordion. Aside from music, I help out at the church kid's club, lead the girls' Bible study and lead Christian Union in college. For several summers I have thoroughly enjoyed working as part of a team with United Beach Missions. I am an avid sportswoman, taking part in triathlons for charity.

I am looking forward to being able to deepen and further my studies of foreign languages, cultures and literature at university, and I am excited about the challenges and opportunities that both study and university life will offer.

Universities applied to:

- Cambridge: Offer
- Durham: Offer
- St. Andrews: Offer
- Edinburgh: Offer
- Warwick: Offer

Good Points:

Through the use of a diverse range of examples, this statement allows the applicant to communicate strong, clear academic information alongside more personal inclusions, which gives this statement life and enthusiasm. While the statement includes clear evidence of achievements, it is energised most intensely by clear motivation, giving it an engaging, warm tone. The applicant is able to give evidence of themselves as a long-standing enthusiast for their subject and can indicate their engagement with languages across a variety of media. The applicant is also able to articulate moments of personal interest in among their discussions of academic research.

Bad Points:

Though the applicant's range of experience is impressive, the anecdotal and meandering style of this statement is at times frustrating. This statement could have been stronger through the use of a clear structure and less of a reliance on storytelling vocabulary and tone. This applicant also has the additional difficulty of applying for a combination of languages; not all of which they already study. As such, it seems as though the statement is somewhat imbalanced in its inclusion of material that isn't relevant to their subject choice. Although there are clear reasons why the applicant would want to include such material as overall evidence of their linguistic capability, the applicant could have worked even harder to make those clear connections. The applicant could have also pushed further with their discussions of their academic interests; their ability to engage with their texts critically could have been made clearer.

Overall:

This applicant represents themselves effectively as a candidate that is seriously engaged in their subject. They also manage to maintain this representation without the statement being devoid of personal intrigue; they include plenty of evidence for how their subject interacts with other extra-curricular activities. Due in part to the nature of their chosen subjects, this applicant does present their statement in a way that dwells only briefly on a wide tranche of different topics. As such, it would have been a more satisfying statement overall had there been scope for the applicant to consider more material in greater analytical depth.

NOTES

HISTORY

Subject: History

To make sense of the chaos and ever shifting perceptions of the past is a task I find enthralling. One may choose to see it as a deterministic narrative or, in the words of Ranke, simply a way of seeing the world 'how it really was'. But what I find most meaningful is that nothing can escape its grasp; and indeed when in all its colour and complexity it is united with the present, it becomes a powerful and compelling world - one that, to me, offers limitless enjoyment and possibility.

This passion has certainly been put into practice during my study of History at A Level. Breaking free from the confines of the syllabus, I went on to read about events preceding Stalin's rise to power. I began with Vladimir Brovkin's 'Russia after Lenin'. His use of songs, jokes, and accounts of the harsh reality of 1920s Russia allowed me to see that History consisted of so much more than textbooks. It suddenly became animated; I found myself imagining with unprecedented vividness the Bolshevik's treatment of those considered 'socially undesirable', as well as the hypocrisy of overthrowing the reigning institutions and creating a new ruling class who swore solidarity with their working counterparts. Chris Ward's 'Stalin's Russia' gave me additional background knowledge of Stalinism and increased my understanding of how a society that had rebelled against Bolshevism with such vehemence could become so deferential and subservient in a matter of years. In studying the French Revolution I developed my awareness of just how historians choose to interpret history - from the ideas of Cobban to Marxist accounts; exposing the contradictions and gaps, but also the exciting prospect of being able to fill them in.

Since beginning my A2 course, I have already begun my wider reading, finding myself enthralled by Richard Aldous' account of Gladstone and Disraeli's parallel careers in the 'Lion and the Unicorn'. A visit to the National Portrait Gallery allowed me to see Sir John Everett Millais' paintings of the rivals firsthand, and spurred in me an interest in art and its authenticity as an historical source . An assignment set on the Black Civil Rights movement inspired me to study Malcolm X, a figure I knew little about beyond the criticisms. I read as widely as I could to develop my own opinion on some of the more positive aspects of his contribution to the cause. This, too, helped me to understand more about history; how figures are so often polarised - and how they can be left a rather unfair legacy , the inverse also being true. My aim was to look at him as objectively as I could and the end product was an essay that I truly feel was a labour of love.

It is my enthusiasm for wider reading that I believe is my strongest academic asset. I read as extensively as I can. Taking English Literature alongside History has extended my empathetic abilities, and I feel studying Economics has enhanced my understanding of an intrinsic factor in historical development. The works of Orwell have also been one of my greatest inspirations, and his frank and clear writing style is something I try to apply to my own work. Reading essays in 'Virtual History ' also exposed me to the intriguing prospect of counterfactual historiography and how it can be used. I was also selected to attend a University Summer School at Eton College for History, helping me to develop my knowledge outside of what is taught in class and affirming my dedication to the subject in a stimulating and academic environment.

By studying History at university I hope I can enrich my perception of just how we came to be where we are today, and apply these lessons of the past in order to help me make decisions about my own life and future. It is complex and rigorous, but therein lies the challenge; a challenge I am highly enthusiastic about experiencing at university level.

Universities applied to:

- Oxford: Offer
- London School of Economics: Offer

- University College London: Offer
- Durham: Offer
- Edinburgh: Offer

Good Points:

The student writes eloquently and with a clear passion for the subject. The statement is well-structured and effectively demonstrates the extra work the student has done to further their interest in History. This is successful insofar as the student shows a clear awareness of the different areas of historical study a degree will entail. The student plays well to the idea that 'less is more' in exploring what they have learnt from the reading they have already done, instead of resorting to a list.

Bad Points:

The statement is well-written but does, at times, need tightening. For example, the first paragraph refers frequently to 'it', so much so that the reader may lose track of what 'it' actually is. The statement also threatens to state the obvious – E.g., 'certainly been put into practice' and 'breaking free from the confines…'; this can easily be implied in what the student goes on to say and does not need to be stressed. The student could elaborate more on how their other studies have reinforced his/her interest in history because, at present, some information on extra-curricular activities lack elements of personality.

Overall:

This is a very strong personal statement, demonstrating intelligence and a real zeal for the subject. The statement speaks with an authority that leaves the reader with no doubt that this student has great potential. The student should consider introducing more personality into the statement – something that is hinted at in the very last paragraph – but otherwise it is a very convincing read.

NOTES

Subject: History

My passion for history can best be explained by discussing the period of German Unification, which displays the most engrossing virtues of studying the subject. Firstly there is great scope for debate and exploration of the interlocking causations, examining the relative importance of Bismarck's own role against the military strengthening of Prussia or the shifting international relations. But most interestingly it is a defining period in the shaping of modern Europe and the way in which it links the past to the present is most fascinating. Studying this period reveals how international relations progressed after the Napoleonic era leading to the way in which Germany was unified through war and thus became a country built around war. It is therefore arguable that this era created the state which would then trigger the two wars which have shaped the modern world. This period shows how history can give us a more rounded understanding of the world we live in, linking our mysterious and intriguing past to our all too familiar present surroundings. It is partly this, which motivates me to study history as in doing so I gain immense satisfaction from learning how our world has evolved.

An understanding of history also provides a fundamental backdrop for any other areas of study. I have found this through my other A-Level subjects, for example historical knowledge of politics in Britain was essential to AS politics, particularly when studying the political situation in Ireland. An understanding of past conflicts is indispensable when it comes to managing contemporary politics. Furthermore, whilst taking French the study of Un Sac De Billes by Joseph Joffo unearthed experiences of living under Vichy France. To learn a language fully it is important to immerse oneself in the culture and history of the country in order to develop a more rounded understanding of the people who live there. Thus it seems that history is inescapable; it not only provides vital background knowledge but also helps bring to life every other academic subject, which is why in my opinion, it is the most important.

During my A Level history course, the Napoleonic era particularly fascinated me and I pursued my interest through further reading, looking specifically at Napoleon's downfall, an area I found most compelling as it offers the greatest exposition of the psychology of this exceptional man. I read Digby Smith's 'The Decline and Fall of Napoleon's Empire' as well as Zamoyski's '1812'. I picked up on several themes throughout Zamoyski's book and developed my own opinions such as sympathetic stances towards General Barclay and the Tsar, but was particularly intrigued by how Napoleon let his ego drive his pre-war diplomacy and how Napoleon's own role in the breakdown of the Treaty of Tilsit perhaps triggered his eventual downfall. The fact that I was so gripped by so many different themes within an historical study of one war also reveals another aspect of history that is so appealing to me. It offers vast numbers of different avenues to pursue in one's research, whether it is Napoleon's diplomacy or the fallibility of the Russian command.

Outside of my academic studies, I am a dedicated sportsman but have particularly flourished musically as a cellist, obtaining a grade 8 standard in year 11 and am a committed member of various ensembles. Music has coloured my historical studies, for example, I played various Shostakovich symphonies coinciding with my study of Stalinist Russia at GCSE, each with a very different feel depending upon his relationship with Stalin, but perhaps most moving was playing his 10th symphony, a purely self-indulgent expression of relief after the death of the dictator. It is impossible to appreciate this great work without its historical context, which transforms the piece into something personal, attaching the listener emotionally. History is not only fascinating in itself, but it enriches our appreciation of all other interests.

Universities applied to:

- Oxford: Offer
- Durham: Offer
- York: Offer
- Bristol: Offer
- Warwick: Offer

Good Points:

The student speaks intelligently and successfully links their interests – both within history and outside of history – to the study of history on a wider scale. The statement is well-organised and reads well. Paragraph three, in particular, has many strong points with a greater focus on what really interests the student and why. The student does well to focus on the different areas of exploration within history, showing a strong awareness of the nuances within historical study.

Bad Points:

The statement focuses too much on what they know, rather than what interests them – the first paragraph in particular reads too much like an essay and less like an exploration of why this candidate actually wants to study history. The student risks falling into a trap of trying to teach and impress the admissions offer with their knowledge instead of offering a more personal approach. The student also needs to try to avoid repetition, for example, 'most interestingly' and 'most fascinating' within the same sentence in order to ensure the whole statement flows better.

Overall:

This is a very strong, well-written personal statement. The student has clearly proved they can both understand and analyse history. The student perhaps needs to focus more on their own motivations behind studying history, but overall, the statement suggests a student with great potential and zeal for the subject. What would make the student stand out, even more, is a stronger closing statement – something to bring the whole personal statement together, and stress the importance of historical study to this student.

NOTES

Subject: History

For me, the Bayeux Tapestry perfectly illustrates the nature of history. People and events are interwoven to create an overall picture, a snapshot in time, but often the facts can be embroidered, as highlighted in Bridgeford's 'Hidden History' of 1066. As time goes by elements fade, or are lost completely, and here lies limitless opportunities for discovery; each historian adds a few more stitches to our understanding of the world, and from newfound evidence we can go beyond the original image to explore whether it shows the full picture. My desire to add my own stitches to this great work is foremost in my decision to pursue the study of history at a higher level.

Incidentally, the Bayeux Tapestry originates from what is, in my opinion, the most enthralling period of British history. Between the Norman Conquest up to the fall of the last Plantagenet on the field at Bosworth were over four centuries of social upheaval and change, from the introduction of feudalism and eradication of Anglo Saxon culture, to the rise of the merchant class, or the greater freedoms afforded to peasants due to the Black Death. These numerous avenues of enquiry are a constant source of interest to me, but most particularly I have learned the value of literature in creating another dimension in which to view our past in ways that other documents cannot provide. I had read much about the fourteenth century before embarking on an epic pilgrimage with Chaucer's characters, but it was the 'Canterbury Tales' which truly brought the period to life through specific examples from every element of society.

My formal education in Russian history instilled in me a continuing fascination with everyday life in Russia in the decades leading up to and following the October Revolution of 1917. I found Orlando Figes' 'The Whisperers' particularly thought-provoking. The use of voices of people who lived through the Stalinist era combined with great sensitivity provided an insight into the personal effect of the regime; the internalisation of Soviet values truly transformed the psyche of a whole nation. However, perhaps most interesting for me were the ways in which some Soviet citizens did not bend to the will of the state, for example through the continued observance of religion and the survival of family ties. This interest has led me to researching ways in which other social groups have rejected imposed values, such as the True Levellers or 'Diggers' under Cromwell.

Studying Sociology has added a new level to my understanding of the importance of history: through teaching the past, the next generation is given an insight into their culture and collective past, which in turn creates greater social solidarity. This has been of particular significance in my life as discovering the history of my own family has given me a sense of heritage and rootedness, but also a greater appreciation for my opportunities, which are far beyond those which my ancestors experienced. Taking a gap year has enabled me to pursue several of these opportunities, including learning French and basic Latin, and studying theoretical perspectives in historiography. A mixture of part time work, home study and involvement in local societies such as the St. Albans Cathedral Textile Conservators has helped me to hone the skill of time management, and given me confidence in my ability to work independently.

I am also looking forward to getting involved with extra-curricular activities at University. I am taking my Grade Eight Flute exam this year, and took an active part in various musical ensembles at my Sixth Form. I also composed a score to Shakespeare's 'A Midsummer Night's Dream', which was performed as a part of the St. Albans Arts Festival in 2011. It was exciting to be involved with a community project, and it has motivated me to take part in others, including an annual festival, 'Folk by the Oak', and a local non-profit theatre company, 'Foot in the Door', in which I have risen to the role of Musical Director.

I believe I will thrive in the challenging environment of a University, and I look forward increasing my historical knowledge and understanding at a higher and more detailed level.

Universities applied to:

- Oxford: Offer
- York: Offer
- Exeter: Offer
- London Holloway: Offer

Good points:

The student writes in a compelling way and reveals a lot about their thought process in the first paragraph, effectively employing the metaphor of embroidery to demonstrate the student's historical interests. They also employ a vast range of historical examples to support their interest in history; this is particularly effective given that many universities require students to take both modern and medieval papers. The statement is well-written and presents a well-rounded student.

Bad Points:

The student needs to pay heed to the idea that 'less is more', for example, the student talks about areas of interest such as the 'Diggers' but does not build enough upon these examples to really merit their inclusion. The student perhaps dwells too much on extra-curricular activities; it would be more worthwhile to make more out of the historical comparisons hinted at in earlier paragraphs. It would also make sense to link the skills learnt in these activities to the study of history overall – this is effectively done in the penultimate paragraph, but less so in the final one.

Overall:

The candidate writes with a certain charm and personality that instantly adds something to this personal statement. At times, however, the student dips into a narrative, but their analysis of this narrative is generally quite strong and so it is not too distracting. They could benefit from tightening some sentences and maybe making more of some of his/her examples, but generally, the statement is strong and well-varied.

NOTES

Subject: History & German

When recently asked to imagine a world without history, I found it difficult. For me there is nothing more relevant to understanding and explaining humanity than the study of history, and it has been something I have explored and enjoyed from an early age. At nine I remember being puzzled when my German friend visited and she was shocked by how much tea we drank. It hadn't crossed my mind that her family didn't as well, but upon investigation I found I'd stumbled upon a very British stereotype. My curiosity was aroused. It was a while before I discovered the East India Trading Company, and how their record imports of tea facilitated the birth of tea culture in Britain, but when I did I was fascinated.

It still delights me that any question I have can be answered with investigation. For example, having watched Hotel Rwanda I was intrigued about the situation and found in Mason's 'Patterns of Dominance' a description of the Rwandan social structure enabling me to analyse reasons for the outbreak of violence. Mason's description then led me to investigate past social structures, whereupon I read 'Ancient Rome' by Baker an analysis of the rise and incredible crumbling of the Roman Empire. This fragility of civilisation was a theme I wished to continue exploring, leading me to choose the topic of my Extended Essay, to what extent the Black Death and its impacts caused the Peasants' Revolt. Writing my essay gave me the opportunity to read primary sources from the era such as eyewitness accounts and rolls of Parliament. I also experienced when researching the Peasants' Revolt the value to the historian of learning another language when I came across the 'Bauernkrieg', a revolt that took place in Germany in 1524 and shared many traits with the Peasants' Revolt. When investigating it much of the material was in German and I was glad to find this didn't stop my research.

This was one of a number of reasons why I chose to apply for German as well as history. Having lived in Berlin during my childhood, attending a British school, I glimpsed the German culture, swimming in lakes and enjoying die Brüder Grimm. When I started German in last year, studying the language for the first time, I stumbled across vocabulary I didn't know I had: Ohrwurm, rechthaberisch, Zartlichkeit. I had always admired the culture and people and the literature didn't disappoint. I was intrigued by the sinister and eerie side to Kafka's die Verwandlung and Süskind's Parfum, and by the dark humour of Durrenmatt's Besuch den alten Dame. Having attended a workshop on German poetry I was further convinced of the need to study the language. When reading Mitchell's translation of the poem Der Panther by Rilke, whilst beautifully written I felt it lacked the essence of the original. This led me to wonder if there is such a thing as translation in literature or whether to truly appreciate a piece of writing one has to read in its original language.

I was convinced of this when, for my English study of foreign texts, I chose to study Mann's Tod in Venedig. Being able to read the original language was an incredible benefit allowing me to explore how rhythm and phonetics added to the meaning of the prose.

Through partaking in the Model United Nations Hague conference I learnt the value of thorough research, in order to be fully prepared for the large debates I took part in. I also welcomed the challenge of seeing the world from the perspective of Senegal, the country we represented. On a recent trip to India, where I worked with various charities I again experienced, through the children we worked with, another view of the world. One particular aspect of their view was all too familiar; when asked what he thought of England, one boy replied, 'lots of tea'.

I hope I have shown that I think it would be an incredible privilege to spend four years studying History and German and I know I'd work my utmost hardest to develop my knowledge, understanding and fondness of both.

Universities applied to:

- Oxford: Offer
- University College London: Offer
- Durham: Offer
- Warwick: Offer
- Exeter: Offer

Good Points:

The statement has a very honest, compelling opening. What makes this statement particularly interesting is the personal, anecdotal quality to it; this makes it stand out compared to all the other, more analytical, statements. They write intelligently and do well to interweave their own personal research to historical debates. The student links the whole statement together well and speaks with a conviction and personality likely to maintain the reader's interest.

Bad Points:

The author could do more to link together their interests in both History and German. The two can easily interlink, and often will in History courses, but the student does not show enough awareness of the ways in which studying both these subjects can reinforce each other. Furthermore, the finishing sentence is much weaker than the rest of the statement – it shows the student's determination but does not read as well as the previous paragraphs.

Overall:

This is a very interesting personal statement that reads with a lot of personality and individual flair. It perhaps risks being too anecdotal, but this is also part of the statement's charm. The student needs to consider more how studying both subjects could prove more beneficial than just one, but at the same time, the statement does successfully demonstrate the student's passion for both disciplines.

NOTES

Subject: History & Politics

History is a subject which has always fascinated me. In my opinion, History cannot be treated as a completely separate domain; it is closely linked to other subjects such as Politics, Economics, Geography, Sociology and Philosophy. For instance, one cannot discuss the causes of WW2 without taking into account the development of radical ideologies, the economic weakness of Germany, Stalin's politics aiming to create a "buffer" of friendly states separating Russia from Europe etc.

I have studied History in several educational systems with Polish, Belgian, and British teachers. The first two focused upon facts and figures, supplying the students with a general background, whereas British teachers focused upon fostering an analytical mind. It is the British approach to history that interests me the most, giving us a better understanding of our world; I think that I will enjoy the system of seminars and group work at the university.

Every historical event has specific causes and consequences, and it is interesting to see how far those can sometimes reach, and to see how today's world was shaped by the past. History is a subject demanding a vast general knowledge and the ability to see 'the whole picture'. It can be seen, for instance, in Norman Davies' God's Playground- A history of Poland where the author stresses the importance of the geographical situation of Poland for its history. This approach to History affords us the possibility to prevent errors in the future, and to understand how every major turn in the history of humanity is a jigsaw made up of multiple factors.

Undergraduate courses in Great Britain, such as 'History and Politics' or 'International History' provide the students with an approach to History from those different points of view, and allow them to improve their analytical, discursive, and argumentation skills. This is why I chose to apply for these studies.

Being in the French section of the European School, I study many subjects in English, including History. This has allowed me to develop my vocabulary and to improve both my written and oral English. I chose the Advanced History and Economics options for my Baccalaureate, which have allowed me to widen my knowledge and my historical analysis skills.

Although Polish is my mother tongue, I speak French and English equally well. My English has improved due to three years of private lessons and six years of studies in the European School. In addition, I have been studying Spanish and Dutch for several years. I also attended the Polish School for eight years where I learnt Polish Literature and History, which not only supplied me with extra information concerning Poland and the World but also gave me an additional perspective from which to analyse the events of the past.

Last year, I participated in two major extracurricular projects: the Young Enterprises and The Model European Parliament. The Young Enterprises project was an excellent exercise, allowing me to develop my sense of responsibility, creativity and organisation, but also to learn more about the functioning of the market in a practical, hands-on sense. Following this I passed the Young Enterprise Examination organised by the University of Cambridge. The Model European Parliament was a project which allowed students to participate in a role play of a parliamentary session. This has been an invaluable experience, giving me the opportunity to learn more about group dynamics and political decision making – something which I hope will be put to further use at university.

Amongst my skills, music is very important. I have been playing the clarinet for eight years, taking classical and jazz lessons and studying guitar for two years. This is something else which I look forward to continuing at university.

To conclude, I believe that both my education and my extra-curricular projects will allow me to not only perform well on this course but to also contribute positively to the university community as a whole.

Universities applied to:

- Oxford: Offer
- Warwick: Offer
- London School of Economics: Rejected

Good Points:

The student plays to his/her strong points, i.e. their experience under different educational systems and knowledge of History outside of the standard British History; this makes the student stand out. Given that English is not the student's native language, the statement is written thoughtfully and eloquently. The third paragraph is particularly strong with an effective analysis of a specific approach to History, showing that the student has clearly thought about what studying History at degree level would entail.

Bad Points:

The first paragraph is weak – it starts clichéd and goes on to a list; this is not likely to fare well. It has no draw for the reader and does not really explain why History – rather than the other disciplines listed – interests the student. The statement, at times, is too fragmented and does not explore fully enough the student's personal interests in History. At times, the statement is far too vague; it is split into small sections, many of which do not add much. The student would be better off focusing on the historical study they have conducted so far and the areas of history that interest them.

Overall:

Compared to other students, the statement is not overly strong but it is clear that the student has great potential – especially given that English is not his/her mother tongue. The student speaks passionately about their interest in History and stands out as a result of their background and previous historical studies. The statement could be better structured but overall creates the impression of a very interesting and dedicated individual.

NOTES

Subject: History & Politics

I am fascinated by the potential for historical events to be revised, as opinions and perspectives change through time. My exploration of the subject has led me to discover how history is an ever-changing field of thought, rather than a static body of facts, on which a historian can have an impact through unique insight and persuasive argument. This has inspired me to interact with historical texts more critically, which complements my intrinsic passion for the stories within history and motivates me to pursue the discipline further.

Studying history at A-Level has strengthened my interest in the subject through learning about periods in time which have tangibly shaped the current state of the world. I supplemented my study of Nazi Germany by reading the Czech historian Dusan Hamsik's biography of Heinrich Himmler; while Paul Preston's 'The Spanish Civil War' expanded my knowledge of the complex international relations which led to Franco's victory in the conflict. Studying 20th century British history alerted me to the importance of individual political figures to the course of history. I pursued this further by attending Vernon Bogdanor's Gresham College lecture on Roy Jenkins which opened my eyes to the effect of personal circumstances on his politics, and subsequently British history.

My interest in the events of history encouraged me to pursue historiography, reading E.H. Carr's 'What is History?'. Although intrigued by Carr's exploration of topics such as the importance of the historian, I was aware of the fact that the book is half a century old, so I decided to read David Cannadine's modern counterpart 'What is History Now?' in order to draw parallels with Carr's magnum opus; and explore the way historiography has evolved. Cursory reading of Herodotus has also been useful in observing how the writing of history has changed since the infancy of the subject.

My A-level Politics course was extremely useful in understanding history better, as well as being an invaluable tool in helping me to understand current affairs. A two-week work experience at the constituency office of Sarah Teather MP had broadened my knowledge of the practical role of a politician; however, the course developed my understanding of political ideologies, processes and participation. Learning about the importance and influence of pressure groups has given me a new outlook on the work I do as vice-chairman of Brent Youth Parliament, as I examined the tangible political change that can be achieved through engaging with youth politics. This has further inspired me to become my school's student governor and engage in a decision-making process with noticeable results and real consequences.

The study of English language and literature has proved invaluable when analysing sources in history as I conditioned myself to pay close attention to detail and linguistic devices which can reveal a lot about the agenda of a source's author. Studying maths developed my logical reasoning ability, which I applied when figuring out causes in sequences of historical events and decisions; while philosophy improved my ability to structure ideas into arguments.

My two greatest extracurricular passions, football and writing, combine through publishing analytical articles on international sports websites; I have also been shortlisted for the national Wicked Young Writers competition. I am a keen observer of modern Egyptian politics, having written an extended essay on Mohamed Morsi as part of the UCL Summer Challenge. My fluency in Arabic and Czech allows me to examine original primary source material such as journals and accounts from family members involved in events such as the Prague Spring or the Egyptian Revolution. My hard work and enthusiasm for history can flourish at a top academic institution, and I look forward to an environment of academic excellence.

Universities applied to:

- Oxford: Offer
- London School of Economics: Rejected
- University College London: Offer
- King's: Offer
- SOAS: Offer

Good Points:

The student clearly shows that they have gone above and beyond to further their interest in History, effectively discussing both an interest in particular periods of history and historiography itself. The student also successfully links their study of other subjects and extra-curricular activities to skills gained which will be applicable to both History and Politics – this is not something every student is able to achieve.

Bad Points:

The statement could do with greater vision – the second paragraph, for example, includes a lot of detail on different parts of history the student has learnt about but does not really expand much on what the student acquired from this and/or how it encouraged them to study History and Politics in greater detail. This is also seen in the following paragraph where the student cites their reading of Cannadine's book but does not give an opinion on their reading and the usefulness of this interpretation. The first sentence is not compelling enough compared to what the student goes on to say.

Overall:

The student has an interest in both History and Politics that is well-explored and demonstrated within the personal statement. What its lacks, however, is a real consideration of why this student wants to study the subject and the way in which History and Politics can weave together. The student needs to focus more on analysing the work they have already done in order to demonstrate their own analytical flair.

NOTES

Subject: History of Art

'History has remembered the kings and warriors, because they destroyed; Art has remembered the people, because they created'- William Morris. History of Art: for me it is a chance to exercise my passion; delving into the past, analysing and concluding, how and why society has cultivated, influenced, and motivated a masterpiece. My curiosity was inspired by the Lady Lever Galleries, particularly as it was the initial attempt to bring a varied and rich culture through art to the tenants of Port Sunlight, and the mixed reception this received. A personal interest in the Palladian architectural movement and its development in Britain inspired me to investigate further the links between the social order and art. I was intrigued by how it evidenced the wealth of the aristocracy and the industrialists.

A level History has whetted my appetite for Art History, as my fascination with human nature leads me to inquire how historical events and characters have influenced artistic figures and society. I am especially interested in the renaissance and how it brought a revival of classical splendour. English Literature encourages me to view information from varying perspectives and to look beyond my initial opinion, giving me the ability to research concisely and deeply into an artist's life and work. An exhibition of Gainsborough's landscapes fascinated me, in particular 'The Mild Evening Gleam'; the poetical style allowed me to increase my understanding of how literature and art combine. Through Theatre studies I have learned to work in depth, in particular from the nineteenth to the twenty first century. It was Ibsen's 'A Doll's House' which provided a snapshot into the structured societal life of the Victorian era resulting in my fascination of the Aesthetic Movement. 'The Cult of Beauty' an exhibition at the Victoria and Albert Museum gave me a taste of the period, proving essential to the development of my understanding towards the movement furthering my belief that it sought the urge to escape from the ugly, materialistic, and oppressive Victorian phase. Outside the classroom, I have an immense yearning to gain a greater knowledge of civilisations' impact on shaping the artist and how an unwritten form of communication can both shape and reflect civilisation, whether it is cavemen recording achievement or Leonardo da Vinci's 'Mona Lisa' where interpretation has been the source of many a nonsensical debate.

I believe that my interest and participation in school debates, and as a founding member of the schools 'Politics and Economics group' will enable me to add value to this course as I will able to use contemporary references within the time span of the artistic piece, and how it influences the public today. As a leading role in school plays, being head of human resources for our 'Young Enterprise Group', raising money for charity, and having been both deputy House Captain, elected by peers and staff, and a prefect, I have developed further my communication, independence and leadership skills. Apart from my studies, my interest for the last ten years has been my love of equestrianism. My greatest achievement has been representing my country for both dressage and jumping, as an individual and in a team, earning me; gold, silver, and bronze medals; and qualifying for the Royal International and Horse of the Year Show. Equestrianism has required dedication, time management skills, utter dependability, quick wit, stamina and extreme motivation. Aspects that I endeavour to achieve throughout all aspects of my life. I am thoroughly looking forward to my university years, focusing on a subject that I am enthusiastic and fascinated by. I have been a student who thrives on challenges, never being happy unless I am busy; History of Art is the natural culmination of my studies and interests. I will be able to test and improve my analytical skills and the desire to discover how art has reflected the changes within society.

Universities applied to:

- Reading: Offer
- Oxford Brookes: Offer
- Leicester: Offer
- Aberystwyth: Offer
- Plymouth: Offer

Good Points:

The student talks intelligently about their interests within History of Art. Perhaps the strongest discussion is on the other subjects the student studies; the exploration of the skills learnt from these subjects should be something replicated throughout the statement. The student is clearly very able and well-rounded and this is effectively demonstrated, particularly in the latter half of the statement. The final paragraph is particularly strong in terms of its analysis of why this specific student is a good candidate.

Bad Points:

The statement begins with an interesting quote, but does not explore what Morris is saying; if you're going to start with a quote, you need to show you've really thought about it and used it for a reason. The same goes for the examples the student later uses – these could be developed and analysed much further. The statement needs to be split into paragraphs to give it some order – at the moment, it is difficult to read. It is always better to write a shorter statement that allows you to include full line breaks than it is to cram in as much information as possible at the expense of that readability.

Overall:

The statement creates the impression of a student with a lot of motivation and determination. It does, however, need a clearer focus. At the moment, the statement introduces ideas but does not fully explore them. The statement's structure could be improved and the student dwells too much on other subjects and extra-curricular activities, but overall the student does show a lot of potential.

NOTES

PHILOSOPHY

Subject: Philosophy

"And if you find her poor, Ithaka has not fooled you. / Wise as you will have become, so full of experience, / You will have understood by then, what these Ithakas mean."

Cavafy was right, indeed. Like any other reflective person, I am essentially a philosophical entity. While most people, perhaps those outside academic philosophy, would consider it a prime example, maybe along with Mathematics, of an established body of a priori truths, of some kind of Ithaka (thus excluding themselves from the possibility of realizing their philosophical essence), I beg to differ. For years, though, unwise as I was according to Cavafy, I was looking for Ithakas like most men, misled by this major misconception. For years, I have been reading Plato and Aristotle, Descartes and Nietzsche always, hastily and impatiently, heading towards truth; towards my rich Ithaka, and always falling on reefs and mythical objections raised by one philosopher against the truths of the other. Always, en route.

When, "wise as I had become" on the road, like old Ulysses, I realized that philosophy is much more than just a truth per se. Instead, philosophy is the pursuit of truth, irrespective of whether that truth is ever achieved; in fact, if and when something ever counts as truth, it does not belong to the realm of philosophy any more. Not until I read Wittgenstein's Tractatus Logico-Philosophicus, had I realized that the aim of philosophy is to designate what can be said and what not, what is non-sense or what might be senseless. This very sub specie aeternitatis realization of philosophy as an activity, a method of approaching truth and reflecting on reality rather than as an established body of justified true belief, was crucial in my selection of philosophy as the subject of my academic study. Since this realization, my chief preoccupation has been to learn as much as possible from the journey to Ithaka, to hone this ability to philosophize effectively, to exercise and engage philosophy as much as possible, whenever and wherever possible.

A culmination of this constant struggle to sharpen my philosophical essence happened this summer in the Epic Questions Summer Institute of U of Va, Charlottesville, Virginia, USA. In this intensive, three-week seminar for high-school teachers, I was the official note-taker and the only high-school student to be accepted among the scholars as an intern of Dr. Mitchell S. Green. Courses in Epistemology, Metaphysics, Philosophy of Mind, Formal Logic, Philosophy of Language, Ethics, Political Philosophy and Bioethics unprecedentedly furthered this philosophical activity and I made the acquaintance of contemporary philosophical thought, reading, such as T. Nagel, R. Chisholm, D. Papineau, B. Williams, along with classical readings.

Hence, to my readings of Plato's Five Dialogues, Descartes's Meditations on First Philosophy and Nietzsche's Übermensch, were added those of the British Empiricists, esp. some of Hume's Enquiries, Kant, B. Rusell's The Problems of Philosophy and Mill's Utilitarianism.

I must admit that I have been uncritically assuming a certain account of human nature (as inherently philosophical), which many may find controversial. And this, itself, thus, turns into a philosophical question. And so on and so forth.

This is exactly the philosophical beauty I live for.

Universities applied to:

- Cambridge: Offer
- University College London: Offer
- Edinburgh: Offer

Good Points:

The statement is well-written and the student clearly demonstrates their passion for Philosophy, as well as their motivation for pursuing further study of it, and something of a personal journey through which their philosophical thinking has developed. The discussion of the nature of philosophical thought ties nicely into their own motivation to study Philosophy.

The statement shows their broad philosophical education, as well as indicating strong self-motivating passions for learning (in a much more subtle manner than simply stating that they are self-motivated), as much of this education is in the form of private study. Acceptance to the prestigious seminar is an impressive achievement and the student is right to stress this, and the 'unprecedented' effect it had on their philosophical activity.

Bad Points:

The statement is vague in what it terms 'philosophy'; though the student clearly has an interest in some vague notion of 'human nature', they don't narrow down exactly what they wish to study at university (Philosophy being such a broad subject that quite a bit of specialisation is necessary). The time spent listing impressive works that they had read would have been better invested in mentioning just one (or even just one subject that they had read around) that had particularly affected them, and expanding on it. Similarly, they could have expanded further on the experience of the seminar (how it affected their philosophical thinking, new ideas encountered while there, etc.), rather than listing the respected philosophers they had met.

The grammar is, at points, questionable, indicating the statement required closer proof-reading prior to being submitted.

Overall:

This statement is average; it conveys a rare passion for the subject and, more importantly, a passion that has been actively pursued in the student's own time. It could, however, benefit from more specificity regarding their thoughts on specific readings and from reading less like a list of books and philosophers. Overall, the statement is intriguing, but leaves you questioning the author's academic ability.

NOTES

Subject: Philosophy & French

I thoroughly enjoy my studies in Philosophy and French at A Level and am now keen to pursue these subjects at degree level. They seem to me to be inextricably linked, and I would love to explore them in tandem.

I feel that philosophical arguments hinge on a shared understanding of terms. I have found in all of my subjects that appreciating written communication requires an awareness of the contextual background of composer, poet, philosopher or playwright. For instance, Bentham's ethical theory of Utilitarianism was developed in response to the powerlessness of the people; Debussy's unconventional use of cadences and 'coloristic' harmony were effective in his display of emotions. The aptitudes involved in a joint honours course, the complimentary skills of communication and analysing arguments, are ones that I immensely enjoy and am keen to continue to develop.

I am intrigued by the ethics of R.E. Studying the subject has made me question the origin of my own morals. While reading 'Think' it struck me that Blackburn has a strong idea of what he believes to be right and wrong (reason is good, blind faith is "bad, or at least suspect"). I personally have a less fixed view of morality. Class discussions often have a profound effect on my personal views and I like to hear the reasoning behind those opinions that differ from mine.

I find it fascinating to explore moral, social or philosophical issues in two languages. I have enjoyed debates in French lessons and like the challenge of defending opinions in both languages. The positions I adopt are fuelled by my philosophical approaches. Books such as Ian Hacking's 'Why Does Language Matter to Philosophy?' provide a selection of case studies over the centuries showing how language has been key to the development of philosophy. The endless play of variations of meanings and interpretations within a culture or situation is what makes the subjects so relevant to real life. I also adore the language of music, one so communicative primarily without the use of words, which stimulates such a large range of personal emotions. Within my French studies I relish the exploration of literature in its original language. I enjoy the opportunity and challenge of grappling with originally intended nuances without relying on someone else's translation, as I experienced upon reading Camus' 'L'Etranger' as well as set texts. I found it rewarding last year to mentor a younger pupil for French and believe she found me helpful and encouraging. I have also seen plays such as 'Lettres de Delation' and 'Le Medecin Malgre Lui'. This has been complimented by my studies of English literature, where developing close reading analysis has enabled me to appreciate the role of context in interpreting the author's meaning.

Apart from my academic work I delight in a range of activities such as extra-curricular music, particularly singing, playing the oboe and piano. I sing in the school chamber choir and in an external semi-professional choir, with whom I make exciting regular appearances in professional venues (Royal Albert Hall, Barbican, Royal Opera House, English National Opera). I have been part of television and studio recordings, as a soloist and as part of a choir, including singing at Wembley Stadium as part of Madonna's choir. I won the school's 2009 Vocal Competition and this term I'm thrilled to be the lead in the school musical 'The Boy Friend'. I have represented the school in sports events including cross-country, athletics, trampolining, cricket and football.

I also take a keen interest in 'ethical' and fair trade, ecological living and small-scale businesses and projects such as the Big Issue. I believe that my interests and skills make me well suited to take full advantage of the opportunities that university has to offer. I am passionate about following a joint honours course and eager to further my appreciation and knowledge of Philosophy and French.

Universities applied to:

- Oxford: Offer
- Exeter: Offer
- King's: Offer
- Sheffield: Offer
- Bristol: Rejected

Good points:

The statement ties Philosophy and French together well and communicates an interesting approach to studying the two in tandem, and their motivation for doing so. The student demonstrates that they are well-rounded both in their balance of interest in French and Philosophy, but also as a person, by devoting some time to talking about their non-strictly academic interests. They make it clear what their main interests in the two fields of study are and explain their inspirations, which also shows off their extensive extra-curricular reading. The statement is excellent in conveying a real passion for their subject as well as an academic background that supports their study of it; it doesn't miss a chance to describe the joy they gain from their studies, while also making it clear how each reading they mention has furthered their thoughts on the study of language.

Bad points:

The statement reads as formulaic and simplistic in its writing style; large parts of it consist of making a point, giving an example, and then moving on with little to tie the piece together as a whole. The language also seems, at times, unnaturally extravagant (see: 'adore', 'delight in'). While these phrases are not inherently problematic, they stand out from the rest of the language used and disrupt the speaker's voice; they seem to be artificial insertions designed to impress the reader (and, obviously, fail to do so). The last paragraph, a list of interests and achievements, while beneficial for the reasons discussed above, ought to be tied in somewhat more to the rest of the statement and to their desire to study Philosophy and French, or to study at university more generally. Without this, the last sentence ("I am passionate about following a joint honours course and eager to further my appreciation and knowledge of Philosophy and French.") is disjointed and jarring and the potential of the paragraph to further the statement's aims is wasted.

Overall:

The statement shows a strong student with a passion for their subject, who has a clear idea of what studying it would involve and why they wish to do so. However, it contains little to make it stand out from the rest and would benefit from being better linked together into one whole, cohesive piece.

NOTES

Subject: Philosophy & Theology

According to Descartes, in order to know anything, we must first doubt everything. To paraphrase him: in order to know why I make such a great candidate to study philosophy, you must first doubt everything you know about what makes a great philosophy student. It's not a perfect exhibit of logic, but then neither was Descartes' Trademark Argument, so I don't think he would criticise me too much. I aim to demonstrate why I would make a great candidate to consider for your university from the foundations up.

As Epicurus might have put it: "Is a great philosophy student willing to work hard, but not able? Then he is not wise. Is he able, but not willing? Then he is lazy. Is he both able and willing? Then whence cometh 2.2's? Is he neither able nor willing? Then why call him a great philosophy student?" My response is that there is a very simple solution – there are only very few great philosophy students. There are many good philosophy students who are either able or willing, but not both – hence cometh 2.2's; therefore, in order for someone to be a great philosophy student, they must be both willing and able.

Recently, I have read Think by Simon Blackburn, and I found it a very useful overview of philosophy. The most interesting part of the book for me was the chapter dedicated towards Free Will, and in particular moral responsibility. One interesting idea was his 'Mini Martian' argument as it highlights the issues with moral responsibility, and the problems raised seem to undermine our whole judicial system, yet we still hold people responsible for their actions. The theologically-centred parts of the book also gave me a chance to contemplate ideas of religion, which spark endless debate.

Despite the fact Singer's arguments lead him to extreme conclusions, for example bestiality, he accepts them and does not attempt to alter his argument, which I find admirable. Singer's views on personhood and the repercussions they have for ethics present a new way for us to view humans and animals that is so radically different, I had to think how to justify why experimenting on infants is wrong. The fact he made me unsure of the morality behind an issue I am so sure about demonstrates his strength as a philosopher.

Both of these writers have intriguing views, but my favourite philosophical author is Phillip Pullman. Pullman's His Dark Materials books were first recommended to me when I was 11, and although unable to grasp the philosophical issues suggested by Pullman at 11, over several readings and years I began to understand the philosophical themes underlying the fantastical plot, i.e. nonhuman persons, dualism, and a tyrannical god to name a few. Pullman's concept of nonhuman persons is similar to the views suggested by Singer, and although fictitious, Pullman's nonhuman persons act as a thought experiment, which justifies some of Singer's ideas. The concept of a tyrannical god also ties in with some of Blackburn's views about an imperfect god. The idea of nonhuman persons was one of the first philosophical issues I considered outside of the context of the novel, and since then I have always found speciesism to be a very thought-provoking topic.

So do you believe I am a great philosophy student? Hume states I can't hope for a miraculous event to persuade you, and Plato would say I'm just a shade of the greatest, but I can apply Swinburne's ideas about logical and metaphysical necessities to the statement 'Great philosophy students are both willing and able'. A philosophy candidate is great if, and only if, they are both willing and able. Therefore it is a logical necessity that anyone who is willing and able (towards philosophy) is a great philosophy student, and so it is also a metaphysical necessity.

Since I have shown that I am both willing and able by discussing some of my favourite philosophies, Swinburne would be inclined to argue that I am a great philosophy student, and I hope I have persuaded you to agree with him.

Universities applied to:

- Oxford: Offer
- Edinburgh: Offer
- Durham: Offer
- Exeter: Offer
- Cardiff: Offer

Good points:

The statement is original and interesting, and will stand out from those around it. It makes for an enjoyable read. The writing is elegant without being overly flowery or showing off, and the writing style reads as very natural and unaffected. The student has used their original approach to demonstrate their broad philosophical readings and highlights some main areas of interest to explain their motivation for further study.

Bad points:

Although the style of the piece is refreshing, it could have been better executed; consider the second paragraph, which, though witty, uses over 100 words just to make the point that a student must be both skilled and hardworking to be successful. The student would have been wiser to make this more concise and to expand on the points in later paragraphs regarding the books that they found philosophically interesting, and, most importantly, why they found them interesting and how they helped develop their ideas. As it is, their exposition of the works they mention is more of a brief overview of some of the books' content, with the additional note that they find them interesting, rather than explaining any particular personal response to them.

Overall:

This statement is refreshing in its lack of pretence; it reads as a genuine insight into the student's personality, way of thinking, and their motivation for applying. Though the style is great, it is let down somewhat by a lack of content. What is included (the works that were read and enjoyed, and theories they find interesting) is mostly good, but there is nothing particularly unique or interesting about the books and theories discussed (since they're all topics and works that are widely studied at A Level). The time spent on each one means the statement suffers from a lack of concision.

NOTES

Subject: Theology & Religious Studies

I have always possessed a desire to further my understanding of what we might describe as 'ultimate' questions. Our secular society has been corrupted by a view that scientific discovery renders theological endeavours obsolete. However, there are so many questions science can't fully address, such as issues raised by morality, meaning and reason behind life, and how we can attend to global disputes that have arisen from religious conflict. It is such meaningful pursuits, as illustrated in Ronald Nash's Life's Ultimate Questions, Simon Blackburn's Think and C.S.Lewis's God in the Dock , that have evoked my emphatic passion to study this fascinating subject.

My enthusiasm for theology is partly founded in the study of ancient scriptures in their original language and, predominantly, context. In depth, critical analysis of the origin of Christian thought, as exhibited in Henry Chadwick's The Early Church, is an exploration I relish as one begins to uncover the origin of what defines much of our culture today. I am fascinated by examining the evidence for a covertly monotheistic Ancient Israelite culture and studying the validity and internal discrepancies between different accounts of the actions and resurrection of Jesus Christ.

John Barton's Ethics and the Old Testament helped ignite a profound interest in moral theology, whilst Keith Ward's What the Bible Really Teaches fuelled and nurtured this passion as well as linking it with biblical interpretation. So much debate surrounds the relevance of religious texts in modern society, with even Barton claiming that the Decalogue only applies effectively to a patriarchal society. But I take great excitement in facing this argument head on by studying the narrative of biblical texts and interpreting their existential force to derive the ethical injunctions so cleverly portrayed through the text.

My sincere aspiration in life is to be at the forefront of key global decisions that contribute to the abolition of conflict and evoke a greater and stronger world. Carl Schmitt's Political Theology made me contemplate the underestimated impact that religion really has in the affairs of our global society. In Meic Pearse's The Gods of War, he contemplates whether religion is the primary cause of violent conflict around the world. This potent question is why I am so intent on studying the diverse, religious teachings found within world religions as this will enable me to gain an insightful understanding of the real motives behind conflicts that baffle so many in the West.

My diverse A level courses have given me the necessary skills required to excel in a degree directed towards deep philosophical and theological thought, as well as portraying me as a versatile and open minded candidate. Religious Studies has provided me with an excellent foundation for a course revolving around religious concepts upon which I wish to greatly build. Music is good for analysing the context in which new ideas in music came about, a transferable skill when studying ancient texts. Geography has helped me to develop a mature understanding of world affairs, whilst biology demonstrates clear, logical thought.

In terms of extra-curricular activities, I am proud to be chairman of my school's parliamentary debating society, demonstrating strong advocacy skills and the ability to analyse respond to arguments put forward to me. My Gold Duke of Edinburgh Award shows tenacity and commitment. This dedication to excellence is further portrayed with 3 grade 8 examinations on Saxophone, Piano and Guitar as well as playing in the National Youth Orchestra of Great Britain, who will be performing at the Proms next year. I also work at a residential care home, run a music school and coach shooting.

I hope that I have conveyed my passion for the subject I wish to commit the next chapter of my life to exploring.

Universities applied to:

- Cambridge: Offer
- Durham: Offer
- Bristol: Rejected
- Exeter: Offer
- York: Offer

Good points:

This student conveys a passionate belief in the worth of Theology as a field of study and their own motivations for pursuing it. In particular, they strongly link what areas of study within Theology they find interesting (scripture studied in its original context to uncover that which still defines our culture and religion as a motivation for conflict) with their broader personal opinions (that secular science cannot explain 'the big questions'), and long-term life plan ("to be at the forefront of key global decisions that contribute to the abolition of conflict"). The writing is natural and unaffected, and for the most part, the statement flows well.

Bad points:

The student fails to go into any depth regarding the writings they've mentioned; the statement reads more like a list of philosophical works that seek to answer questions they're interested in with no explanation to why these works, in particular, moved them. (The exception to this is the exposition of The Gods of War, which is done excellently). The manner in which they hope to portray themselves as a student has a weak approach.

Rather than describing the development of their theological beliefs, their reasons for studying what they do, their extra-curricular activities, etc., the student states that "My diverse A level courses... [portray] me as a versatile and open minded candidate" and "I hope that I have conveyed my passion for the subject", rather than letting the statement stand on its own.

They would do better to describe the ways in which they are versatile, open-minded, and passionate (which they do go on to do but should, ideally, be done in a little more depth – how is the study of music transferrable to ancient texts, for example? The student could expand on this rather than briefly listing three somewhat obvious points). They should let the readers draw their own conclusions, rather than simply stating these qualities.

Overall:

Though the student is passionate, their statement suffers from a lack of evidence for the qualities they claim for themselves as a student. They do this in a brief list of unsubstantiated claims. Rather than simply stating that, for example, their Duke of Edinburgh award necessarily shows commitment, they ought to explain what this experience taught them or what skills were necessary to complete it. The student is, however, well-rounded and clearly committed to excelling in a wide variety of areas, both academic and otherwise, and this comes across well.

NOTES

ECONOMICS

Subject: Economics

The right answer - does such a thing even exist? When considering the field of mathematics, my response would be an unequivocal yes - indeed, I find its simplicity and elegance some of its most attractive qualities. For economics, however, the question of a right answer is not so straightforward. My interest in economics was sparked when I read "Freakonomics" and "SuperFreakonomics". I found the search for a logical explanation behind seemingly illogical behaviour intriguing, and the idea that small changes to incentives could effect such large changes to those behaviours fascinating.

To further my understanding, I attended lectures at the LSE, including one given by Ha-Joon Chang. His arguments challenged much of what I had learned - deregulation and trade liberalisation would not, apparently, stimulate competitive growth, while education, it turned out, could not be counted on to increase entrepreneurship or productivity. These contradictions made me eager to read his "23 Things They Don't Tell You About Capitalism" and "Bad Samaritans". Although relishing his controversial stance on almost everything, I found his central thesis - that by using protectionism to support fledgling domestic industries, other poor nations can emulate South Korea's success - overly optimistic and one-size-fits-all. As Paul Collier argues in "The Bottom Billion", many are trapped by conflict or bad governance, with even bleaker prospects after "missing the boat" on which many Asian economies sailed away to prosperity.

While economics is rooted in the world around us, with all its fascinating, messy complexities, mathematics derives its beauty from its abstract nature. It is unique in that it can lead us to an answer that is not merely the right one, but is true in an absolute sense. This was emphasised by G. H. Hardy in "A Mathematician's Apology", where he spoke of a mathematical reality distinct from the ordinary one, of which we can only ever hope to produce a "partial and imperfect copy". Another of the appeals of mathematics is its breadth of application. I was able to explore this over the past three years in a series of Royal Institution master classes covering topics from graph theory to the mathematics of juggling. My decision to continue with mathematics was confirmed when I undertook the AEA; I found it challenging but immensely satisfying to be able to use simple concepts from the A-level core modules to solve even the most daunting problems.

Over the past year, I have mentored two students in mathematics. Explaining concepts to them helped deepen my own understanding and led me to explore proofs behind theorems I had previously accepted. In addition, acting as a primary school classroom assistant inspired me to set up my own volunteering scheme, in which I and other students help children learn to read. I have enjoyed competing in the UKMT Mathematics Challenge, in which I won a medal at Olympiad level, and the UK Linguistics Olympiad, in which I twice progressed to the selection round for the national team. I have also represented my school in the Hans Woyda competition, and am excited to be doing the same in the Target 2.0 challenge later this year.

Despite their differences, the authors I mentioned above hold something in common: their use of empirical methods to reach conclusions. It is here that the attraction of combining the study of mathematics and economics becomes especially apparent. Without mathematics, economics risks beginning to earn its title "the dismal science", reducing to speculation and rhetoric without even the emotional investment enjoyed by politics. This is not to dismiss the importance of normative economics, but to say that it draws meaning from a basis in fact. I am not arguing for sound bite solutions to complex questions, but rather that, even in a field as hotly debated as economics, the right answer is still a worthwhile goal, reachable through the use of data and copious amounts of trial and error.

Universities applied to:

- Cambridge: Offer
- London School of Economics: Offer
- Warwick: Offer
- Bristol: Offer
- Durham: Offer

Good Points:

This statement is thoughtful, interesting, and conveys clear motivations for studying Economics, as well as demonstrating a good level of preparation for university study. The student elaborates on their response to each preparatory activity they engaged in, rather than falling into the trap of simply listing books read and lectures attended. They are clearly passionate about the subject and show promise as an economist, which they demonstrate in, again, not only listing their achievements but explaining what they took from the experience; subtly indicating what this says about them as a student.

Bad Points:

There is little to say in criticism of this statement except that, perhaps, it could come across as a little cliché. Questioning whether there is such a thing as 'the right answer' in the introduction and concluding that pursuit of the field to which they're applying for further study is worthy, are both very common.

Overall:

This is an exceptional personal statement. Not only is the student accomplished, they convey this without bragging and in enough detail that we gain insight into their abilities, motivations, and personal interests, rather than simply receiving a list in prose form. Although the ideas with which the student begins and concludes the statement are somewhat unoriginal, the explanation found in-between is exceptionally strong and justifies the unoriginal sentiments – they're clearly not being added just as throwaway lines.

NOTES

Subject: Economics & Management

The world has changed greatly over my lifetime and Economics seems to me to offer explanations for many complex occurrences in a simple, elegant manner. This is what draws me to the subject and is why I chose to study it at A Level. It allows us to trace events such as the credit crunch back to an ever-expanding supply of credit. But at the same time, the fact that there is rarely a right answer means that there is always scope for further study. When shale gas was discovered in America in 2005, it revolutionised the country: energy prices plummeted while thousands of jobs were created. This situation demonstrates how market mechanisms can act to lower prices, but it is the global consequences that are of most interest to me.

While representing my school in ICAEW's BASE competition at the national finals, I gained more of an understanding of how reliant businesses are on others, miles away from themselves, which encouraged me to read Joseph Stiglitz's 'Making Globalisation Work' in which he calls for reforms to how globalisation is managed. I found it interesting that he believes globalisation is failing because of the way governments are guiding it rather than inherent failures and also how dominant the USA appears in global governance.

The government's role in influencing globalisation was highlighted to me during a work placement with a UKTI dealmaker for India. Through various meetings with Indian entrepreneurs in need of help trading in the UK, I saw how governments could entice talent, and the money it generates, into their own country from around the world. However, it was the number of bureaucratic and cultural obstacles these entrepreneurs faced that struck me most.

The turbulent economic climate we live in makes the subject even more interesting. As we now climb out of recession, there is a debate over how best to tackle the government's burgeoning debt pile without slipping back into recession. Despite George Osborne's attempt to reduce the deficit, it is more than twice the Euro-area average. Monetary policy is also under scrutiny with the BofE needing to strike a fine balance. It needs to ensure that the money supply contracts gradually as growth is established to prevent inflation taking off. I got first hand experience of this challenge while representing my school during the Target 2.0 competition.

As a long-term volunteer at Cancer Research UK, I am now trusted to help managers do tasks such as stocktaking and measuring KPIs. Whilst working there I have noticed that store managers deal well with day-to-day issues but as you venture further up the chain of command, the management becomes more distant and less involved. For instance, it would take a quick visit to establish that there is a flat above the shop I work in, owned by Cancer Research, but used only for storage. The rental income forgone surely exceeds the utility derived from its current use. Arguably this system of management has led to an inefficient allocation of resources. This insight was one of the reasons for wanting to study this course.

I have always been prepared to challenge myself and as such sat two GCSEs and one AS a year early while managing to juggle various sports, both in-school and out, including playing rugby for the Second XV along with cricket and swimming for the School and Potters Bar Swimming Club. Along with sport I am working towards my Grade 6 Clarinet and Duke of Edinburgh Gold. I am a Lance Sergeant in CCF through which I command 4th year students and am also preparing for a forthcoming expedition to Tanzania, where we will help improve local orphanages both physically and through fundraising. I feel that I am ready to tackle the challenges that this academically rigorous course offers.

Universities applied to:

- Oxford: Offer
- Warwick: Offer
- Durham: Offer
- Bath: Offer
- York: Offer

Good Points:

This statement is particularly good in that it integrates the student's extra-curricular activities into their interest in economics, rather than discussing the academic areas they're interested in and then listing their other interests, as a lot of personal statements do. This allows them to discuss their merits as a student – how their study so far has influenced their decision to study economics, and how it has prepared them for it (e.g.: the first-hand experience they got from participating in the Target 2.0 competition). They clearly express their particular academic interest in macroeconomics while allowing the rest of their statement, including non-academic activity, to portray them as a well-rounded individual.

Bad Points:

The statement is perhaps overly focused on practical economic activities, with no mention of any formal study of economic theory outside of GCSEs and AS levels (which are standard for someone applying for an economics degree). While mentioning participation in events like Target 2.0 is great, competitions like these, while giving some insight into the application of economic policy, are far removed from university study. Some evidence of research more suited to a degree would assuage any worries about the student's preparedness for university.

Overall:

This is a very strong statement – the student is accomplished, eloquent, and passionate. It could be improved by discussing some academic interests (discussing theory they've read or going into more detail about the one the student did mention).

NOTES

Subject: Economics & Management

Economics is the study of now. I view it as the study of the psychology of the people who dictate our lives. The world around us is shaped by the fundamental concept of supply and demand, wants and needs, goods and services. What grips me is that everything I have studied I can apply to real life. Discussions about inflation, for example, are so applicable since its current status is active in the world of pricing; the price of a Big Mac and "Burgernomics" is something to which I can relate from my travels.

The statistical aspect of economic analysis is closely linked to my interest with Mathematics, thus I will take an Econometric route on option modules. This scientific approach to what is otherwise a field based solely on individual theories and concepts interests me, as I find quantitative analysis much more accurate and reliable than qualitative theories. As an example, I relish analysing more Econometric models on the A Level Course: like Profit Maximisation calculations.

Despite this, Economics intertwines both Maths and Philosophy on a regular basis. I recently read an article from the Guardian by George Monbiot, which discussed the cost-benefit analysis model and whether nature could be quantified as a tangible asset, and how this would benefit neo-liberals in their perpetual quest for profit. This is just an example of how Econometric analysis does not always deliver such verisimilitude where the figures given are ambiguous. This is what is unique about Economics: there is no right answer to the question 'Is there a right answer?' The concept of there being methods of analysing the psychology of and nature behind the way that the interface between consumers and producers operates seems to exceed all other subjects in terms of interest.

I find it peculiar that a subject that has such a ubiquitous undercurrent in our society is so undefined and obscure; it is undoubtedly this which draws me to it. Consequently I strive to keep up with Economics in the modern world by reading the "I" and "Guardian" newspapers, and "The Economist" magazine regularly. For wider background reading I have read Marx's "Communist Manifesto", Tim Hartford's "The Undercover Economist" and "Too Big To Fail" by Andrew Ross Sorkin.

Sorkin's book provided a gripping, in depth insight into the world of investment banking and entrepreneurship – I finished the book in a matter of days. His book has inspired me to enter the investment sector. Upon graduation I would like to become an investment banker or negotiator, hence I am in the process of trying to arrange some work experience with the London Metal Exchange.

I completed a programme of work experience with Linden Homes this summer, through the Career Academy Programme on which I am enrolled. It was a six week internship during which I gained a firm understanding of a construction company's place within the national economy. I enjoyed spending valuable time in a variety of departments within the firm. I also have work experience planned in Belgium 2013.

Additionally, I participate in a multitude of extracurricular activities. My team and I finished second in the national UMPH Business Competition; in Year 11 my team set the school record for the Enterprise Day Challenge and for three consecutive years my team won the Grimsby Inter-School Quiz without loss. Furthermore, I am part of both the Franklin College Debating Team and the weekly "Blue Sky Club", where students meet to discuss current affairs.

Recently, a particular subject of interest has been the US election. We frequently discuss the debates and the candidates, covering subjects like their political viewpoints and how it will affect both our lives and those of the American public – plus the potential Economic ramifications of the possible outcomes.

With a genuine zeal for the subject and an ability to relate my studies to the real world, I am convinced that I will thoroughly thrive at degree level Economics.

Universities applied to:

- Oxford: Offer
- London School of Economics: Rejected
- York: Offer
- Birmingham: Offer
- Leeds: Offer

Good Points:

The student gives a good insight into their academic interests and what's inspired them to develop over time. They also demonstrate a passion for the subject, not only by stating their interest in it but by further explaining what interests them and why they would make a good candidate to study it at university. The student is already accomplished and explains well what they've gained from their various extra-curricular activities.

Bad Points:

The writing is weak and, at points, unnatural. The forced interjections of examples and unusual adjectives make it read like a student attempting to write a formal and formulaic exam essay. They would do better to write in their usual style, even if it is somewhat informal; this will allow them to better express themselves and they will come across as more interesting to those reading it. More importantly than this, however, at times, the student fails to keep up their otherwise good level of detail, and the writing becomes list-like.

This is particularly prominent when they discuss books they've read to develop their understanding of economics. Although they expand on one of these, they do so in little detail. Interviewers are unlikely to be impressed by simply mentioning that you've read a book – any student applying for degree-level economics is able to read The Communist Manifesto, for instance – but they will be impressed by your response to it and what you gained from the experience of reading it. Unless you expand on these details, a list of books you've read does nothing to contribute to the statement, or your chances of selection.

Overall:

This statement is very strong, except where it discusses academic work. The detail here was most likely sacrificed in favour of expanding further on their extra-curricular activities and their particular areas of interest. However, they've limited discussion of their study of various classic economic works so severely that it fails to add anything to the piece. The statement would, therefore, benefit from a more balanced approach to the various areas of the student's life.

NOTES

Subject: Economics

My motivation to study economics actually came as a surprise, as I had expected the subject would be mainly concerned with acquiring money. However, from our first lesson I realised that economics is truly about maximising the happiness of society. Good economists advocating policies which are just a fraction more effective can make positive differences to the lives of huge numbers of people. This is what excites me about economics, and constantly thinking in terms of economics has become second nature to me. The best way I can demonstrate this is through my blog. It has been rewarding to use knowledge acquired from extensive reading outside the course in the formation of more complex arguments, such as how universities should be funded.

My two favourite books so far have been Thomas Friedman's "The World is Flat" and Philip Ball's "Critical Mass", which I chose by cross-referencing university reading lists with website reviews. I enjoyed Friedman's demonstration of seemingly small policy changes making a large difference through "reform retail". I also gained a much firmer grounding in the history of globalisation and, surprisingly, logistical systems. Most importantly, Friedman highlighted some major choices that the world will have to make as it becomes ever more globalised, particularly the balance between efficiency and tradition in developed economies. Wal-Mart seems to be a metaphor for this debate, and perhaps the way in which it ends up doing business will be symbolic of the future of our flat world.

I also found "Critical Mass" very thought-provoking because I had to incorporate skills from all of my AS levels, even Chemistry for the Maxwell-Boltzmann distribution curves, in order to understand the book. I found the thought processes that lead scientists to study trends rather than individual "peoploids" very revealing, as it is the core of economic rationale. However, the topics I became most immersed in were the models of Axelrod, particularly the study of the formation of alliances. I believe that a similar technique could be employed in economic models in order to better account for external influences and chaos theory. Moreover, I have been able to apply his display of the effectiveness of "Tit for Tat" as a strategy in game theory to my A2 history course on the Cold War.

Despite being very interested in theoretical economics, I am well aware that a good knowledge of current events is just as important. I read both "The Economist" and "The Sunday Times" weekly in order to stay up to date. At school, I actively take part in the economics, politics and debating societies. These have been great outlets for topical discussion and, on the whole, a very constructive way to spend my lunchtimes. I also play hockey for my school and West Herts Hockey Club, which has been great for keeping fit and improving my teamwork skills.

A very challenging application of these skills has been the Target 2.0 competition, which I was chosen to enter after competing with nine other applicants to represent my school. It has been gratifying to use data and quantitative reasoning in order to reach a definite conclusion, which is something I had not expected to have the opportunity to do until econometrics and statistical economics modules at university. I am very much looking forward to studying the more mathematical side, because I have always had an affinity for maths. Target 2.0 has also given me an increased sense of perspective on not only the intricate workings of monetary policy, but also news relating to central bankers such as the "Monetary Illusions" article featured recently in the economist. Most importantly, I now know that I would love a career in which I can employ economic theory to my work, and the best chance I have of achieving this is by continuing to study economics at a higher level.

Universities applied to:

- Cambridge: Offer
- Bristol: Offer
- Warwick: Offer
- Bath: Offer
- Nottingham: Offer

Good Points:

This student has an interesting insight into Economics as a subject and into their particular motivation for studying it, which is well backed up. The details regarding how they chose what to read, as well as their response to their readings and why they've chosen to discuss these particular books (that is, why they're their favourites) make the statement stand out, as it gives a personal response to the works, rather than reeling off an impressive list of books or simply summarising the ideas expressed in them to show some academic ability. The student is well-rounded and shows an interest in a variety of economic pursuits (and, moreover, actively acknowledges that the area in which they have the most interest is not the be-all and end-all of Economics, which is unusual for a personal statement, and benefits the image of them as a good candidate for university study).

Bad Points:

The statement only discusses academic pursuits. While this time is well-spent and the student comes across as very accomplished, universities often like to see the non-academic side of students too, to show that they are individuals capable of managing a balanced life, rather than devoting all of their time to work in order to maintain the high-level of academic accomplishment expressed in their exam results and personal statements.

Overall:

This is a strong statement because the student has found a great level of detail in discussing what's inspired them to apply for Economics and what makes them a good student. It could be improved by being balanced with some discussion of the student's non-academic interests.

NOTES

Subject: Economics

In Year 11, I fell in love with Economics. I followed a basic introduction course where I discovered the greatness of economists such as Adam Smith. I was at first convinced by the invisible hand theory, but my convictions were challenged by Keynes' work: government spending can, in certain cases, induce growth by boosting demand.

Economics advances rational explanations of an irrational world. I find this paradox amazing. In the case of Veblen goods, the higher the prices, the higher the demand. This shows that Economics is a social science: human behaviour and ways of thinking come into play. For a long time, microeconomics, with the utility function theory, assumed that individuals were rational. Today some economists are working under different assumptions. As Kahneman, whose work fascinates me, put it, people have cognitive bias.

I also love the fact that because Economics is not an exact science, it is open to controversy: if you put three economists in a room, you will have three different analyses of the same situation. France's GDP resisted better the 2008 recession than the UK's. Today, UK's growth is back while France's is still flat. This could be explained by automatic stabilizers (more social transfers in France), but also by the different monetary policies (more accommodative in the UK than in the EU) or budget policies (UK cut spendings, France increased taxes).

Paradoxically, I also like the fact that Economics relies heavily on the precision and objectivity of Mathematical models. Behind every economic principle lies logical reasoning, and I believe my taste and talent for Maths can help me greatly in my studies. In 2012, I finished in the top 1.5% in a national French logic competition (Concours Kangourou). During my Year 12, I finished second in my school in the UK Maths Challenge, and in the top three in the French Maths Olympiads. I have chosen an additional Maths option in my curriculum, and I believe that studying a wide range of subjects such as Ancient Greek, Geography, History, or even Philosophy (in addition to my scientific disciplines) has helped me gain valuable general knowledge.

At the end of Year 11, obliged to make a choice between Economics and Maths, I chose the latter as I knew I would need a good foundation in Maths to study Economics. However, I have sustained my keen interest in Economics, reading the book "50 Economic ideas" by Edmund Conway, and attending an Economics Summer School (DebateChamber, 2014). In a course on economic growth, I studied the Solow-Swann model, which gave me food for thought. Does a country's growth depend solely on the capital-output ratio of the economy? In the long term, does an economy really reach a state of equilibrium where GDP cannot increase further?

After having been class delegate for three years, I was elected by all the students as their representative on the Lycée council. I have taken part in numerous debates about the Lycée's organisation with adult board members. This role has taught me to defend my opinions whilst listening to others' and given me a sense of responsibility. I am a motivated person and love leading projects: two years ago I founded a football club, the Newstars, which now competes in an official League.

Moreover, I spent two weeks in Ghana last summer setting up sustainable sporting activities for young children. I saw the extent of poverty and underdevelopment and was amazed by the omnipresence of corruption, affecting everything from parking spaces to police work. As a result, I became interested in development models and learnt that economic aid to Africa can have unintended consequences, such as reinforcing fraud and market distortion, bringing potentially more poverty.

This made me realise that Economics is not only compelling intellectually, but can also make a practical difference in people's lives, thus I am eager to develop my understanding of the subject and its practical applications further at degree level.

Universities applied to:

- Cambridge: Offer
- London School of Economics: Rejected
- University College London: Offer
- Bath: Offer
- Warwick: Offer

Good Points:

This statement gives a good personal insight into the development of the student's economic thought and their personal motivation for the further study of Economics, as well as explaining their conception of Economics as a discipline, which will allow universities to decide if they're suitable for their institution. The student shows a genuine interest in the subject, evidenced by their reading around a wide range of economic theories and leaving questions open to indicate what questions they hope to develop answers to as a student of Economics. They clearly convey both their academic and personal accomplishments and, importantly, they link these specifically to the study of Economics.

Bad Points:

The views expressed are somewhat unoriginal. While this is not inherently a bad thing if discussing their own economic stance (an A level student, after all, is unlikely to come up with an original economic model), but can be a let-down if discussing their reasons for studying Economics. Stating that Economics is not an exact science, for instance, is quite a trite point to make that is unlikely to make the statement stand out from the crowd. The student could improve this by discussing exactly why they personally are suited to a subject filled with such controversy, and how they hope to resolve this controversy for themselves to develop a clear economic stance, for instance.

Overall:

This is a very strong statement. Even the unoriginal and underdeveloped aspects mentioned above do not let the statement down hugely because the student so clearly expresses their interest in Economics, and what makes them a strong candidate.

NOTES

Subject: Land Economy

My interest in economics has grown out of two diverse sources. On the one hand, an international perspective and a critical attitude to global issues is my lucky inheritance, given my mother's engagement in international media and my father's interest in Latin American culture. As I grew up my mother was employed by the International Herald Tribune and euronews while my father worked as a Spanish translator. This background has given me a particular openness to the world around me, a fondness for understanding different cultures and a critical sensitivity towards social issues. On the other hand, from an early age I enjoyed the benefits of having an aptitude for mathematics and the pleasure of abstract problem solving. After long speculation I have come to the idea that I should combine these two diverse interests, in the social world and that of abstract rational thought, through the discipline of economics.

The fact that my initial interest in mathematics grew with time is due to the excellent education I received at Berzsenyi Daniel, one of the top grammar schools in Hungary. I benefited from the advanced math classes (8 hours a week) and summer math camps with knot and game theory being this years theme. These intense learning experiences were valuable not only due to the content taught, but also as teaching was structured around improving presentation skills, developing source analysis and the rules of academic writing. The warm and encouraging atmosphere of these camps as well as the inspirational, if competitive attitude taught at Berzsenyi has set me onto a trajectory of exploring mathematical and economic issues during my own time. As such, I ended up reading some works by John Harsanyi and audited lectures at ELTE's first year applied economics course, with units that included microeconomics and basic function analysis. An additional dimension where Berzsenyi provided a privileged educational focus was the area of languages.

Emphasis was placed not only on the idea that students should become adapt speakers (of English and German in my case), but also that they become open to the cultural background and history of the nations where these languages originate.

It is from these classes that my interest in English and German literature springs, with Oscar Wild and Thomas Mann taking top spot.

There has been additional influence that remained a persistent factor in my personal development. This has been the importance of community based team work. I grew to understand the significance of this, partly by getting elected co-chairman of the Student Council and partly by having played water polo. The first experience taught me the importance of political representation and responsibility, while the second the significance of discipline as well as creativity when treading collectively towards a common goal. Extracurricular activities also played an important role at my school. I took part in a UNESCO competition which focused on climate change and scarce natural resources. While the team achieved third place, the competition was an invaluable experience that further propelled me towards wanting to understand the relationship between national economies and environmental issues.

I feel that exploring the discipline of economics would be the most ideal way to combine my interests as well as develop the skills I have gained during my education so far. While the diverse multicultural environment of the UK has remained an important factor in my choices, it is the historic tradition of higher education that has attracted me the most. I strongly believe that it is this tradition; with its central focus on the individual student, with high expectations, excellent resources and internationally renowned scholars and teachers, which would be the best place for me to develop my natural abilities and ambitions.

Universities applied to:

- Cambridge: Offer
- St. Andrews: Offer
- London School of Economics: Offer
- Edinburgh: Offer
- Aberdeen: Offer

Good Points:

The statement portrays the student as capable and well-educated, with a clear and developed interest in Economics. They seem to have a good grasp of what studying Economics at degree level will involve, and are confident they will be able to handle the work (in particular, the mathematical aspects of it); a claim that is supported by their academic accomplishments. They address the particular environment of university study, which is unusual, but beneficial to the image of a mature, competent student who has made a clear-headed decision to study Economics, on the basis of interest and ability.

Bad Points:

The student emphasises their excellent education. While it is perfectly fine to admit the advantages a good education has given you, this does little to stress your own accomplishments as a student or to demonstrate that you'll be a good candidate for further education in Economics (it might even have the opposite effect since a much larger portion of learning at university is done through independent study). This time would be better spent discussing their own efforts, the way their interests have developed, and how they've pursued them, rather than discussing the structure of courses they've been lucky enough to attend. Where they do discuss their own interests (their favourite authors, for instance), they do so in little depth.

The writing is clunky and forced and reads as trying to be impressive by inserting superfluous adjectives and connectives, e.g.: "There has been additional influence that remained a persistent factor in my personal development. This has been the importance of community based team work." Sentences like these are clearly not written in the student's natural writing style but, rather, the style they've developed for A level essays, which require formulaic structures involving making a point, giving an example, and expanding on it. More naturally, it would read something like "The importance of community has been a persistent factor in my personal development".

Overall:

The student ought to take a more personal approach to their statement by focusing on their interests and achievements they've secured through their own efforts, as well as relying on their natural writing to convey their personality, as opposed to wording the statement in an attempt at academic speech. Despite this, the essay is strong; they elaborate well on how their education has benefitted them and why they want to study Economics further.

NOTES

POLITICS, PHILOSOPHY & ECONOMICS

Subject: Politics, Philosophy, Economics (PPE)

By the time of the 2012 elections, my country, Greece, was facing a profound political, financial and social crisis with far-reaching consequences. The volatility of the situation intensified my interest in Politics, Philosophy and Economics, as I wished to deepen my understanding of society and the causes of such a crisis.

During this period, I watched the political campaigns of all major parties to better comprehend their agendas, which increased my awareness of the situation in Greece in relation to the rest of the world. This led me to participate in the Harvard Model Congress Europe, a simulation of US parliamentary procedures, where I debated with students from around the world on possible solutions to improve US-Venezuela relations. Apart from enhancing my problem-solving skills, this experience acquainted me with the formal US procedures and confirmed that politics is a subject I want to learn more about. Being interested in intergovernmental relations, I completed an internship at the Greek Consulate of Izmir, which helped me develop insights into the political agendas behind the issuing of visas, for example.

Last year, during my internship at the Human Resource department of a major healthcare product manufacturer, I gained first-hand experience of the severity of unemployment in Greece and its sweeping consequences. This experience made me interested in investigating the root cause of unemployment. Varoufakis' "The Global Minotaur" helped me see how an unsustainable and imbalanced economic system could instigate a global crisis, one that Europe tried to remedy with austerity measures, which led to a reduction of economic activity and less need for employed labor. The accuracy with which macroeconomic theory can depict reality spurred my interest to further study this subject and learn more about how these phenomena can be prevented.

My interest in philosophy was further cultivated by my involvement in a volunteering activity where I taught Greek at a shelter for Syrian refugees for three months. Given the fact that the Syrian Civil War made these people seek a better future in Athens with no assets or connections, I started reading about whether war could ever be justified. This led me to seek answers as to whether there are universal moral rules that everyone should follow. I was particularly captivated by the utilitarian perception of morality that J.S. Mill argues, explaining that any action leading to the "greatest happiness" for the "greatest number" is justified. Although this theory can have considerable ethical implications if the minorities are repressed for the benefit of the majorities, it serves as a useful guide to show that the death and destruction provoked by war cannot be justified. Debate, which I have been heavily involved in in the past few years, helped me delve deeper into ethical issues, such as prisoners' rights and bodily autonomy and earned me an invitation for the tryouts of the Greek National Debate Team that will be held shortly, where I will compete for a place in the team.

My determination and patience were further cultivated through chess, my other passion. Last year, the third place among all Greek schools gained by the team I put together and trained made my leadership and co-operation skills all the more tangible. I also enjoy learning about life in space. Studying Physics on my own and investigating the possibility that life might have existed on Venus enhanced my analytical skills and helped me win the third place in the Physics competition during the International Space Olympics in Moscow.

All in all, PPE is ideally suited to my interests as I was able to ascertain during a PPE program I attended last summer at the Oxford and Cambridge Summer Academy. Seeking answers as to how politics, philosophy and economics affect our everyday lives and shape our decisions is an ongoing enquiry that gives perennial rise to fresh questions, which I would love to explore at University.

Universities applied to:

- Oxford: Offer
- London School of Economics: Offer
- Durham: Offer
- York: Offer
- Warwick: Offer

Good Points:

This statement shows off an impressive history of political extra-curricular activities in such a way as to not only list the achievements and experience the student wants to show off, but also to highlight how they have benefited from the experiences and how it has shaped their desire to study PPE. The statement is well-balanced in devoting time to all three subjects, causing one to reasonably conclude that PPE is an ideal subject of choice for them and that they are an ideal student to study it. The student conveys their passion for particular areas of study (e.g.: macroeconomic theory and predicting economic activity in order to prevent disaster).

Bad Points:

The statement doesn't flow particularly well and the student does little to tie the three subjects together. The student could conclude that all of politics, philosophy, and economics could be appropriate for them to study, but the particular combination of the three is one offered by few British universities for a reason. The student should devote some time to discussing why they wish to study the three together and how the study of one affects the others, rather than keeping their passion for each completely separate. The penultimate paragraph, listing interests outside of PPE, is also somewhat disjointed from the rest of the statement and interrupts the flow of the piece as a whole, but this is perhaps unavoidable (and the paragraph does contribute well to the image of the student as a well-rounded individual). Still, they would do better to focus it somewhat on how these skills directly link to university study or the study of PPE.

Overall:

This is a very strong statement. Their background in the three subjects is diverse and interesting, and they convey well how this has affected them as a student. Although they do this for each of the subjects discussed, they could improve it by tying their experience in the three fields together, so as to explain why they wish to study PPE specifically.

NOTES

Subject: Politics, Philosophy, Economics (PPE)

I have been fortunate enough to have spent half my life overseas and to have attended eight different schools in five different countries and as a result I have engaged with people from a wide range of cultures and backgrounds. Having enjoyed these experiences immensely, I am determined to build on this foundation by studying for a degree that will increase my understanding of how trans-national and cross-cultural transactions work. One of the key factors in these transactions, undoubtedly, is human nature.

I was very interested, therefore, to read Jonathon Wolff's 'An Introduction to Political Philosophy', particularly the contrasting interpretations of the 'state of nature' that rose dependent on the interpretation of mankind. In my experience there is a parallel between inter-personal and international relations and I want to understand the ways in which states and people operate. My background has made me more aware of complex international issues, such as Australia's current problem in reconciling the fact that its major trading partner has the potential to become its biggest adversary.

Because of my interest in this situation I delved deeper into China's rise, through the medium of an extended project which discussed whether China poses any threat to the USA. Research for this project caused me to question whether there is any justification for the Western ethical preference for a 'free' economy over command economies. This work made me realise that I need economic knowledge in order to better understand the complexities of international relations and encouraged me to fast track an A level in economics.

My research touched on the question of the apparent commonality of cultural morals and delving into this issue led me to reflect on the arguments for universal morality that J.S. Mill presents in 'Utilitarianism'. His claim that public convictions and general happiness are the basis for a viable moral authority appears to reflect the operation of democratic governance. I would argue, however, that there is a strong, external ethical pressure that acts regardless of happiness, a knowledge of base morality that is followed for its own end. The complexity of such issues has always appealed to me, which is perhaps why I was so enthused by the mathematical elements of philosophical logic that Blackburn presents in 'Think'. The notion of reducing rational questioning to formulaic equations was completely new to me and I found it very compelling. I was equally intrigued by the attempts, particularly of Descartes in 'Meditations' and Anselm in the 'Proslogian', to develop an irrefutable argument based purely on reason; the notion of an a priori argument that could establish what empiricism cannot is a profound possibility. I thoroughly enjoy immersing myself in unknown and foreign situations. This probably stems from my travels across the globe, which took me from childhood in Moscow to my more recent time in Canberra.

Through school and college, I have sustained an ability to balance my academic studies with a hectic social life, part-time jobs and my sporting commitments. I have been elected to the captaincy of two football teams and have played a consistent role in promoting youth involvement, through coaching a junior football team and being involved in the Olympic FLAMES programme. I am happy to lead or work within a team and can negotiate with difficult individuals, whether they are complaining customers or disaffected youngsters. I am eager to pursue a career path that will take me into an international and cross-cultural environment. This is why I feel strongly drawn towards a degree where I can use my experiences and ambitions to better prepare myself for the multinational market of the future. I want to develop an academic arsenal which will best establish me as a positive contributor in an increasingly trans-national, interlinked world - where global understanding looks set to become an essential attribute.

Universities applied to:

- Oxford: Offer
- Warwick: Offer
- London School of Economics: Rejected
- York: Offer
- Manchester: Offer

Good Points:

The student demonstrates a clear interest in all three subjects and does especially well in linking the three together, detailing how their interest in one politics issue lead to studying Economics, which lead to readings in Philosophy. They give the impression of an individual who has naturally come to the conclusion that PPE is the right area of study for them and they back this up substantially with both their personal history and academic studies. The balance between discussing their academic interests and other areas of their life is just right, and they use the latter to reinforce their worth as a student. The statement flows naturally while the conclusion rounds it off nicely with a look to the future and what they wish to do with their degree.

Bad Points:

At times, the student dwells on explaining their exact response to each book mentioned and their current position on each area of study. This is not particularly useful as those reading it will be more interested in how you think and how your reading developed your thought, rather than whether you, for example, tend towards consequentialism or deontology, as you don't have nearly enough space in a personal statement to back up a philosophical position in any substantial or interesting way.

The statement also ought to be broken down into smaller paragraphs. This will improve the overall structure and will make for a much more natural read.

Overall:

This is an excellent statement; it ties the three subjects together and clearly conveys why each is personal to the student and what they want to achieve by studying them. They ought, however, to focus more on how their background has affected their way of thinking, rather than listing their positions on various issues.

NOTES

Subject: Politics, Philosophy, Economics (PPE)

Living in London, I have witnessed numerous political and economic problems affecting people's every day lives: the threat of terrorism after 7/7, lack of council housing and the disaffection demonstrated in the riots. Seeing governments' failure to tackle these problems directly has fuelled my desire to both understand and find solutions to such problems.

Studying A Level History I looked at the totalitarian regimes of both Mussolini and Hitler. I read 'The Republic' by Plato and Machiavelli's 'The Prince', to look at how dictatorial states can develop. I find Plato's ideas of a 'perfect' society, such as the lack of class mobility, chillingly reminiscent of the totalitarian states which I studied. On the other hand, I find 'The Prince' a perceptive study of ways to gain and hold power. The political dominance of leaders described in the books seemed similar to the legacy of Tony Blair which I explored through my Extended Project Qualification on 'How can the Labour Party rebrand in order to win the 2015 election?' I researched the opinions of the general public pertaining to the party and discovered that raising economic confidence was the main area on which Labour needed to work.

'The Return of Depression Economics' by Krugman highlighted the difference between Krugman's proposals of Keynesian solutions to the economic issues we currently face and George Osborne's recent budgets. The way the markets have intensified inequality through the crisis shocked me into reading Wolff's 'An Introduction to Political Philosophy' which cemented my conviction on the moral importance of state action to alleviate poverty. To further my knowledge, I attended an Economics Summer School with the Debate Chamber and studied aspects of economics which I had not previously encountered, such as game theory. I enjoyed the logical aspect of game theory combined with the moral side of problems such as the Prisoner's Dilemma. Carrying out research into the Black-Scholes equation, as part of a maths presentation on the effect of maths on the current economic crisis, highlighted how important maths is to the study of economics.

Taking my French A Level at the time of the French presidential election piqued my interest in French politics, and I used my French language skills to appreciate the presidential debate and Hollande's acceptance speech. As a violinist, I have had the opportunity to visit France, Germany and Finland with Bromley Symphony Orchestra and Chamber Orchestra. The different political tasks that face other countries, whether it is reconciling cultures in France or leading the European economy in Germany, provide a contrast to everyday British politics. In addition, I was able to play at the Royal Albert Hall and I have gained the time management skills needed for practising, rehearsals and concerts. I looked at the politicisation of music as part of a feature for the website, Sound Influx, and concluded that while it raised awareness, music no longer has a true influence on politics.

As Student Subject Leader for Politics, I have promoted the subject within the school by explaining the basic ideas relating to British political parties to year 9 students and by teaching year 10s about Marxism, for which I had to express ideas clearly. Within the next year I intend to help year 8s set up and run their own political campaigns, in order for them to develop an interest in the subject. I collaborated with a teacher at my school for a research project, sponsored by Canterbury Christchurch University, looking into ways of making cross-curricular links between different subjects, particularly investigating the effect Maths can have across the curriculum. We discovered the benefits of making such links, with students being able to use their skills and enthusiasm for one subject to improve their understanding of other areas of learning. It was this which confirmed to me that I want to study an interlinking degree such as this at university.

Universities applied to:

- Oxford: Offer
- Durham: Offer
- Warwick: Offer
- London School of Economics: Offer
- York: Offer

Good Points:

This student's approach makes for a fairly unique and interesting read. They focus on a fairly narrow set of issues and spend the first three paragraphs discussing books and schools of thought that have influenced their thinking.

This demonstrates a passion for exploring an issue they're interested in and shows off their extra-curricular activities, as well as showcasing their ability to tackle fairly advanced texts. They also demonstrate a broad background in all three subjects without separating their discussion of the three or taking note of the different 'classifications' of the texts discussed. This subtly conveys a predisposition towards not only the three subjects separately but towards studying the three in tandem. The points they discuss are suitably detailed and convey their particular interests within the fields of Politics, Philosophy, and Economics. They also devote an appropriate amount of time to discussing areas of their life that are not directly linked to PPE, but demonstrate their worth as a student.

Bad Points:

The first and last paragraphs are a little weak, mostly because of their lack of connection to the rest of the statement, and at times, the piece doesn't flow as well as it could have. The ideas discussed so well in the second and third paragraph ought to be linked back to their personal experience of observing issues in London or else the first paragraph is somewhat useless. The last paragraph, though fine, makes quite a weak case for studying a joint degree and is the only part of the statement that reads as forced, rather than a natural conclusion. This is especially true given how well the interlinking nature of the three subjects is handled earlier in the statement – if the student wants to make their predisposition towards a joint degree explicit, it is here, and with regards to the interplay of their study of the three subjects, this ought to be done.

Overall:

This is an exceptional personal statement, finding the right balance between broadness and specificity, between the subjects, and between academic and non-academic areas of their life. Its only downside is that it suffers, as many personal statements do, from some disjointedness and superfluous content.

NOTES

Subject: Philosophy, Politics, Economics (PPE)

Political policy and institutions, economic circumstance and philosophical debate permeate our everyday lives, as Keynes said "The world is ruled by little else". Their nuances and intricacies impact lives universally and thus their study is thus both riveting and indispensable.

The notion that "human progress is neither automatic nor inevitable" spurred my desire to question the validity of the beliefs we hold and the policies we live under. Hearing Professors Kay and Chang lecture on the future of capitalism and its potentially calamitous impact on the world economy, led me to question the validity of this influential economic policy. This drew me to Stiglitz's 'Price of Inequality' through which I began to appreciate the plethora of ways neoliberalism and capitalism affect our lives; influencing political representation, social circumstances and behaviour. Inspired by this I pondered whether politicians betray their obligations and catalyse the economic inequality and social injustice faced as a result of such policy rather than alleviating hardship and suffering; seeking answers in the political system of the USA for which I have a passion. Developing an interest in radicalism, I investigated the radicalisation of the GOP and the repercussions this is having for political and economic stability for my extended project. Through their actions in congress and framing of the debate it is clear that radical Republicans are politically preventing any amelioration of US domestic difficulties. Lieven's book 'America: Right or Wrong' supports this however I would further argue that the antiquated constitution and anachronistic political system are culpable and it would be wrong to blame individuals for an institutional failure to secure the wellbeing and financial security of the American people.

Perceiving the swathes of injustice in Western societies led me to probe for examples elsewhere and through attending a SOAS summer school I became gripped with the manifestations of justice in tumultuous regions in Africa such as the Rwandan 'Gacaca' trials; an amalgamation of punitive and restorative justice. Such a philosophical concern led me to question the nature of true Justice and whether Rawls, in 'A Theory of Justice', is justified in claiming that it is optimally applied from behind a "veil of ignorance". Conversely I hold that true justice requires a full knowledge of societal and individual circumstance since the values and aspirations that define who we are allow us to determine what justice truly is.

Seeking answers to philosophical questions has become an outlet for my natural curiosity. In preparation for an essay competition I theorised whether the happiness we all experience is true happiness and whether it is the only thing humans ever pursue. I built upon my knowledge of ethical systems particularly that of Mill's Utilitarianism and Aristotle's Nichomachean Ethics and concluded that happiness is the "simple harmony between man and the life he leads". I further felt that moral codes exist only to justify one's actions to oneself and hence act as mere vehicles for true happiness.

While the social sciences are often discussed in global terms and focus on societies as a whole, it is equally important to appreciate their quotidian impact on individuals. Driven my by desire to broaden my horizons I work extensively with London Citizens Community Organising and on other community projects allowing me to discover the crucial socioeconomic issues facing people and the means of assuaging these matters.

I feel that studying social sciences in isolation limits appreciation of their complex nature and only through holistic analysis and investigation can one seek the answers to the questions of the past, present and future. Hence I feel that my insatiable thirst for knowledge and my desire for understanding the imperative concerns of our world mean that such a combination is suited to both my academic and personal passions.

Universities applied to:

- Oxford: Offer
- Warwick: Offer
- Durham: Offer
- Bristol: Offer
- St. Andrews: Rejected

Good Points:

This statement is especially strong in its lack of superfluous content: each point is well-developed and contributes to the image of the student and their academic interests and abilities. It shows a well-rounded student with a passion for political economics. They clearly convey their areas of interest and use each book mentioned to its full advantage, detailing why they chose to read it and how it affected their thinking.

Bad Points:

The student focuses overwhelmingly on politics and some related economics, with only a cursory exposition of some philosophical ideas that interest them, which was not linked to the rest of the ideas discussed. The student also suffers somewhat from a lack of extra-curricular activity. While their political interests seem to be broad, they don't discuss anything non-academic, which can be worrying for tutors reading the statement. Discussing hobbies, responsibilities, and interests outside of PPE gives an impression of a well-rounded person and shows a healthy balance between academic and non-academic pursuits. Discussion of these parts of their life can also be used to show time management, leadership abilities, and other desirable qualities.

Overall:

This statement would be exceptional if the student were applying for a Politics and Economics degree. The philosophical parts discussed, however, are poorly integrated and the student appears to have put far less time into their study of this discipline. They also fail to discuss anything besides academic pursuits. The political and economic interests mentioned, though, are discussed excellently, and clearly demonstrate the student is more than capable to take on a joint honours degree.

NOTES

Subject: Philosophy, Politics, Economics (PPE)

I have always had a fascination with risk and whilst I enjoy a good game of poker, managing an imaginary portfolio of stocks has proved to be a more sustainable long-term strategy. Whilst the use of trends and technical indicators is important, an overall view of the economy is vital and I read the news in print and online daily to stay on top of it. The financial crisis of 2008 was when I first became aware of the economy and I have closely observed it since. The various measures put in place to produce the subsequent period of austerity and recovery have slowly but surely succeeded, ultimately achieving a rate of recovery unmatched since WWII. The past half a decade or so has been an interesting time to live through and is sure to serve as a case-study for years to come.

The intrinsic link between politics and economics became particularly obvious recently with the turbulent scene in the UK surrounding the referendum for Scottish independence. Aside from the pound's decline and rally at the time, there were far-reaching potential consequences for the country as a whole both politically and economically. In particular, had it not been for the economic quagmire predicted for an independent Scotland, it's likely that the Yes voters would have come much closer to a majority. Looking at politics through the lens of philosophy has enticed me and studying Hobbes' state of nature, contemplating a time when the states that run the world today didn't exist, is both thought-provoking and useful for modern thinking. The premise of the pursuit of felicity caught my attention and reading into the concept of egoism, I was amazed by the parallels with the theory of evolution and The Selfish Gene made long before Darwin's time. All these ideas reduce the human to a selfish vehicle for genes and reveal the deterministic nature of our actions. Ultimately, they demonstrate that there has been no transcendence between us and the matter from which we are made.

This conclusion ties in with Nihilism, the mesmerising doctrine that drove me to look into philosophy as a whole. I thought Blackburn's "Think" was a fantastic introduction; the highlight for me was the discussion of senses as primary and secondary. Seeing the secondary senses of smell, taste etc. washed away by objectivity and even the primary senses of extension, motion etc. eradicated by the lack of a proper idea of solidity reminded me of Nihilism. I found the doctrine analogous to this transition to the realm of the noumenal because, in essence, Nihilism simply suggests that purpose and morality, among other things, are human abstracts that do not exist in any objective sense. Furthermore, just as Hume and Berkeley go on to refute the most basic property of the world around us – solidity – some nihilists additionally negate knowledge and reality as impossible and non-existent respectively.

During my free time, I was an editor for my school's weekly paper, contributing opinion articles and also writing a column that I started, with one of my articles being featured in the XZR International magazine. Additionally, I won one of my school's essay prizes with a piece on ethics and went on to present my ideas at an interschool lecture event. An avid public speaker, I have debated economics and given numerous talks. I have also had a strong involvement in voluntary work, helping at Mencap, the Patients Association and my local hospice. Furthermore, I have honed my leadership and teamwork skills, completing all three Duke of Edinburgh awards and captaining my house's football team.

Although my formal education has been based in science, my aptitude for questioning and analytical thinking in tandem with my keen interest in the way that society functions ought to serve me well in the study of PPE. The transition from definite answers to more abstract concepts and conclusions has given me great satisfaction outside of classrooms and I look forward to further embracing it within them.

Universities applied to:

- Oxford: Offer

Good Points:

The writing style is natural and flows well. The student does well in linking the three subjects together and explaining why studying them all as a joint degree is a worthwhile pursuit. They have a clear idea of what areas of Philosophy they're interested in, and demonstrate a relatively developed understanding of some of the ideas they discuss. Though some aspects of the statement are impersonal (as discussed below), the chronological nature of the progression of their private study is a nice insight into exactly how these ideas have developed, which is a telling insight into them as a student. They adequately address their formal academic background in the sciences and emphasise the private study they've done that leads them towards a degree in the social sciences and humanities.

Bad Points:

Although the student shows a good grasp of the economic climate that has surrounded them for the past few years, they do little to make it personal or to why this has made them want to study PPE. Instead, the statement reads more like a summary of recent political events and how they relate to some schools of philosophy. The third paragraph lets down the rest of the statement; its ideas are confused and expresses rather simplistic philosophical ideas in an academic language that tries to impress. It summarises ideas with no attempt to link them to the student's particular interest in them or to their desire to study PPE. They would also do better to discuss in a little more detail what they have gained from their extra-curricular activities, rather than simply listing them.

Overall:

This statement shows an intelligent student who has already actively developed their views in some areas relevant to their degree and a good understanding of how current events relate to it. Their statement is somewhat impersonal, however, and reads as a list of schools of thought in politics and philosophy with some brief explanation of how they relate to each other, rather than an explanation of why they personally are interested in them.

NOTES

Subject: Philosophy, Politics, Economics (PPE)

Studying economics, I found that its analysis is most effective when considered in the context of other disciplines such as politics and philosophy. The strong links between economics and these fields is the most appealing aspect to me of studying PPE at Oxford.

Reading Gigerenzer's 'Risk Savy', I was particularly interested in the irrational decisions that can be made when a common concept such as risk is misunderstood. His call for a simplification of risk portrayal by specialists, such as converting probabilities into natural frequencies, and a revolution of the way risk is taught in schools struck me as a convincing thesis in how to reduce the damaging decisions that ignorance of risk can lead to. My interest in the way human behaviour affects our economic decisions led me to read 'Irrational Exuberance' by Robert Shiller that proved helpful in developing my economics prize essay. There I analysed the debate between Shiller and Fama over whether the market price was always the best indicator of an asset's value and if so whether we could predict asset price bubbles. I found Fama's belief that all economic agents are rational when faced with new information on the worth of an asset was undermined by Shiller whose persuasive analysis of situations in which human nature leads us to act irrationally therefore aiding the occurrence of bubbles.

Equality as a concept that can be approached through all three subjects is one that I became concerned with. Pickett and Wilkinson's 'The Spirit Level' advocated a much more equitable society emphasising the economic benefits to future sustainable growth, and although I found this convincing I was sceptical of the tenuous link between inequality and social problems such as mental illness and teenage pregnancies. These doubts were reinforced by Snowdon's 'The Spirit Level Delusion' where he demonstrates that many social wrongs such as homicides are not linked to inequality and have in fact been falling as inequality rises.

I attended Picketty's recent talk at the LSE, and although I agreed with his call for greater equality I was not persuaded by his proposal for a heavily progressive tax system, as it appeared politically implausible. On the other hand Nozick's equally extreme belief that redistributive taxation is akin to forced labour, I perceived to be unfair because that it would result in wealth being concentrated in the hands of the skilled, leading to great inequality that would be detrimental to the whole of society.

After reading 'An Introduction to Political Philosophy' by Wolff and 'Justice: What's the right thing to do?' by Sandel, I have become increasingly more concerned with the relationship between the citizen and the state and the question of the power the state has over the individual. This led me to read Mill's 'On Liberty' in which I found his view that the individual is sovereign over his body and thus his liberties, an unrealistic state in which individuals could live. The potential clashes that would occur between individuals over their desire to retain all their liberties seemed contradictory to an ideal society. However I found the view of Rousseau, in his 'The Social Contract', that the individual must sacrifice his natural rights to the community in order to preserve his liberties, a more compelling view on the relationship between the citizen and the state, allowing the state to limit our rights in order to preserve our other liberties and society as a whole. The 'moral and collective body' that this association creates seems to me a more persuasive representation of the ideal relationship between the citizen and the state.

I am an active member of the school community playing 1st XI football and being a school prefect. I am on the committee of the schools Economics Society where I invite, and have the opportunity to discuss with influential professionals in their respective fields.

Universities applied to:

- Oxford: Offer
- Bristol: Rejected
- Edinburgh: Offer
- Exeter: Rejected

Good Points:

The student makes it clear why they wish to study PPE as a joint honours, all the while underlining their passion for Economics and how it informs their study of the other two subjects. They show a wide range of reading around the subjects and mention a few more unusual books that they've found interesting (though students shouldn't aspire towards obscure readings above all else, it helps not to only mention books on the Oxford recommended preparatory reading lists – Think by Blackburn is mentioned by a huge number of PPE applications, for instance). More importantly, they outline their particular areas of interest, show a good understanding of the ideas they discuss, and outline why they found them interesting.

Bad Points:

They completely separate their discussion of political, economic, and philosophical ideas. While they mention in the introduction why they wish to study them together, they fail to go on to make a particularly compelling case for this. Instead, it reads like three mini-personal statements – one for each of the disciplines. Although they show an interest in various areas of PPE, they say very little about why they want to study them further or, more importantly, what makes them a good candidate for study. This is particularly evident in the paragraph outlining their non-academic interests, which is simply a brief list of things they do in their spare time. The statement reads more like a summary of their political, philosophical, and economic views, rather than a proposal to study at a university. Most egregiously, the candidate makes explicit mention of wanting to study at Oxford in their statement, this is an unnecessary inclusion which all-but ensures that universities besides Oxford will reject the application, and Oxford may also (as this indicates poor critical thinking skills on the part of the applicant.)

Overall:

It is evident from the statement that this is a very capable and well-developed student, however, the statement could be improved by tying the three subjects together more substantially opposed to just a throwaway line in the introduction. The student could have also spoke more about who they are as a person and a student, their strengths, and why they, in particular, should study PPE.

NOTES

Subject: War Studies / Politics

This world is a bleak place; and a change is what it needs. Not the type offered during the General Election Campaign of 2019, but the type offered by the inspirational Mahatma Ghandi and Martin Luther King Jr. It was between the ages of four to seven, during my stay in Bangladesh, that I saw poverty at my door step and corruption at every corner. Then I did not understand why this was so and honestly, I still do not. Today, as a passionate member of the pressure groups Amnesty International and Avaaz, I have tried to find my voice and channel it into something that is productive by signing many e-petitions against International Government actions such as stoning women and freeing political prisoners.

My interest in Politics was initially provoked by the daily reading of national newspapers during my GCSE years, the study of Hitler's Germany as well as the Middle East crisis; the complexities of such international conflicts also further intrigued me. This then led me to study both History and Politics at 'A' level. However, I had never anticipated that I would come to admire them both so much. Politics has taught me to be cynical, but has also shown me that it can also be the path to positive change. Meanwhile, History has taught me some painful truths and that there is no end to knowledge; we can never know enough. Studying Sociology at 'A' level as well, has helped me attempt to understand why society does what it does while my English Lit. 'A' level gives me the words and skills to artfully explain myself.

During the General Election of 2019, I found myself supporting a political party with such loyalty, that after the election I had joined the party. Through this membership I have attended local meetings to understand the issues of my constituency and get more involved. I have also attended a conference in London before the election with guest speakers including Nick Clegg and Jack Straw the then Justice Secretary. During this conference I led the way to scrutinising their claims by questioning their policies; to which I was given a much expected diplomatic reply. This then only enhanced my curiosity for the subject.

I wanted to experience the Political workings to see if I was truly made for this and so I ran for the Charities Officer post in the Student Council. This required three weeks of campaigning just like the politicians during an election, making public speeches and publishing my own mini manifesto. I kept to my morals and still managed to have won. This confirmed for me that studying Politics at a greater depth and becoming a Politician was what I wanted with a serious passion. Furthermore, as a member of the Council, I have learned a great deal; how to organise my time effectively so I could reply to every request made by students and staff promptly as well as helping to organise social events such as the Summer Ball. I am also held accountable, just like MPs, by the electorate and therefore I have to take every step in my decision making very carefully so that it is justifiable.

Along with the responsibilities I have in the council, I am also a member of the Politics Society in which I am continuously leading very heated debates about current political issues. I am also a member of the Amnesty Society within college and a member of the Jazz Choir as singing has always been a hobby. My political debates do not end in college, but continue over the dinner table and even on social networking sites. Even during my part time work as a sales assistant on Saturdays, I find myself teaching my colleagues and even my manager how politics works and what is happening right now worldwide. I see the future that I want and the world needs, and I am willing to give it my all. I am an ambitious, responsible, independent young woman with determination to bring about change; all I need is the opportunity.

Universities applied to:

- King's: Offer
- SOAS: Offer
- Queen Mary's: Offer
- Cambridge: Interview + Rejected

Good Points:

This statement is intensely personal and makes for an interesting read, which offers a telling insight into the student's life. They explain their personal reasons for wanting to study War Studies / Politics and makes a compelling case for their worth as a student by explaining what they've gained from both their formal education and their political activity. They also describe in detail what they want to gain from the further study of Politics and what they hope to do with their degree.

Bad Points:

It would have been nice to see them discuss the development of their political thought through their academic and political activities, as this is more relevant to study at university and would give the student an opportunity to discuss any more focused academic work they had done in preparation for the demands of further education (reading around the subject outside of class, for instance). The writing is also somewhat clunky. Additionally, the line in the introduction regarding channelling political beliefs into signing e-petitions is weak; remember that this is going to be viewed alongside, and compared to, hundreds of other statements from students who may be channelling their political beliefs into more direct action. By contrast, signing petitions is very little evidence of political drive and seems especially superfluous given what they go on to discuss.

Overall:

This student excels in demonstrating their passion for the subject. Their extensive political activity makes for a very strong statement and presents them as a well-developed young adult, which will interest, in particular, universities who interview candidates. It could, however, benefit from some content on their political beliefs, or at least their way of thinking, and on more academic work they had done to prepare. That said, this is very common in personal statements and their extra-curricular politically-driven activities are sure to stand out.

NOTES

FINAL ADVICE

- Start early
- Use the examples to see what successful applicants did
- Write too much and then cut it down
- Focus on your work experience and personal skills
- Illustrate with plenty of examples
- Get as many different opinions as possible
- Aim to finish comfortably before the deadline

Afterword

A strong personal statement is the perfect way to push your application onto the front foot. As with any piece of writing, the hardest part is the very first step – so start early. Take inspiration from this rich collection of successful statements, focus on your strengths, follow our top-tips and you *will* write an amazing personal statement.

Good luck!

Acknowledgements

Many thanks to each and every graduate who kindly provided their personal statements for use in this book – this unprecedented resource would not have been possible without them. I also thank my family for their support, in particular, my dad, Anil, for his keen eye for detail and razor-sharp focus.

Rohan

ABOUT US

UniAdmissions is the UK's leading provider of preparatory resources for university. We currently publish over 100 titles across a range of subject areas — covering specialised admissions tests, examination techniques, personal statement guides, plus everything else you need to improve your chances of getting on to competitive courses such as medicine and law, as well as into universities like Oxford and Cambridge.

Outside of publishing we also operate a highly successful tuition division. This company was founded in 2013 by Dr Rohan Agarwal and Dr David Salt, both Cambridge Medical graduates with several years of tutoring experience. Since then, every year, thousands of applicants and schools work with us on our programmes. These programmes offer expert tuition, exclusive course places, online courses, best-selling textbooks and much more.

If you've found this book helpful, or if you would like to find our more about our courses, programmes, and teaching, reach us at:

Website (UniAdmissions): www.uniadmissions.co.uk

Facebook: www.facebook.com/uniadmissionsuk

Your Free Book

Thanks for purchasing this Ultimate Book. Readers like you have the power to make or break a book —hopefully you found this one useful and informative. *UniAdmissions* would love to hear about your experiences with this book. As thanks for your time we'll send you another eBook from our Ultimate Guide series absolutely <u>FREE</u>!

How to Redeem Your Free eBook

1) Find the book you have on your Amazon
purchase history or your email receipt to help find the book on Amazon.

2) On the product page at the Customer Reviews area, click 'Write a customer review'. Write your review and post it! Copy the review page or take a screen shot of the review you have left.

3) Head over to www.uniadmissions.co.uk/free-book and select your chosen free eBook!

Your eBook will then be emailed to you – it's as simple as that!
Alternatively, you can buy all the titles at

Manufactured by Amazon.ca
Bolton, ON

36437481R00219